Fundamentals
of
Tourism and Travel Management

Fundamentals
of
Tourism and Travel Management

J C Dua
Madhulika Bhargava

Kaveri Books
New Delhi – 110 002

First Published in 2017
ISBN: 978-81-7479-161-0

Published by
Kaveri Books
4832/24, Ansari Road
New Delhi-110002 (India)
Tel: 011-2328 8140, 4707 2321
E-mail : info@kaveribooks.com
kaveribooks@gmail.com
Website: www.kaveribooks.com

Typeset in AGaramond Font at
Delta Book World, New Delhi - 110 002.

PRINTED IN INDIA

Preface

Over the decades, tourism has experienced continued growth and deepening diversification to become one of the fastest growing economic sectors in the world. Modern tourism is closely linked to development and encompasses a growing number of new destinations. These dynamics have turned tourism into a key driver for socio-economic progress.

Today, the business volume of tourism equals or even surpasses that of oil exports, food products or automobiles. Tourism has become one of the major players in international commerce, and represents at the same time one of the main income sources for many developing countries. This growth goes hand in hand with an increasing diversification and competition among destinations.

This global spread of tourism in industrialised and developed states has produced economic and employment benefits in many related sectors–from construction to agriculture or telecommunications.

The contribution of tourism to economic well-being depends on the quality and the revenues it offers. UNWTO assists destinations in their sustainable positioning in ever more complex national and international markets. As the UN agency dedicated to tourism, UNWTO points out that, particularly, developing countries stand to benefit from sustainable tourism and acts to help make this a reality.

This work has been in the offing for a long time. During the past several years, friends, within the department have been asking me to write a text book on tourism which would bring together recent thinking and research on the subject, and could be of use both for the general readers and students.

The work, 'Fundamentals of Tourism and Travel Management' broadly covers the first semester of the undergraduates. I have adopted the traditional divisions, but have tried to bring out self-imposed topics and understanding of broader concepts.

We are grateful to Miss Arushi Malik, the computer expert, Lala Bhagwandas Goyal and Mrs Anita Dua for their constant help and encouragement without whose help it was almost impossible to complete this book.

The present book would hardly have been possible without the friendly, prompting and personal interest of Mr Rakesh Goel of Kaveri Books, New Delhi.

Dr. J C Dua
Madhulika Bhargava

Contents

UNIT–III:
TOURISM DEVELOPMENT: ISSUES AND PROBLEMS

UNIT–IV:
IMPACTS OF TOURISM

UNIT–V:
TOURISM RESOURCE POTENTIAL OF INDIA

Introduction

The basic concepts and methods of tourism modelling and forecasting is introduced to equip visitors with the following information: what is the tourism demand analysis, how to construct statistical models, which model should be used, and how to generate accurate forecasts, etc.

Tourism is a socio-economic phenomenon comprising of activities and experiences of tourists and visitors away from their home environment, serviced by the travel and tourism industry and host destinations. The sum total of this activity, experience and services can be seen as the tourism product.

Recent developments in tourism demand modelling and forecasting entailing–

- Concepts and measures of tourism demand
- Data description
- General procedure of tourism demand forecast

The increasing interest in tourism demand studies has been motivated by rapid growth of the tourism industry across the globe since the ending of World War-II. The last four decades have seen great developments in tourism demand analysis, in terms of diversity of research interests, depth of theoretical foundations, and advances in research methodologies. Modeling tourism demand in order to analyze the effects of various determinants, and accurate forecasting of future tourism demand, are two major focuses of tourism demand studies.

Understanding the interrelationships between several parts of the system enables all tourism stakeholders to improve planning and management effectiveness and enhance the likelihood of success.

Essentially, the tourism system can be described in terms of supply and demand. Tourism planning should strive for a balance between demand (market) and supply (development). This requires an understanding not only of market characteristics and trends but also of the planning process to meet these market needs.

Furthermore, the context of the supply and demand sides needs to be carefully monitored and managed, e.g. ecological, political, social, cultural and other factors in the external and internal environments of the visitor demand destination supply components must be carefully considered.

Often tourists from core generating markets are identified as the demand side; the supply side includes all facilities, programmes, attractions and land uses designed and managed for the visitors. These supply side factors may be under the control of private enterprise, non-profit organizations and/or governments.

The developments in tourism forecasting methodologies fall into two categories: quantitative and qualitative methods. The latest quantitative forecasting literature is dominated by three sub-categories of methods: non-causal time-series models, the casual econometric approaches and other emerging methods such as Artificial Intelligence (AI) techniques. The difference between the first two categories is whether the forecasting model identifies any causal relationship between the tourism demand variable and its influencing variables.

New and innovative forms of partnerships are also evolving to ensure the sustainable development and management of tourism-related resources.

The supply and demand side can be seen to be linked by flows of resources such as capital, labour, goods and tourist expenditures into the destination, and flows of marketing, promotion, tourist artifacts and experiences from the destination back into the tourist-generating regions.

In addition, some tourist expenditures may leak back into the visitor-generating areas through repatriation of profits to foreign tourism investors and payment for imported goods and services provided to tourists at the destination. Transportation provides an important linkage both to and from the destination.

For planning purposes, the major components that comprise the supply side are:

- Various modes of transportation and other tourism-related infrastructure.
- Tourist information.
- Marketing and promotion provided.
- The community or communities within the visitor destination area.
- The political and institutional frameworks for enabling tourism.

The dynamic nature of tourism systems makes it critical to scan the external and internal environments of the destination on a regular basis and to be prepared to make changes necessary to ensure a healthy and viable tourism industry. The tourism system is dynamic and complex due to many factors and sectors linked to the provision of the tourist experience and the generation of tourism revenues and markets. A large number of stakeholders are involved in this system. There is growing recognition that the interdependence of these stakeholders is essential for sustainable pro poor tourism.

Tourism development can no longer work in isolation from the environment and local communities or avoid the social and cultural consequences resulting therefrom.

The Impacts of Tourism

Establishing or developing a tourism industry has both benefits and costs. If these impacts are understood from the outset, planning, strengths and opportunities can be maximized while weaknesses and threats can be minimized.

A list of potential costs and benefits is presented below:

- Each destination will be different in terms of tourism characteristics.
- The costs and benefits of tourism will vary in each destination and can change over time, depending on tourism and other activities in a destination's local and regional context.

Economic Impacts of Tourism

- Tourism generates local employment, directly in the tourism sector and in support of resource management sectors.Tourism stimulates profitable domestic industries, hotels and other lodging facilities, restaurants and food services, transportation, systems, handicrafts and guide services.
- Tourism generates foreign exchange for the country and injects capital and new money into the local economy.
- It helps to diversify the local economy.
- It leads to improved road systems and infrastructure .

Econometric approach plays a very important role in tourism demand studies, which is able to interpret the causes of variations of tourism demand, support policy evaluation and strategy making, and predict future trends in tourism development. Compared to the studies between the 1960s and 1980s, more advanced econometric techniques, such as the Cointegration, Error Correction Model (ECM), Vector Autoregressive (VAR) Approach, Time Varying Parameter Model (TVP), and Almost Ideal Demand Systems (AIDS), have been applied to tourism demand studies in the 1990s and early 2000s.

These methods contribute to improvements in the understanding of international tourism demand. In particular, the CI/ECM approaches identify the differences between the long-run and short-run demand elasticities, and the TVP model demonstrates the evolution of elasticities over time. The performance of alternative models is situation-specific, and many factors may influence their forecasting accuracy.

In general, the TVP model and the STSM perform relatively well, especially for short-run forecasting. Where advanced econometric models compete with their univariate time-series counterparts or the conventional benchmark no-change model, the econometric models tend to outperform the others, especially as far as annual data are concerned.

Fundamentals of Tourism

Tourism subject serves to identify the visitor as a person who satisfies their needs during the travel and stay outside their residence by consuming tourism goods. In practical life, many times, visitor is also called as a tourist or excursionist. Tourism enjoys a love-hate relationship with its host community since it is both a much sought after and much reviled activity. On one hand, it has been identified as an economic saviour, generating employment, income and tax revenue and acting as a catalyst for regional development. On the other hand, it has been described as a pariah that destroys host societies and cultures and cuts a swath of environmental destruction. But tourism, or more precisely the process of tourism development, is a much misunderstood activity.

Some schools of thought consider tourism as an industrial activity since tourism consumes resources, creates waste and has specific infrastructure needs. While looking at this point critically, we must take certain characteristics of the tourist as a consumer of resources. Tourism, as a resource dependent industry, must compete for scarce resources to ensure its survival. Tourism, by and large, is a private sector dominated industry, with investment decisions being based predominantly on profit maximisation. Tourism is a multi-faceted industry, and as such, it is almost impossible to control activities associated with it. Tourists are consumers, not anthropologists. Tourism is an entertainment.

Unlike other industrial activities, tourism generates income by importing clients rather than exporting its product. The recognition and understanding of these 'fundamental truths' can play key role in developing future sustainable tourism policies. As a minimum, acknowledging their existence will offer valuable insights into understanding the causes and nature of most impacts. More importantly, by accepting their inevitability as a condition of tourism development, planners, policy makers and industry leaders can begin to develop effective policies and programmes to minimise impacts. Moreover, an awareness and understanding of these 'fundamental truths' can play a critical role in reducing community animosity to tourism.

Factors such as cultural distance and environmental malleability will influence the level to which some 'truths' affect impacts. In a similar fashion, it may be possible to harden host communities and environments to make them more resistant to adverse impacts. It may be observed that strong similarities between mass tourism and other heavy industries exist especially in respect to the search for economies of scale and in the necessity of transforming backward societies into modern industrial ones.

Tourism is essentially dependent on three discrete types of natural resources with land, air and water as one type, and man made resources including the built up heritage and cultural resources being the other two. The developments located in areas with unique and fragile ecosystems can cause a permanent restructuring of environments, often effectively destroying the original ecosystem. In addition, the construction of roads and the provision of electricity can increase the environmental impacts of tourist developments far behind the development site.

The most common tourist activities viz., shopping, sightseeing and souveniring, can be the most invasive, especially when the perception exists that they are imposed on host communities. Added to this is the historic lack of willingness of the industry to assume responsibility for the activities of tourists themselves. Moreover, tourism produces waste products that are more typical than the type of waste produced by urban communities, which are normally associated with traditional industrial activity. Sewage, garbage and automobile exhaust are among its most common and most problematic by-products. Tourist destinations are under stress. Research exhibits a wide range of social, cultural and environmental impacts that can result from the over use of the resource base.

The working group for ecologically sustainable tourism in India has made various recommendations for the preservation and enhancement of the social and cultural integrity of tourism communities, including their environmental protection. Tourism, as a resource-dependent industry must compete for scarce resources to ensure its survival. Tourism is a fiercely resource competitive activity. To survive, it needs to gain supremacy over its competitors. Unfortunately, all too often, tourism's demands are in direct competition with the wants and desires of residents of host communities.

One should not forget that tourism is a private sector dominated industry, with investment decisions based predominantly on profit maximization. While tourism may be influenced by government, it is essentially a private sector driven industry. As such, development decisions will be based on the ability of the enterprise to function at a profitable level. At the same time, although government plays a significant role in the promotion, development and marketing of the tourism product, it plays an inadequate role in policing these developments to ensure they operate in an ecologically appropriate manner.

The quest for profit maximization spurs investment in profit-incurring centres like swimming pools instead of cost-prone centres like sewage systems. The very nature of the tourism industry makes voluntary compliance with environmental protection programmes virtually impossible. Wide variations in the type and application of environmental protection legislation across state and national boundaries often act as a disincentive for industry to act in a more environmentally sound manner.

It is a widely accepted fact that tourism is a multi-faceted industry. In India, tourism is a state subject. As such, the central government does not have much control on the implementation of the government policies. Thus, due to the fragmented nature of tourism, uncoordinated and ineffective government controls, it is almost impossible to control this sector. Under the circumstances, the industry can not be effectively controlled as far as the action of the tourists are concerned. As a result, the only real regulatory role that trade associations can play is one of policy provider. The problem is exacerbated by the fragmented nature of government involvement in control over tourism activities.

Tourism is a source of entertainment. Tourism, especially many forms of 'cultural' and 'environmental' tourism, is entertainment, striving to satisfy tourists' needs, wants and demands. To be successful and, therefore, commercially viable, the tourism product must be manipulated and packaged in such a way that it can easily be consumed by the public.

Tourists are consumers, not anthropologists. It is a mistake to assume that most tourists are anything more than consumers, whose primary goal is to have merely tourism experience.

To satisfy the tight schedules of tour operators and sightseeing coaches, the product must often be modified to provide regular show times and a guaranteed experience.While these forms of pseudo events have been assailed by some members of the sociological fraternity, they remain a necessary, if somewhat distasteful, requisite for efficient tourism operations.

Learning opportunities can be created from the tourism experiences provided. But, in spite of protestations, the primary role of tourist attractions is to entertain. Even large museums and art galleries that are ostensibly developed to provide educational and cultural enlightenment opportunities have recognized that they are in the entertainment business and have arranged their displays accordingly.

Conclusion

Tourism has been accused of leading to the bastardisation of local cultures through the comodification of traditional cultural activities. This assertion is unfair. Entertainment provided for the enjoyment of the tourism industry must not be confused with the preservation and continuation of traditional cultural activities.

Tourism is an industrial activity that exerts a series of impacts that are similar to most other industrial activities. It often consumes of scarce resources, produces waste by-products and requires specific infrastructure and superstructure needs to support it. As a huge, broadly based, diverse industry, that lacks clear market leaders and a clear legislative focus, tourism defies attempts to control its impact. However, for sustainable tourism to occur, it must be closely integrated with all other activities that occur in the host region.

Since tourism represents the system, there are links not only between its sub-systems (subject and object) and its components, but also between tourism and other systems, that create external environment. Tourism is influenced by economic, social, cultural, technical-technological, political, legislative and ecological environment.

Tourism destination can be a tourist resort, tourist region or country as a target of tourists. Tourism destination has to possess suitable natural and cultural potential for tourism development. This potential is an incentive to travel and stay for the visitors. Tourism potential is not equally located and according to its singleness it can be of local, regional, national or international importance.

Tourism businesses are organisational units, that create set of establishments (e.g. transport, accommodation, catering, sport-recreational, wellness, travel agencies) that offer products to satisfy the needs of visitors.

Tourism institutions take care of synchronisation of tourism offer with tourism demand in tourism destination. This function is carried by public sector bodies at local and regional level. They serve organisational and co-ordination functions in tourism. Often, institutions based on public and private partnership are also active.

In everyday practice, we experience different forms and types of tourism. If we take as a base motivation of visitors, that means purpose for which the tourists travel and stay temporarily in foreign place, than we are speaking about the sorts of tourism. If we take as a base for consideration of different reasons, that influence tourism and implications that tourism brings, than we are speaking about the different forms of tourism.

Among the elementary sorts of tourism we can name recreational, sport/adventurous, cultural, balneal/health and business tourism. Sorts of tourism are in practical life variously combined and complemented at the same time; with one sort as dominant e.g. recreational tourism is most of the times combined with sport and cultural tourism; balneal tourism is most of the times combined with cultural and health tourism, and business tourism is combined with cultural tourism, and so forth.

UNIT – I

CONCEPTUAL FRAMEWORK OF TOURISM

1

Conceptual Framework and History of Tourism

Tourism is concerned with the nature of professionalism within the field. Universities, colleges, and technical schools throughout the world have become aware of the increasing importance of the industry and are seeking to provide programs to train and educate prospective professionals in the field of tourism.

A wholesome tourism carries the feautures as: "Tourism that takes full account of its current and future economic, social and environmental impacts, addressing the needs of visitors, the industry, and the environment and host communities".

Tourism scholars believe that local perception has been an important subject of research involving tourism industry, despite the fact that there is a great deal of article–writing and studies on local perception of tourism development. The question is how we can balance preserving the tradition and making the necessary adjustment to provide the needs of the place as a tourist destination without exploiting the local community and distracting their life.

Researchers have identified tourism as one of the biggest and fastest growing industry around the world. In addition, there are great deals of discourses on cultural tourism which is an extremely important component of the industry. Currently, most experts in the field of tourism are concerned with the impact of uncontroled and unorganized development of tourism. Tourism scholars believe that local perception has been an important subject of research involving tourism industry.

Accordingly, the environmental, economic, and socio-cultural aspects of tourism development are the most important dimensions of sustainable development. Moreover, an acceptable balance between these three conditions is essential to guarantee long-term sustainability.

While tourism has attracted much critique and discussion, much less attention has been paid to these practical problems, the mundane "what and how" of how tourists arrange and what they do. Although the visit to 'exotic' places, and the effects on those places by tourists have been a fertile area for research, in the literature it is difficult to find answers to straightforward questions such as: How do tourists find out about what to visit? How do they travel between different places within an area? How do they decide what to do?

It should be given priorty along with an ethnographic study that attempts to take these problems seriously. The focus should be on the 'work' of tourism, the organization and arrangement of the experiences by tourists and the resources they use. Using an ethnomethodological approach, we explore the different ways in which tourists collaboratively find solutions to their problems.

In an article Barry Brown writes, "Recent research has attempted a more sympathetic and detailed engagement with the bodily practices, feelings and thoughts of tourists themselves. In a similar way this paper attempts to engage directly with these mundane practices of tourism. It explores the 'work' involved in tourism, not in terms of paid employment whereby tourists are seldom paid for their visits – although sometimes they are in the form of the organized purposeful activities which are part of visiting. There is much 'work' in tourism, in the sense of organization, management, planning and directing. Looking at the 'work' of tourism also explores MacCannell observation that tourism can be *hard work*."

He further says, "In visiting a city, tourists' problems are that they need to decide what to do and how to do it. The solutions tourists develop are varied – here I explore four of them: sharing the problem with others, putting guidebooks in their place, moving with maps and pre- and post- visiting. Each of these solutions describes a different way in which tourists can apply the available resources to arrange their visit. These descriptions present a view of tourists as active producers of their holidays, while constrained by the services provided – yet still holiday *makers*."

Apart from this, the environmental, economic, and socio-cultural aspects of tourism development are the most important dimensions of sustainable development. Moreover, an acceptable balance between these three conditions is essential to guarantee long-term sustainability. Accordingly, the environmental, economic, and socio-cultural aspects of tourism development are the most important dimension of sustainable development. Moreover, an acceptable balance between these three conditions is essential to guarantee long-term sustainability.

Furthermore, they help to maintain, keep and store cultural traditions and values of societies. We can observe the growing importance of stakeholders and local communities in heritage management and planning. In addition, involvement of all stakeholders in planning and decision making it fundamental to preserving and conservation of cultural resources.

The balance between conservation and the use of heritage sites is essential for the latter because tourism is one of the core income-generating activities. Therefore, increasing tourism activities may result in vital issues for heritage conservation.

So the focus is on how do we balance between preserving the tradition and making necessary adjustments to provide the needs of the place as a tourist destination without exploiting the local communities and distracting their life.

TOURISM THROUGH THE AGES

The desire to know and see the unseen regions of the world is as old as human civilization. Travelers, voyagers, expeditionists, pilgrims, preachers, all could be in a way considered as precursors of modern tourists. Tourism is widely accepted as a term to describe a kind of travel which has two chief characteristics: that the travelers concerned mean to return home after a comparatively short time, and that the money they spend abroad is money derived from home, not money earned in the places visited.

Wealthy people have always traveled to distant parts of the world to see great buildings or other works of art, to learn new languages, to experience new cultures, or to taste new cuisines. The ancient Greek philosophers thought that leisure was a necessary component of human flourishing even though freedom from the demands of necessity was possible only for a few people.

Apart from satisfying the urge to see new places and witness various types of social and cultural activities going on in different parts of the world, the modern day stressed, industrial, and materialistic society forces the man to evolve ways and means to escape from the humdrum of modern life. Hence, tourism.

Moreover, the tremendous development of means of transport and communication has made the world much smaller, making it easier to move from one part of the world to the other in a very short time.

A tourist, through the ages, would normally travel from one place to another for three basic reasons namely, ***tirthatana***—going out to the places of religious merit or pilgrimage; ***paryatana*** – going out for pleasure and knowledge; and ***deshatana*** – going out of the country primarily for economic gains.

From historical perspective, the term 'tourism' is believed to have originated in the beginning of the nineteenth century, but this should in no way be taken as to disguise the fact that what the concept 'tourism' connotes today has, indeed been occurring much earlier.

Tourism as a word appeared in 1811 and was associated for "mobility" for recreation. Burton and Noad have opined that recreation is not easily defined homogenous entity. It includes all the pursuits other than those associated with the work necessary, which are of personal and social nature. The essence of recreation is free choice. It embraces wide range of diverse pursuits. The recreation is not always dominant motive for conditioning the travel and therefore, "tourism" is to be associated with all the motivators of travel.

The main elements in the process of tourism are man, space and time. In the modern literature available on tourism management, Seeking J. especially touches on 'widespread confusion (even within travel industry) over the meaning of the word 'tourist'. In contrast to the precise definitions used in government and international organizations (such as the ones by the WTO), Samuel Pegge for the first time reported the use of 'tourist' as a new expression.

The concept 'tourism' connotes today has, indeed been occurring much earlier for traveler in 1800 and later the same was brought in by the England's sporting magazine in 1811. Drawing on the studies of Neil Leiper (1979-90), it becomes evident that the terms 'tourist' and 'tourism' did not exist before sixteenth century. Nevertheless, the word 'tour' was in use in the French context of tower. It is further backed up by the fact that one does find the expressions like 'journeying', 'travel' and its original form along with the terms denoting particular forms of travel such as 'pilgrimage' in the travel literature of the medieval era. Leiper comes out with hypothesis, called the 'de la tour' hypothesis respecting the etymology of tourism that the world tourism was evolved from a family name, from an unsigned article in 'International Tourism History'.

The essay reveals that the Duke of Burgundy signed a business treaty with England in 1516 which led to an unforeseen increase in the number of the English traveling across the channel. The Duke favoured a family named 'de la tour' by granting it a monopoly in the lucrative venture relating to effecting provision for travel and accommodation as representative of the visiting English.

Shortly, the English travelers were found giving voice to 'taking a tour' which over time turned into 'tourist' and 'tourism'. It is also believed that the word 'tour' in the context of tourism became established in the English language by the 18th century. On the other hand, according to the Oxford English Dictionary, the word 'tourism' first came to light in English in the early 19th century (1811) from a Greek word 'tornus' meaning a round shaped tool.

However, if the de la tour hypothesis is true, it suggests that the pre-arranged packaged tours did exist even in those days. According to Burkart and Medlik, travel implies "journeys undertaken from one place to another for any purpose including journeys to work and as a part of employment, as part of leisure and to take up residence. All tourism includes some travel but not all travel is tourism". Ritchie, Brent and Goeldner in their title 'Travel, Tourism and Hospitality Research' highlight that "It is common practice to use the words 'travel' and 'tourism' either singly or in combination to describe three types of concepts:

(a) the movement of people;

(b) a sector of economy or an industry; and

(c) a broad system of interacting relationship of people, their needs to travel outside their communities, and services which attempt to respond to their needs".

The purpose of travelling could also include business, study, and exploration, looting/pirating, or, as was the case with the earliest man, to gather food. However, it is basically the motivation which creates an activity force, an urge, force from within that builds pressure within the man, and the desire for leisure and pleasure which a makes a person to travel. Moreover, travel is a very popular concept and is applicable to persons in all walks of life.

The terms *tourist* and *tourism* were first used as official terms in 1937 by the League of Nations.

The history of tourism can perhaps be said to originate with the pilgrimage. In India, Hindus were expected to visit sacred sites, including some now in Pakistan, Bangladesh, and Nepal. There are also Buddhist, Sikh, and Muslim sites in the same region; for all Muslims the international pilgrimage to Mecca (the *hajj*) is a lifetime goal. The history of European tourism can also perhaps be said to originate with the medieval pilgrimage.

Although undertaken primarily for religious reasons, the

pilgrims quite clearly saw the experience as a kind of holiday (the term itself being derived from the 'holy day' and its associated leisure activities). Pilgrimages created a variety of tourist aspects that still exist – bringing back souvenirs, obtaining credit with foreign banks – in medieval times, utilizing international networks established by Jews, and making use of space available on existing forms of transport. Pilgrimages are still important in modern tourism.

Historical Relevance

Tourism being an age-old phenomenon, one finds references of tourism and of the efforts made by the rulers of different countries to provide facilities for travel and tourism from the history and books written during the ancient period.

There are references to this effect in the ***Ramayana, Mahabharta, Puranas*** etc. Similarly, the history of ancient India, ancient Rome, Mesopotamia etc. are witness to the efforts made by the rulers to promote tourism in their respective countries.To cite a few examples, Emperor Shulgy Babylonia is known to have made roads and rest houses for travelers that gave rise to tourism in that country.

The work done by Emperor Ashoka in the field of construction of roads, rest houses, wells, hospitals and the provision of shady and fruit trees is already well known. He did it to remove the difficulties faced by the people travelling from one place to another. The facilities continued to exist even during the later periods.

The cultural relations between India and China can be traced back to very early times.

There are numerous references to China in Sanskrit texts, but their chronology is sketchy. The ***Mahabharata*** refers to China several times, including a reference to presents brought by the Chinese at the *Rajasuya Yajna* of the Pandavas; also, the ***Arthasastra*** and the ***Manusmriti*** mention China. According to Terence Duke, martial arts went from India to China. Fighting without weapons was a specialty of the ancient *Kshatriya* warriors of India. Both

Arnold Toynbee and Sir L. Wooley speak of a readymade culture coming to China. That was the Vedic culture of India.

Incredible India is one of the very few countries that offer different categories and kinds of tourism. A little bit of history, a dash of medical, a pinch of adventure and a lot of soul– the Indian tourism *thali* offers it all. Thus the tourist visiting India has a variety of choices among spiritual tourism, historical tourism, medical tourism, adventure tourism, etc. ***Atithi Deva Bhava***, a saying in Sanskrit that loosely translated means that 'guest is like God', has been part of the Indian culture since long. This saying has been used in advertising campaigns by the Tourism Ministry aiming at creating awareness about India's culture of extending warmth and hospitality to outsiders.

The old **Roman Empire** has the credit of making first known pleasure travel. Relay horse system was introduced. 'Spas', i.e., hot water springs dotted the whole of Italy. They had very good roads to popularize and smoothen travel. One can also not forget the introduction of Olympic Games (originally from the 8th century BC to the 5th century A.D.). However, with the fall of the Roman Empire in the 5th century A.D., there was decline in tour and travel. It was followed by, what is known in history, the Dark Ages when travel had become unsafe, though it was more so in case of the erstwhile Roman Empire than in the case of other countries, especially India.

Nature of Tourism

The tourist attractions provided by the Roman Empire did attract common masses. The travel in India remained, by and large, confined to pilgrimage or trade or to some extent for educational and religious purposes. There was a regular travel and trade between India and the south-east Asian countries and Europe, and also between Arab countries and India, especially the Malabar Coast. It had also resulted in large migrations making travelling a more common feature. Chinese traveller Fa-hien, the first Chinese pilgrim to India, stayed here during the Gupta period for some years. Che-mong, another monk accompanied by a few others spent 20 years (404-424 A.D.) in the pilgrimage of India. The visits of Hieun Tsang and I-Tsing during the 7th century are well-known. No doubt, they travelled to India for their own limited purpose.

13th to 15th Century

The period from first half of thirteenth century to the end of the fifteenth century is known in the history as an era of great travellers. The most important travellers of this period included Marco Polo, Kublai Khan, Ibn Battuta, Christopher Columbus, Vasco da Gama, etc. As a corollary to this era, travelling, though mainly religious one, got slightly pushed upwards. A number of Christian missionaries started travelling to different parts of the world for the spread of Christianity.

The Bhakti movement in India also gave a further boost to inland travelling. Fabulous wealth and scope of spreading a particular religion amongst a large population and area provided attraction to many tourists to travel in India and China.

Upto 18th Century

Italy, which remained the centre of European art, architecture and literature from the late Middle Ages to the 18th century, attracted many travellers. The Grand Tours – which meant travel to Italy, were undertaken especially during the 17-18th centuries. The tours were primarily for the learning of art, literature and architecture and to exchange ideas on the subjects.

During this period, it became fashionable in England to undertake a Grand Tour. The sons of the nobility and gentry were sent upon an extended tour of Europe as an educational experience. The eighteenth century was the golden age of the Grand Tour, and many of the fashionable visitors were painted at Rome by Pompeo Batoni. A modern equivalent of the Grand Tour is the phenomenon of the backpacker.

Health tourism has always existed, but it was not until the eighteenth century that it became important. In England, it was associated with spas, places with supposedly health-giving mineral waters, treating diseases from gout to liver disorders and bronchitis.

The most popular resorts were Bath, Cheltenham, Buxton, Harrogate, and Tunbridge Wells. Visits to take 'the waters' also allowed the visitors to attend balls and other entertainments. Spas attracted many fashionable travellers by the nineteenth century.

It could be argued that Britain was the home of the seaside holiday. In travelling to the coast, the population was following in the steps of Royalty. King George III made regular visits to Weymouth when in poor health. At the time, a number of doctors argued the benefits of bathing in sea water, and sea bathing as a widespread practice was popularised by the Prince Regent (later George IV), who frequented Brighton for this purpose.

The concept of tourism upto the end of the 18th century was very limited and for a specific purpose. As such, tourism could not get a big boost during this period. Even though people had money, most of the factors that could encourage them to go for tourism were missing. There was lack of motivation and desire for leisure and pleasure or perhaps a big majority could not afford this luxury. Following are the reasons which acted as constraint to tourism in those days:

- A large number of people belonging to middle income group, upto the end of the 18th century, neither had sufficient time nor money for undertaking tourism.
- People lacked adequate information about geography, accommodation, travel, flora and fauna, types of people, language etc. – the most important pre-requisites for tourism.
- The transport system was very slow and the journey not very safe.
- People, by nature, were not very much mobile nor did they have the desire to move.
- Movement from one place to another required extensive preparations, and necessity of carrying heavy luggage made travel very cumbersome.
- Wars during those days were very common.
- Due to the lack of technological advancement, not only the work was slow, but also mental and physical fatigue was at the utmost level.
- People could hardly afford to have luxury of tourism nor could they have or give paid holidays.

- Women during this period were, by and large, not part of the work force or bread earners.
- The men folk would find solace at home and ladies did not have the urge or convenience to move out.
- The amenities at home were very limited and the housewives had not much time to spare.
- The average family used to be a large one and the large families were considered to be an aspect of entertainment unto them.
- The social philosophy believed in the concept of saving as a virtue.
- The enjoyment and relaxation for self, wife, and children were never accepted virtues during those periods and people would never borrow for self-enjoyment.
- The concept of next life would always burden their minds.
- There was not much of urbanization; as such, the life was not a fast moving one.
- The facilities like insurance, travel agents etc. were absolutely absent.

Leisure travel was associated with the industrialisation of United Kingdom – the first European country to promote leisure time to the increasing industrial population. Initially, this applied to the owners of the machinery of production, the economic oligarchy, the factory owners, and the traders. These comprised the new middle class. Cox & Kings were the first official travel company to be formed in 1758. Later, the working class could take advantage of leisure time.

19th and 20th Century

The nineteenth and the twentieth centuries have witnessed a complete change in the concept of tourism. Tourism has slowly emerged to be an industry. Nations are competing with each other in trying to provide more and more facilities and attractions to make tourism an attractive and profit-making industry. Hardly a day passes when one does not hear of something new at national or international level relating to tourism. A number of factors, facilities, changes in the social and economic scenario and efforts made by different nations, independently or in collaboration with one another, have contributed in major way in giving a new and modern concept to tourism.

The **industrial revolution** has proved to be one of the most important causes in not only giving a modern concept to tourism but also contributed to its development as well. The industrial revolution caused monotony in one's life that made tourism popular.

Thomas Cook was the founder of World Wide travel agency Thomas Cook and son. In 1841, a temperance meeting was to be held in Loughborough and Cook arranged for the Midland Railway to run an excursion train from Leicester and back, charging passengers a shilling for the return journey. This was to be the first ever public excursion train journey in England. From this he began to arrange excursions for pleasure, taking a percentage of the railway tickets. In 1844, the Midland Counties Railway Company agreed to make a permanent arrangement with him provided he mustered the passengers. He was working from London by this time. In 1856, he introduced a railway tour of Europe and in the early 1860s, he began the travel firm of Thomas Cook and son, which now included tours of USA. His firm undertook military transport and postal services for England and Egypt during the 1880s.

Winter sports were largely invented by the British leisured classes, initially at the Swiss village of Zermatt (Valais), and St Moritz in 1864. The first packaged winter sports holidays took place in 1902 at Adelboden, Switzerland. Winter sports were a natural answer for a leisured class looking for amusement during the coldest season. At first, the annual holidays and paid holidays was the other factor that made it easier to travel.

'Holiday with Pay Act 1938' passed by the English government was the first such move which made travel easier and comparatively affordable.

Now almost half of the population in Europe, 30% in America and small portion of population in Asia and other regions get paid holidays. New destinations for and forms of tourism are being marketed. Different nations have started paying serious attention towards the infrastructural developments in order to provide tremendous boost to tourism.

In India, tourism of modern form is comparatively a recent concept. During the Raj, the period of British rule over the Indian subcontinent, nontraditional appreciation for historical, cultural and natural sites of India was encouraged by institutions such as the Archaeological Survey and the Monuments Commission, and by the development of transportation in the country.

The British not only visited historical sites such as the Taj Mahal; they established seasonal resorts in cool mountainous areas such as Simla, Darjeeling, and Pune (Poona). These resorts also attracted wealthy Indians and are still favored destinations. Some of steps taken towards promotion of tourism and its evolution since the British times are mentioned below.

- The Sargent Committee on Education was the first move which diverted the attention of the government to the promotion of tourism. Its recommendations included sales promotion, publications, guides, liaison with other countries and UNO, hotels, collection of tourist statistics, etc.
- In 1949, Tourist Traffic Branch was started in the Ministry of Transport.
- In 1955-56, this Branch witnessed the expansion of its working in the whole of India.
- The work was divided into different sub branches, *viz.* (i) *Tourist Traffic Section* – to make out plan, deal with travel agencies, UNO and Tourist Spots; (ii) *Tourist Administration Section*, and regional offices established in various states; (iii) *Tourist Publicity Section* – for printing of pamphlets and organizing exhibitions etc.; and (iv) *Distribution Section* – for the distribution of literature.
- Tourist Information Centres were established in several countries/places like New York, Los Angeles, London, Paris, Frankfurt, Melbourne, Perth, etc.
- On 1st March 1958, Ministry of Tourism (within the Ministry of Transport) was established.
- ITDC was established in 1963 in which were amalgamated the Hotel Corporation of India, Indian Tourism Corporation, and India Travel Undertaking.
- Establishment of separate Ministry on 14th. March 1967 provided tourism a competitive look.

- This resulted into management of aerodromes, youth hostels, safety of aircrafts, carrying of passengers by air, compilation of tourist data, various regulations, setting up of several advisory bodies like wild life, Director General Civil Aviation and so on.
- In recent times, public-private partnership actively promoted tourism and gave tourism a new appearance of profit-making industry status.
- A number of national and international tourism organizations have also been influencing the scope and concept of tourism for the past nearly half a century.

In brief, one can discuss a number of reasons or motivations that have accounted for a massive growth of tourism. These are:

- The vacations; desire for 4 "S" – Sun, Sand, Scene and Sex; business meetings; health; adventure; sports; study; and special desire are some of such reasons.
- A large middle income group which is having money and time has targeted tourism. They have money or have the sources of getting money (like LTC).
- Earlier governments would spend much more for providing facilities for the foreign tourists in the form of Five Star Hotels, etc. Now, the stress is on the middle income groups or budget tourism and creation of accommodations like Yatri Niwas, etc.
- Pacific Asia Travel Association (PATA), Asia Business Forum emphasized the need to adopt new strategies to cater middle class traveller to take advantage of the travel boom.
- In the recent past, the neo-rich class has emerged in the upper level of middle income group. They have lot of money and would like to travel and ape the higher income groups.
- The information technology has advanced tremendously. The computer provides the information not only about the place but also facilities on the way, the time taken, tourist attractions, whether one gets guide or not, and hotel accommodation, etc.
- The transport system is fast progressing. Airtaxi operation, private airlines, coast travel and many other transport facilities are being used for travel.
- Due to technological advancements, mental and physical fatigue has decreased. Now there are many and different types of holidays leading to availability of lot of leisure time and there is a tendency to increase it further.

- Life standards have changed to a great extent. Travel is now least cumbersome and one can move without extensive preparations in the shape of heavy luggage.
- Due to an increase in women work force, the concept of tourism has further changed. With both husband and wife working, they have more urge to move out.
- With small family being the norm, a child especially the girl child is becoming a big motive force for tourism.
- A drastic increase in the amenities at home has provided a lot of time for the families and things have become easy.
- Accumulation of wealth no more provides merry making. Now spending is a virtual materialism i.e. enjoy now and today – enjoy to the fullest possible extent. The new concept 'borrow and never pay' and 'search for happiness' have become an accepted norm.
- Urbanization and facilities have become an accepted norm like banking, credit cards, insurance, travel agents, service industry and tele-communication service, etc. are other developments which have made tourism a sunrise industry.

Recent developments in tourism: There has been an upmarket trend in tourism over the last few decades, especially in Europe where international travel for short breaks is common. Tourists have higher levels of disposable income and greater leisure time and they are also better-educated and have more sophisticated tastes. There is now a demand for a better quality product in many quarters. This has resulted in the following trends:

- The old 'sun, sea, and sand' mass market has fragmented. People want more specialised versions of it, such as 'Club 18 -30', quieter resorts with select hotels, self-catering, etc.
- People are taking second holidays in the form of short breaks/city breaks, ranging from British and European cities to country hotels.
- There has been a growth in niche markets catering for special interests or activities.

The developments in technology and transport infrastructure (particularly the advent of jumbo jets) and low-budget airlines have placed some types of holiday in the affordable mainstream.This has facilited:

- The development of a mass cruise holiday market.
- The advent of affordable holidays to long-haul destinations such as Thailand or Kenya.
- The phenomenon of the low budget airlines, utilising a new generation of small regional airports.

This has been made easier by internet purchasing of tourism products. Some sites have now started to offer dynamic packages, in which an inclusive price is quoted for a tailor-made package requested by the customer upon impulse. There have been a few setbacks in tourism, such as the September 11, 2001 attacks and terrorist threats to tourist destinations such as Bali and European cities. Some of the tourist destinations, including the beach resorts of the Costa del Sol, the Baleares and Cancún have lost popularity due to shifting tastes. In this context, the excessive building and environmental destruction often associated with traditional "sun and beach" tourism may contribute to a destination's saturation and subsequent decline. Spain's Costa Brava, a popular 1960s and 1970s beach location is now facing a crisis in its tourist industry. With only 11 per cent of the Costa Brava now unblemished by low-quality development (Greenpeace Spain's figure), the destination now faces a crisis in its tourist industry.

The terms tourism and travel are sometimes used interchangeably. In this context travel has a similar definition to tourism, but implies a more purposeful journey. The terms tourism and tourist are sometimes used pejoratively, to imply a shallow interest in the cultures or locations visited by tourists. Sustainable tourism is becoming more popular as people start to realize the devastating effects that poorly planned tourism can have on communities. Receptive tourism is now growing at a very rapid rate in many developing countries, where it is often the most important economic activity in local GDP.

In recent years, second holidays or vacations have become more popular as people's discretionary income increases. Typical combinations are a package to the typical mass tourist resort, with a winter skiing holiday or weekend break to a city or national park.

This proposition is equally relevant to tourism involving the activities of humans travelling to and staying in places outside their usual habitat and environment for different motives and purposes– be it education, experiences, enrichment, or enjoyment.

Two universally accepted yardsticks have traditionally been used to measure the tourism index in any country or region: International Tourism Arrivals and International Tourism Receipts.

New tourism is a transition from the existing type to the tourism of the future. However, it is typified by flexibility, segmentation, more authentic tourism experiences, thrust towards diagonally integrated organizations, and management of the tourist industry. Today, there are clear and apparent manifestations that the tourist industry is beginning to take on a different configuration, a type of tourism based on a new commonsense. The emerging new best practice is the result of a number of factors. These factors include the diffusion of a system of new information technologies in the tourist industry, deregulation of the airline industry and financial service, the negative impact of mass tourism on host countries, the moving away from sun-lust tourists, environmental pressures. technology competition changing, consumer tastes, leisure time, work patterns and income distribution.

The economics of new tourism is quite different from the old, with system economies acting as determinant of profitability rather than the scale economies. In other words, system gains, segmented markets, designed and customized holidays are evolving into more and more significant criteria for profitability and competitiveness in tourism. Tourists, of their own, are shifting from 'tinsel and junk' (anything sham, showy and trash) to more 'natural services' with to high tech, high touch and greater care, concern for and conservation of the natural environment. There is, indeed, a shift towards ecotourism, green tourism, rural tourism, farm tourism, sustainable tourism, etc. with perpetual opportunities of benefit from this new tourism.

Conclusion

The new tourism has a number of profound implications for survival and competitiveness in tourism. There are new techniques and trends to be followed by the industry players. To gain competitive advantage, the actors of the industry will have to Put consumers first, Be leaders in quality, Develop radical innovation, and Strengthen the firm's strategic position within the industry's value chain. And for tourist destinations to be competitive, certain key principles need to be incorporated in the policy framework. Some of these are Put the environment first, Make tourism a lead sector, Strengthen the distribution channel in the market place, and Nurture a formidable private sector. An efficacious and successful implementation of these strategies will place tourist destinations firmly in the camp of new tourism – a tourism that is sensitive to the environment as well as inhabitants of the region or area; a tourism that is sustainable; a tourism that is capable of transforming tourism-dependent and vulnerable areas' economies into viable entities.

2

Tourism: The Dynamics of Definitions

Tourism, which generally in everyday conversation is used, interchangeably with Travel, is, in fact, a much broader term. In spite of the fact that Travel is an essential ingredient of Tourism, the latter concept encompasses much more within its meaning. In a significant sense, every traveler is a 'potential' tourist. Specifically, there has been a definitive transition from the 19th and early 20th century tourism as a indulgence in leisure and pleasure to tourism as a more or less particularly economic activity having a consumption, or demand aspect and a production, or supply aspect, especially during the last quarter of the twentieth century.

Tourism, a service-oriented industry, has emerged to be a revolutionizing phenomenon, especially in the second half of the twentieth century, outpacing the manufacturing and extractive industries as a catalyst of the development process at the national and at global levels. Tourism has come to be one of the world's largest growing industries with immense potential.

The whole concept of tourism has been transformed from the Mass, Rigid and Packaged tourism (MSRP) to the present neo-tourism, which is Flexible, Segmented and Diagonally Integrated (FSDI). Moreover, in the wake of enforcing economic liberalization and globalization, the development policies of no sector can be independent and/or operative in isolation, remain static and unrelated to the broad national perspectives. This proposition is equally relevant to tourism involving the activities of humans travelling to and staying in places outside their usual habitat and environment for different motives and purposes – be it education, experiences, enrichment, or enjoyment.

Tourism is travelling for predominantly recreational or leisure purposes or the provision of services to support this leisure travel. The World Tourism Organization defines tourists as people who "travel to and stay in places outside their usual environment for not more than one consecutive year for leisure, business and other purposes not related to the exercise of an activity remunerated from within the place visited"

Tourist: The term Tourist is believed to have been derived from the Latin word, "TORNUS' which means a tool, a circle or a turner's wheel. In the sense of the word of the origin, tourist is a person who undertakes a circular trip, i.e., ultimately comes back to the place from where he sets about his journey.

Tourism is the act of travel for the purpose of leisure, pleasure, relaxation, recreation and business, and the provision of services for this act.

Tourists are people who are "travelling to and staying in places outside their usual environment for not more than one consecutive year for leisure, business and other purposes not related to the exercise of an activity remunerated from within the place visited".

In a general way, **Tourism** can be defined as the temporary movement of people to destination(s) away from their usual or normal habitat, the activities entered upon during their stay in those destinations and the facilities developed to provide for their requirements/needs. The conceptual and operational meanings of Tourism have remained ambiguous and enigmatic.

Even a cursory survey of the extant literature on Tourism, both of the theoretical-analytical variety and of the applied-operational variety, would leave one wondering as to the precise and unique meaning being ascribed to Tourism.

There certainly is a need for evolving and adopting a precise definitive meaning to the term, which may be valid in all contexts. A more comprehensive definition would be that tourism is a service industry, comprising a number of **tangible** and **intangible** components.

The **tangible** elements include transport systems — air, rail, road, water and now, space; hospitality services – accommodation, foods and beverages, tours, souvenirs; and related services such as banking, insurance and safety and security. The **intangible** elements include: rest and relaxation, culture, escape, adventure, new and different experiences.

One of the earliest definitions of tourism was provided by the Austrian economist in 1910, who defined it as, "sum total of operators, mainly of an economic nature, which directly relate to the entry, stay and movement of foreigners inside and outside a certain country, city or a region."

Hunziker and Krapf, in 1941, defined tourism as "the sum of the phenomena and relationships arising from the travel and stay of non-residents, insofar as they do not lead to permanent residence and are not connected with any earning activity." In 1976, Tourism Society of England defined it as "Tourism is the temporary, short-term movement of people to destination outside the places where they normally live and work and their activities during the stay at each destination. It includes movements for all purposes." In 1981, International Association of Scientific Experts in Tourism defined Tourism in terms of particular activities selected by choice and undertaken outside the home environment.

In the second quarter of the twentieth century, 1937, League of Nations proposed a definition of the tourist as "one who travels for a period of 24 hours or more in a country other than that in which he usually resides". The major limitation of the definition is in terms of neglect of movement of people within the country/ area of origin i.e. domestic tourists.

The definition by Hunziker and Krapf was later accepted and adopted by the International Association of Scientific Experts in Tourism (AIEST). However, thereafter the International Union of Official Travel Organizations (IUOTO) broadened the concept through the inclusion of various forms of business and vocational travel.

Taking over the thread, the International Union of Official Tour Operators (IUOTO), now the World Tourism Organization (WTO) gave certain recommendations in this context in the United Nations Conference on International Travel and Tourism, held at Rome in 1963. In the conference, it was conceded to introduce the term 'visitor' to describe 'any person visiting a country other than that in which he has his usual place of residence, for any reason other than following an occupation, remunerated from within the country visited'.

This definition was held to include two genera of visitors: **Tourists**, categorized as temporary visitors staying at least 24 hours with a purpose classified as leisure (recreation, sport, holiday, health, study or religion), or business, family, mission or meeting; **Excursionists**, classified as temporary visitors staying less than 24 hours, including cruise travelers but excluding travelers in transit.

Institute of Tourism in Britain now christened as Tourism Society, tried to interpret the concept of tourism in 1979. Tourism is deemed to include any activity concerned with the temporary short-term movement of people to destinations outside the places where they normally live and work and their activities during the stay at these destination.

There is nothing particular to the UK about this definition. Five important points should be noted in relation to the definition:

- There is nothing in it that restricts the total market to overnight stays.
- It includes same day visits.
- There is nothing in it that restricts the total market to travel for leisure or pleasure, and
- It includes travel for business, social, religious, educational, sports and most other purposes provided that the destination of travel is outside the usual routines and place of residence or work.
- The definition excludes all routine commuter travel and purely local travel, such as to neighborhood shops, schools or hospitals.

The definition was further worked out while retaining its naivety at the International Conference on Leisure-Recreation-Tourism held in 1981.

According to the reformulated version, 'Tourism may be defined in terms of particular activities selected by choice and undertaken outside the home environment. It may or may not involve overnight stays away from home'.

In the definition without proper specification may entail involvement of certain undesirable and uncalled for activities such as burglary, eve-teasing, prostitution, and many others of the type. Moreover, there is no mention of the minimum distance travelled from the home base (origin) to term the traveller a tourist.

Mathieson and Wall have tried to define tourism, as 'the temporary movement to destinations outside the normal home and workplace, the activities undertaken during the stay and the facilities created to cater for the needs of tourists'.

The main elements of the definition are:

- The movement to destinations is of temporary nature and short-term in character.
- It is distinct from migration as the aim to all intents and purposes is to be back home within a short span of time – a few days, weeks or months.
- The purpose of the visit to the destinations can be any except seeking permanent residence or employment.

WTO organized yet another International Conference on Travel and Tourism Statistics at Ottawa, Canada in June, 1991. WTO endorsed the statement that tourism comprises the activities of persons travelling to and staying in places outside their usual environment for not more than one consecutive year for leisure, business and other purposes, (WTO 1992 - subject to ratification by the UN). In March 1993, the United Nations Statistical Commission adopted a set of administration on tourism statistics prepared by the World Tourism Organization (WTO).

Tourism is defined as comprising 'the activities of persons travelling to and staying in places outside their usual environment for not more than one consecutive year for leisure, business and other purposes'.

Melntosh and Goeldner in the process of defining tourism have identified four different perspectives of tourism:

(i) *The tourist* – The tourist/visitor looks for diverse psychic and physical experiences and satisfactions from the tourism activity. In addition, the nature of these experiences will mostly find out the destinations chosen and the activities experienced and enjoyed or participated in.

(ii) *The business catering tourist goods and services* – Business people behold tourism as an opening to make profit by furnishing goods and services demanded by the tourist market.

(iii) *The government of the host community or area* –The government looks on tourism as a capital and megabucks factor in the economy. Its outlook/attitude bears upon the income and employment generation capabilities of this business for its citizens apart from the foreign exchange earnings from international tourism and the public/ government revenue in the form of tax receipts from tourist expenditures, directly and/or indirectly.

(iv) *The host community* – Local residents most often consider tourism as a cultural and employment factor. It is primarily the effect of interaction between large numbers of international visitors as guests and the local residents as hosts which may be promising or unpromising, or both that is of significance and interest to this group.

In the twenty seventh session of the United Nations Statistical Commission held in February/March, 1993, the general agreement over the distance travelled from the usual place of environment was fixed around 80 km. Nevertheless, the issue of distance travelled one-way away from home is open to debate as it is variable ranging from 40-160 km in different countries and agreed upon by different organizations on different counts.

- Thus, tourism may be defined as the sum of the phenomena and relationships arising from the interaction of tourists, business suppliers, host governments and host communities in the process of attracting and hosting these tourists and other visitors.
- In a general way, tourism can be defined as the temporary movement of people to destination(s) away from their usual or normal habitat, the activities entered upon during their stay in those destinations and the facilities developed to provide for their requirements/needs.
- In the modern scenario, travel and tourism is the industry of moving, housing, feeding and entertaining people as they go from a place of their habitat to another for business and/or pleasure.

Five main characteristics of tourism may be identified from the definition:

(i) Tourism arises from a movement of people to, and their stay in various destinations..

(ii) There are two elements in all tourism: the journey to the destination and the stay including activities at the destination.

(iii) The journey and the stay take place outside the usual place of residence and work, so that tourism gives rise to activities, which are distinct from those of the resident and the working population of the places, through which the tourist travels and in which they stay.

(iv) The movement to destinations is of temporary, short-term character, with the intention of returning to the usual environment within a few days, weeks or months.

(v) Destinations are visited for purposes other than taking up permanent residence or employment remunerated from within the places visited.

Sometimes ***Tourism* and *Travel*** are used interchangeably. In this context travel has a similar definition to tourism, but implies a more purposeful journey. Tourism is travel for predominantly recreational or leisure purposes or the provision of services to support this leisure travel.

Tourism must be distinguished from other kinds of and motivations for travel.

Economic and political migration, for example, is not new, but its increased extent is considered a significant element of globalization.

Contemporary economic migration includes the journeys made by migrant laborers and travel for business purposes in a postindustrial age of transnational corporations and labour markets, prompted also by international disparities in wealth and movement, especially between less developed countries and Organization for Economic Cooperation and Development (OECD) countries. Political migration includes refugees from crisis or conflict areas. Tourism, in contrast, has no material imperative.

In brief, it can be stated that Tourism is:

- **Temporary,** to distinguish it from permanent travel of migrants, nomad and gypsies;
- **Voluntary,** to distinguish it from the forced travel of the exile and refugee;
- **Round up,** to distinguish it from one-way journey of the migrant;
- **Relatively long,** to distinguish it from the recurrent trips of the holiday house owner.

Tourism Classification

The United Nations classified three forms of tourism in 1994 in its Recommendations on Tourism Statistics: Domestic tourism, which involves residents of the given country travelling only within this country; Inbound tourism, involving non-residents travelling in the given country; and Outbound tourism, involving residents travelling in another country. The UN also derived different categories of tourism by combining the three basic forms of tourism:

- Internal tourism, which comprises domestic tourism and inbound tourism;
- National tourism, which comprises domestic tourism and outbound tourism; and
- International tourism, which consists of inbound tourism and outbound tourism.

As per WTO definition, Tourism may be classified into the following types:

- **Inbound international tourism:** Visits to a country by non-resident of that countr – for example, when an American citizen, Ms. Clinton comes to India to see the Qutub Minar, she is an inbound tourist for India.

  Inbound tourism is a term coined by the Korea Tourism Organization and widely accepted in Korea. Intrabound tourism differs from domestic tourism in that the former encompasses policy making and implementation of national tourism policies.
- **Outbound international tourism:** Visits by the residents of a country to another country, for example, when an Indian citizen goes to America to visit California is an outbound tourist for India.
- **Internal tourism:** Visits by residents of a country to their own.
- **Domestic tourism:** Inbound international tourism + internal tourism.

- **Interntational tourism:** It comprises of inbound tourism and outbound tourism.

Recently, the tourism industry has shifted from the promotion of inbound tourism to the promotion of intrabound tourism because many countries are experiencing tough competition for inbound tourists. Some national policymakers have shifted their priority to the promotion of intrabound tourism to contribute to the local economy. Examples of such campaigns include "See America" in the United States, "Get Going Canada" in Canada, and "Guseok Guseok" (corner to corner) in South Korea.

Before people are able to experience tourism, they usually need disposable income (i.e. money to spend on non-essentials); time off from work or other responsibilities; leisure time tourism infrastructure, such as transport and accommodation; and legal clearance to travel.

Individually, sufficient health is also a condition, and of course the inclination to travel. Furthermore, in some countries there are legal restrictions on travelling, especially abroad. Certain states with strong governmental control over the lives of citizens (notably established Communist states) may restrict foreign travel only to trustworthy citizens. The United States prohibits its citizens from travelling to some countries, for example Cuba.

The principal character in the phenomenon called Tourism, is the'Tourist', and without his being around, the tourism phenomenon is meaningless. The WTO in a conference held in 1963 introduced the term 'Visitor'. A Visitor is defined as 'Any person visiting a country other than that in which he has his usual place of residence for any reason other than being interested in an occupation remunerated from within the country visited.

The term includes two types of visitors:

- Tourist is a temporary visitor staying for a period of at least 24 hours in the country visited and the purpose of his/her journey can be classified under one of the following heads :

  * Leisure (recreation, holiday, health, study, religion or sport)

  * Business, family, mission, or meeting.

As per the WTO's definition, following persons are to be regarded a tourists:

(i) Persons travelling for pleasure, for domestic reasons, for health, etc.

(ii) Persons travelling for meetings or in representative capacity of any kind (scientific, administrative, religious, etc.).

(iii) Persons travelling for business purposes.

(iv) Persons arriving in the course of sea cruises, even when they stay for less than 24 hours (in respect of this category of persons, the condition of usual place of residence is waived off.

However persons belonging to the following categories are not considered as tourists:

(i) Persons arriving with or without a contract to take up or engage in any business activity in that country.

(ii) Residents in a frontier zone and persons domiciled in one country and working in an adjoining country.

(iii) Students and young persons in boarding establishments of schools/ colleges.

(iv) Travellers passing through a country without stopping, even the journey takes more than 24 hours.

(v) **Excursionist** is a temporary visitor staying for a period of less than 24 hours in the country visited. (Including travellers on the cruises).

The drawback of the definition of a Visitor as per WTO is that it does not talk about the visits made within the country. For these purposes, a distinction is drawn between a Domestic and an International Visitor.

Domestic Visitor – A person who travels within the country he is residing in, outside the place of his usual environment for a period not exceeding 12 months.

International Visitor – A person who travels to a country other than the one in which he has his usual residence for a period not exceeding 12 months.

After we have discussed the definition of a visitor, tourist, and excursionist as per WTO and made a distinction between a Domestic and an International Visitor, we now come to definitions used in India for the purpose of collecting tourism statistics.

Definitions followed in India

In relation to the definitions provided by the WTO, those followed in India are different in some ways.

International Visitor – has been defined as a person holding a foreign passport, visiting the country and the main purpose of whose visit is other than the exercise of an activity remunerated from within the country visited.

International Tourist – An international tourist has been defined as a person visiting India on a foreign passport, staying at least 24 hours in India and the purpose of whose journey can be classified under one of the following headings:

- Leisure (recreation, holiday, health, study, religion, or sport).
- Business, Family, Mission or Meeting.

The following are not regarded as foreign tourists:

- Persons arriving with or without contract to take up an occupation or engage in activities remunerated from within the country.
- Persons coming to establish residences in the country.
- Nationals of Nepal entering India through land-routes along India-Nepal border.
- All foreigners entering India from Bhutan by land and children aged less than three years.

Excursionist – He is a visitor staying less than 24 hours in the country including cruise passengers.

Cruise Passenger – He is a visitor who arrives in the country aboard cruise/ships and who does not spend a night in an accommodation establishment in the country.

Domestic Tourist – A person who travels within the country to a place other than his usual place of residence and stays at hotels or other accommodation establishments run on commercial bases or in *dharamshalas* or stays with friends and relatives and uses sightseeing facilities, or goes on a pilgrimage for a duration of not less than 24 hours or one night and not more than 6 months at a time for any of the following purposes:

- Pleasure (holiday, leisure, sports, and so on)

- Pilgrimage, Religious and Social functions
- Study and Health.

The following are not regarded as domestic tourists:

- Persons arriving with or without a contract to take up an occupation or engage in activities remunerated from within the state centre.
- Persons visiting their home town or native place on leave or a short visit for meeting relations and friends, attending social and religious functions and staying in their own houses or with relatives and friends and not using any sightseeing facilities.
- Foreigners, resident in India.

Having observed the Indian definition, we must also know a traveller must hold a foreign passport to be included in the category of an International Visitor; this implies that Indians settled abroad and holding Indian Passports will not be counted as International Visitors when they come to India for recreation, business or other such purposes. However, nonetheless they are counted as Domestic Visitors and so here we see that categorisation is based on nationality rather than place of residence. But as per WTO definition they should have been included in the list of International Visitors. From this we can clearly see the difference in the Indian definition and the one given by WTO.

The immediate **challenge to nations** in this era of global travel is to retain their own identity and yet adopt modernism. Environmental issue is probably the most burning issue in this context today. The likely long-term environmental losses due to tourism need to be weighed against its short-term gains. In fact, we find ourselves in the midst of a business paradigm transition where the traditional/conventional norms for profitability and sustainable success are becoming obsolete.

And a new paradigm, primarily characterized by the focus on achieving profitability through system economies (quality tourism per se that destroys the environment), it is poor tourism planning and ineffective management that does it. Managed efficiently and effectively, tourism can definitely be far less destructive than the non-tourism industries while being no less earning.

Many countries depend heavily upon travel expenditures by foreigners as a source of taxation and as a source of income for the enterprises that sell (export) services to these travellers. Consequently, the development of tourism is often a strategy employed either by a Non-governmental organization (NGO) or a governmental agency to promote a particular region for the purpose of increasing commerce through exporting goods and services to non-locals.

However, there are some irritations connected with the spread of tourism.There are different levels of tourist irritation.

(i) *The level of euphoria* : People are enthusiastic and thrilled by tourist development. They welcome the stranger and there is a mutual feeling of satisfaction. There are opportunities for locals and money flows in, alongside tourist arrivals.

(ii) *The level of apathy* : As the industry expands, people begin to take the tourist for granted. They rapidly becomes a target for profit-taking and contact on personal plane begins to become more formal.

(iii) *The level of irritation* : This will begin when the industry is nearing the saturation point or is allowed to pass a level at which the locals cannot handle the number without expansion of facilities.

(iv) *The level of antagonism* : The irritation has become more overt. People now see the tourists as the harbinger of all that is bad. Taxes have gone up because of the tourists. They have no respect for property. They have corrupted our youth. They are bent on destroying all that is fine in our town. Mutual politeness has now given way to antagonism and the tourist is ripped off.

(v) *The final level* : All this while people have forgotten that what they cherished in the first place was what drew the tourist, but in the wild scramble for development, they overlooked this and allowed the environment to change. What they now must learn to live with: the fact that their ecosystem will never be the same. They might still be able to draw tourists but of a very different type from those they so happily welcomed in early years. If the destination is large enough to cope with mass tourism, it will continue to survive.

Conclusion

Tourism can be defined as a practice of touring or travelling for pleasure or recreation and the guidance or management of tourists as a business. Tourism, which generally in everyday conversation is used interchangeably with Travel, is, in fact, much a broader term. In spite of the fact that Travel is an essential ingredient of Tourism, the latter concept encompasses much more than travel alone. In a significant sense, every traveller is a 'potential' tourist.

3

Forms of Tourism

Forms of tourism can be discussed in terms of the displacement of persons under certain conditions. These trips always take the visitors outside their usual environment, but might take them also outside their country of residence into another economy. Forms of tourism can also be discussed in terms of the different types of tourism in a particular country, i.e., ecotourism, sports tourism, health tourism, etc.

Tourism is basically travelling to another destination for the purposes of recreation, leisure, or business. A person who travels to a destination and stays outside of, where they usually live for more than 24 hours but less than one year, is recognized as a tourist by the World Tourism Organization.

In economic measurement, countries are usually interested in looking separately at effects whether they occur on their soil or within other economies. This issue is particularly relevant in the case of tourism which by nature supposes that individuals displace from one place to another.

In order to make this analysis possible, it has been necessary to develop concepts which associate tourism and its activities with the residence of the individual taking the trip, that is, developing his/her tourism activities, and the place where these activities occur.

There are two ways we can look at this activity. One is visiting some place for a reason and then go as a tourist or you can directly go as a tourist. You already know that tourism is an activity done by an individual or a group, moving from one place to another, from a country to another for performing a specific task, or a visit to a place or several places for entertainment which leads to an awareness of other civilizations and cultures and history. Tourism is an important industry that depends on culture and science and has a direct impact on the national revenue for all touristic countries.

Tourism is the movement of the tourists from one place to another place. It is the temporary short-term movement of people to destinations outside the place where they normally live and work, and includes the activities they indulge in at the destination as well as all facilities and services specially created to meet their needs. Tourism does not only mean travelling to a particular destination but also includes all activities undertaken during the stay. It includes day visits & excursions.

It is what is meant by this series of definitions relating to what are called the "forms of tourism" which are relatively outspoken.

The type of tourism depends on the reason for travel. Travel can be to destinations that are domestic or international.

Domestic tourism: is the tourism of resident visitors within the economic territory of the country of reference. Domestic tourism involves residents travelling only within their country.

Inbound tourism: is the tourism of non-resident visitors within the economic territory of the country of reference. Inbound tourism involves non-residents travelling within a country.

Outbound tourism: is the tourism of resident visitors outside the economic territory of the country of reference. Outbound tourism involves residents travelling within another country.

Inbound and Outbound tourism both describe types of international tourism.

Internal tourism: is the tourism, of both resident and non-resident visitors, within the economic territory of the country of reference.

National tourism: is the tourism of resident visitors, within and outside the economic territory of the country of reference. It may vary:

- according to time period of short-term (up to 3 days) and long-term (more than 7 days)
- according to way of organization — organized (by travel agency) or individual (families on their own)
- according to place of destination —international tourism (prevails in Europe) or domestic tourism (prevails in large countries – USA, Canada, etc.)
- according to direction of tourist flows — incoming tourism or outgoing tourism

Leisure Tourism

Tourists may travel to experience a change in climate and place and learn something new, enjoy pleasant scenery, or to know more about the culture of a destination. Tourists, who seek break from the stress of day to day life, devote their holiday to rest and relaxation, refresh themselves. These tourists prefer to stay in some quiet and relaxed destination preferably at a hill resort, beach resort or island resort. Nowadays tourists undertake various adventure sports activities for leisure and to refresh themselves after working hard. This tourism includes following forms based on the activities undertaken:

Cultural Tourism

India is known for its rich cultural heritage and an element of mysticism, which is why tourists come to India to experience it for themselves. The various fairs and festivals that tourists can visit in India are the Pushkar fair, Taj Mahotsav, and Suraj Kund mela.

It is also called as heritage tourism. People are curious to know about foreign lands and their cultures. Culture is most important factor which attracts tourists to a destination.

Cultural tourism gives insight into:

- Historical sites, buildings and monuments;
- Places of historical events, e.g., battles (Waterloo), catastrophes (Pompeii);
- Way of life of the people of distant land;
- Dress, jewellery, dance, music, architecture;
- Customs and traditions;

- Fairs and festivals;
- Religions;
- Culinary delights.

Religious Tourism

It is also called as Pilgrimage tourism/Spiritual tourism. It is a form of tourism, where people travel individually or in groups for pilgrimage. The world's largest form of mass religious tourism takes place at the annual Hajj pilgrimage in Mecca, Saudi Arabia. Modern religious tourists are more able to visit holy cities and holy sites around the world. The most famous holy cities are Jerusalem, Mecca and Varanasi.

India is famous for its temples and that is the reason that among the different kinds of tourism in India, pilgrimage tourism is increasing most rapidly. The various places for tourists to visit in India for pilgrimage are Vaishno Devi, Golden temple, Char Dham, and Mathura-Vrindavan.

Family Tourism

Family tourism involves the family unit and their participation in diverse forms of tourism activity. This includes visiting one's relatives and friends for interpersonal reasons. Many people in India travel for visiting their friends and relatives. While visiting friends or relatives, people also visit tourists' attractions in and around the city.

Health Tourism

Health tourism is also called as Medical tourism. People have been travelling for centuries to improve and rebuild their health and stamina. Today, many people travel great distances to visit exotic locations or avail health care facilities in faraway countries, in search of medical treatment and care.

Tourists from all over the world have been thronging India to avail themselves of cost-effective but superior quality healthcare in terms of surgical procedures and general medical attention. There are several medical institutes in the country that cater to foreign patients and impart top-quality healthcare at a fraction of what it would cost in developed nations such as USA and UK. The city of Chennai attracts around 45% of medical tourists from foreign countries.

Medical tourism is an age-old concept that has gained popularity in the recent times. Many developing countries are emerging as hot medical tourism destinations capitalizing on low cost advantages. Many hospitals have specially designed packages including resorts facilities. Thus health tourism covers one or more of the following aspects:

- Change of climate
- Alternative therapy – Ayruvedic treatment, hot sulphur springs, naturopathy and art of living
- Medical treatment

Wildlife Tourism

India has a rich forest cover which has some beautiful and exotic species of wildlife – some of which that are even endangered and very rare. This has boosted wildlife tourism in India. The places where a foreign tourist can go for wildlife tourism in India are the Sariska Wildlife Sanctuary, Keoladeo Ghana National Park, and Corbett National Park.

Sports Tourism

Sports Tourism refers to travel which involves either viewing or participating in a sporting event staying apart from their usual environment. Sport tourism is a fast growing sector of the global travel industry. Sports tourism refers to people travelling to participate in a competitive sport event. Normally these kinds of events are the motivators that attract visitors to visit the events like Olympic Games, FIFA World Cup. Sports tourism can be adventurous also. Adventure sport tourism is also called as Adventure tourism. Adventure sport tourism is more challenging because it takes the tourists into regions which are less frequently visited and may not have easy access. According to the National Tour Association, adventure tourism is a "tour designed around an adventurous activity such as rafting, hiking, or mountain climbing." Advanture tourism comprises of sports like:

- winter sports – skiing, snowboarding, cross-country skiing
- summer sports, extreme sports (rafting, paragliding, sky diving, etc.)
- sport events (world championships)

Adventure sports tourism is a package of:

- Recreation
- Enjoyment
- Education
- Thrills of participating in an adventure

Adventure Tourism

As a kind of tourism in India, adventure tourism has recently grown in India. This involves exploration of remote areas and exotic locales and engaging in various activities. For adventure tourism in India, tourists prefer to go for trekking to places like Ladakh, Sikkim, and Himalayas. Himachal Pradesh and Jammu and Kashmir are popular for the skiing facilities they offer. Whitewater rafting is also catching on in India and tourists flock to places such as Uttranchal, Assam, and Arunachal Pradesh for this adrenalin-packed activity.

Educational Tourism

Educational tourism developed, because of the growing popularity of teaching and learning of knowledge and the enhancing of technical competency outside the classroom environment. In educational tourism, the main focus of the tourist visiting another country is to learn about the culture, such as in case of Student Exchange Programs and Study Tours, organizing specialized lectures of the eminent personalities, and for research.

Business Tourism

The business traveller's main motive for travel is work. Tourists visit a particular destination for various reasons pertaining to his/her work such as attending a business meeting, conferences, selling products, meeting clients. Business tourism is popularly called as MICE (Meetings, incentives, conferences, and exhibitions) tourism.

Alternative Forms of Tourism

Alternative tourism aims at seeking a change from impersonal, traditional tourism to establishing cardinal rapport between visitors and the local community. Instead of using touristic commodities, these tourists prefer to use or share the services of local people. The focus in these travels is the preserved natural environment, authentic atmosphere and cuisine, and local traditions. Alternative tourism is nowadays regarded as a key to sustainable development. It is also known as special interest tourism. It is of various types:

- Ecotourism
- Food tourism
- Agro-rural tourism

There are also many other types of tourism that fall under a "niche" or specialty travel category. This category of travel has evolved in recent years, and describes the various reasons why people travel for recreation, business or leisure.

Sea-side Tourism

Recreation by the sea, water sports (swimming, rowing, sailing, surfing, windsurfing).

Mountain Tourism

Mountain hiking, climbing, biking.

Shopping Tourism

To go for shopping abroad due to lower prices of goods.

Conclusions

The types of tourism in India have grown and this has boosted the Indian economy. For that to continuously grow, efforts must be taken by the Indian government, so that the tourism sector can contribute more substantially to the nation's GDP.

Nowadays, people are more aware of destinations and attractions, have money to spend, and need break from their routine stressful life. They take breaks to refresh and relax or may travel for some psychological and social needs. Tourism service providers need to understand what motivates a person to travel. Various purposes have been categorized and these have led to different forms of tourism. The popular and most basic form of tourism is leisure tourism, under which family tourism, cultural tourism, religious tourism, sports tourism are included. Business tourism is also getting momentum.

All types of tourism in India have registered phenomenal growth in the last decade ever since the Indian government decided to boost revenues from the tourism sector by projecting India as the ultimate tourist spot.

The reason why India has been doing well in all types of tourism is that India has always been known for its hospitality, uniqueness, and charm – attributes that have been attracting foreign travellers to India in hordes. The Indian government, in order to boost tourism of various kinds in country, has set up the Ministry of Tourism and Culture. This ministry recently launched a campaign called 'Incredible India!' in order to encourage different types of tourism in India.

The result was that in 2004, foreign tourists spent around US$ 15.4 billion during their trips to India. Being a country with tremendous diversity, India has a lot to offer in terms of tourism and related activities. The diversity that India is famous for, ensures that there is something to do for all tourists in India, no matter what their interests are.

4

Forms and Types of Tourism Products

Tourism, basically, is an infrastructure based service product. The nature of the service here is highly intangible and perishable offering a limited scope for creating and maintaining the distinctive competitive edge. The effective marketing of tourism needs constant gearing up of infrastructure to international standards and presupposes in it coordination with the tourism suppliers. In strategic terms, it calls for the action of an integrated approach management and marketing.

The product for the tourist covers the complete experience from the time he leaves home to the time he returns. The tourist product today is developed to meet the needs of the consumer, and techniques like direct sales, publicity and advertising are employed to bring this product to the consumer.

In operational terms, it means the implementation of better defined, better targeted, market-driven strategy for realizing the defined objectives. The important point to note here is that marketing is applied to situations where the choice can be limited to a relatively small number of brands giving the consumer a reasonable choice. The process of selection, thus becomes easier. In the field of tourism, this process is taking place by the increased use of "package tours".

A consumer can combine incdividual products in a large number of ways. There would be many possible destinations, each with a number of hotels, each to be reached by more than one airline. Thus, the potential choice facing the consumer is very large. The nature of the service here is highly intangible and perishable offering a limited scope for creating and maintaining the distinctive competitive edge. The effective marketing of tourism needs constant gearing up of infrastructure to international standards and presupposes in it coordination with the tourism suppliers.

There are many tourism products that are available to the consumes today. In modern times, these products, whether traditional in nature like culture and pilgrimage, or modern like adventure, conventions and conferences, health, medical, etc. are being packaged, promoted and priced appropriately to woo as many tourists as possible. The tourist product is a composite product, whether it is sold as a package or assembled by the individual himself or his travel agent.

Tourism Production Process

Tourism products are the dealings in which a visitor takes a vigorous factor and which often utilize the natural and cultural resources of a nation.The tourism product is the result of a complex production process. Although the lists are relatively long, they are not exhaustive. The process begins with primary inputs of resources, raw materials, and other components such as construction materials, fuel, and agricultural products to create the facilities and equipment needed by the tourism industry. These are then converted through additional processing, manufacturing, or construction into intermediate (processed) inputs or tourism facilities.

Intermediate inputs include attractions such as national parks, museums, galleries, historic sites, and convention centers, as well as tourism supports and facilitators, such as hotels, restaurants, gift shops, and car rental companies. The intermediate inputs are then further refined through managerial expertise, technical services, scheduling, and packaging into intermediate outputs.

Intermediate outputs are those services normally associated with the tourism industry such as commercial accommodation, tour services, foodservices, and festivals. At this stage, however, the tourism product is still effectively just a potential commodity.

Rooms may be offered by a hotel, but they do not become a part of the product–the tourist's experience–until the guest stays in the room. Restaurant food doe not become a meal until it is ordered, cooked, and consumed.

The services of the tourism industry must be refined by consumers to form the final output-personal experiences. In the final stage, the tourist utilizes the intermediate outputs (services) to generate the final output; intangible but highly valued experiences such as recreation, business, and social contacts.

Product development is a prerequisite for satisfying tourists' changing demands and insuring the long-term profitability of the industry. Ideally, tourism products meet marketplace demands, are produced cost-efficiently, and are based on the wise use of the cultural and natural resources of the destination. Despite the importance of product development, relatively little work has been done to examine the nature of the generic tourism product. The purpose of this paper is to fill that void. The tourist product can be analysed in terms of its attraction, accessibility and accommodation.

Attractions

Attractions are those elements in a product which determine the choice made by particular tourist to visit one particular destination rather than another. The attractions could be cultural, like sites and areas of archaeological interest, historical buildings and monuments, flora and fauna, beach resorts, mountains, national parks or events like trade fairs, exhibitions, arts and music festivals, games, etc. Tourist demands are also very much susceptible to changes in fashion. Fashion is an important factor in the demand for various tourist attractions and amenities. The tourist who visits a particular place for its natural beauty may decide to visit some other attractions due to a change in fashion. For instance, for Theatres, Night Life and Cuisine and other facilities like Health resorts, Spas. Possessing unique characteristics not available elsewhere.

Accommodation

The demand for accommodation by tourists away from one's home is met by a variety of facilities. The range and type of accommodation is quite varied and has undergone considerable change since the last half century. Larger hotels are increasing their share of holiday trade, especially in big metropolitan areas and popular spots. In recent years, some changes have been reflected in the type of accommodation. There has been an increasing demand for more non-traditional and informal types of accommodation. The latest trends in accommodation are holiday villages.

In fact, a large number of tourists visit a particular destination or town simply because there is a first class luxury hotel or resort which provides excellent services and facilities. Many hotel establishments elsewhere in various countries, especially the resort hotels have gained a reputation for their excellent cuisine, services and facilities.

Amenities

Amenities can be of two types; natural, e.g. beaches, sea-bathing, possibilities of fishing, opportunities for climbing, trekking, viewing, etc. and man-made, e.g. various types of entertainment and facilities which cater to the special needs of the tourists. Certain other natural amenities such as spacious waters for the purpose of sailing or the opportunities for fishing and hunting are also very important.

The tourism product is not a simple combination of the five elements, but the result of synergistic interaction among all the components. To borrow a well-worn phrase, the tourism product is more than the sum of its parts. However, to begin to understand the product, the elements need to be separately and objectively identified. The core of any tourism product is the physical plant comprising:

- a site,
- natural resource,
- facility such as a waterfall,
- wildlife,
- resort.

It may be either fixed property such as a hotel, or mobile equipment such as a cruise ship. The physical plant also refers to conditions of the physical environment such as weather, water quality, crowding, and the condition of the tourism infrastructure.

Land, water, buildings, equipment, and infrastructure provide the natural and cultural resources on which any form of tourism is based.Their physical design has a major impact on the consumer's experience.

The quality of the physical plant can be assessed by whether the design enhances the user's experience, protects the environment, and makes the product accessible to tourists with a wide range of physical abilities or limitations.

Tourism products can be classified as under for a better understanding of each of peculiar characteristics, so that they can be marketed and positioned appropriately:

NATURAL TOURISM PRODUCTS

These include natural resources such as areas, climate and its setting, landscape and natural environment. For example:

- country side;
- climate – temperature, rains, snowfall, days of sunshine;
- natural beauty – landforms, hills, rocks, gorges, terrain;
- water – lakes, ponds, rivers, waterfalls, springs;
- flora and fauna;
- wildlife;
- beaches;
- islands;s
- spas;
- scenic attractions.

Millions of tourists from countries with extreme climates visit beaches in search of fine weather and sunshine. The sunshine and clear sea breeze at the beaches have attracted many people for a very long time. In fact, development of spas and resorts along the sea coasts in many countries were a result of the traveller's urge to enjoy good weather and sunshine.

The climate of a tourist destination is often an important attraction. Good weather plays an important role in making a holiday. Millions of tourists from countries with extreme climates visit beaches in search of fine weather and sunshine. The sunshine and clear sea breeze at the beaches have attracted many people for a very long time.

Destinations with attractive winter climates, winter warmth and sunshine are also important centres of tourist attraction. Many areas have become important winter holiday resorts attracting a large number of tourists.

Around these winter resorts, winter sport facilities have been installed to cater to the increasing needs of tourists. People coming from warm climates travel for snowfall and cold climate. In countries with tropical climates, many upland cool areas have been developed as 'hill stations'. Hence climate is of great significance as a tourism product.

Spas offer the unique advantages of taking the best from the West and the East, combining them with the indigenous system and offering best of the two worlds. For example, Swedish massages work well with the Javanese Mandy, lulur, aromatherapy, reflexology and traditional ayurvedic procedures. Now various spa products are being combined with yoga, meditation, and pranayama, giving a holistic experience to tourists. Spa treatments are now combined with other medical treatments to treat blood pressure, insomnia, depression, paralysis and some other diseases. People are now travelling to spas and clinics for curative baths and medical treatment.

Tourists of all age groups, backgrounds, cultures and countries enjoy this tourism product. Besides attraction and saleability, beach holidaying has lead to overall development of tourism in many parts of the world. The basic importance of beaches is that they provide aesthetic and environmental value of the beach such as beautiful natural scenery with golden sands, lush green vegetation and bright blue sky. The water should be clear, free of currents and underwater rocks.

A beach resort needs to be developed as an integrated complex to function as a self-contained community.

Environmental management should also ensure the availability of necessary infrastructure in the immediate hinterland to the coastal region in support of the development on the coast to maintain its ecosystem. Islands abound with natural beauty, with the rare flora and fauna and tribes. This makes islands an ideal place for adventure, nature and culture lovers to visit. This tourist product has great scope as these islands are being developed as tourist paradises.

The topography is generally undulating and they offer natural scenic beauty with exotic flora and fauna. Most of these islands have places of worship like churches, temples, etc. As an added attraction, some of these islands have developed as tax havens thereby encouraging commercial development of these economies. They offer social and cultural attractions, as tourists can experience the local lifestyle, local food, fairs an festivals, etc.

Many areas have become important winter holiday resorts attracting a large number of tourists and are also important centres of tourist attraction. Around these winter resorts, winter sport facilities have been installed to cater to the increasing needs of tourists. People coming from warm climates travel for snowfall and cold climate.

MAN-MADE TOURISM PRODUCTS

Man made tourism products are created by man for pleasure, leisure and relaxation of tourists. It consists of :

(A) **Culture,** which includes different aspects of culture – (a) Sites and areas of archaeological interest; (b) Historical buildings and monuments; (c) Places of historical significance; (d) Museums and art galleries; (e) Political and educational institutions; (f) Religious institutions.

(B) **Traditions,** which includes – (a) Pilgrimages; (b) Fairs and festivals; (c) Arts and handicrafts; (d) Dance; (e) Music; (f) Folklore; (g) Native life and customs.

(C) **Entertainment** – (a) Amusement and recreation parks; (b) Sporting events; (c) Zoos and oceanariums; (d) Cinemas and Theatre; (e) Night life.

(D) **Business** – (a) Conventions; (b) Conferences.

(A) Culture:

Cultural tourism is based on the mosaic of places, traditions, art forms, celebrations and experiences that portray the nation and its people, reflecting the diversity and character of a country. A growing number of visitors are becoming special interest travellers who rank the arts, heritage as the reasons for travelling. Today, we can witness large masses of people travelling to foreign countries to become acquainted with the usages and customs, to visit the museums and to admire works of art. Two significant travel trends will dominate the tourism market in the next decade:

- mass marketing is giving way to one-to-one marketing with travel tailored to the interests of the individual consumer;
- a growing number of visitors are becoming special-interest travellers who rank the arts, heritage and/or other cultural activities as one of the top five reasons for travelling.

Tourists acquainted with the usages and customs, visit the museums and to admire works of art taking that the preservation of its culture is one of the basic responsibilities of any community. Hence mass tourism can contribute unique benefits to the exploiting of the cultural heritage of a nation and can serve indirectly to improve the individual cultural levels of both citizens and travellers. A lot of tourists visit historical cities like Varanasi in India due to its status as one of the oldest cities of the world.

Cultural resources have another specific characteristic, which many tourists want to experience the exotic. There will be a great urge on the part of the tourist to visit and become acquainted with the ancient civilization in their quest for novel human knowledge.

Culture means the prospect of contact with other civilizations, their original and varied customs and tradition with their distinct characteristics. This entire process creates a powerful motivator towards travel.

Various museums also attract tourists like, National Museum of India, New Delhi, Madame Tussauds Museum in London, the Louvre Museum in Paris, Smithsonian Washington Museum.

Museums of famous painters like Salvador Dali, Pablo Picasso, Natural History Museum, British Museum, Museum of Modern Art are also popular tourist products, including the sites of archaeological interest, such as remains of Mohenjodaro and Harrapan civilizations, museums for fossils and dinosaurs, Historical buildings like Warwick, etc.

(B) Traditions:

A pilgrimage is a journey to a sacred place or shrine of importance to a person's beliefs and faith. A person who makes such a journey is called a pilgrim. Secular and civic pilgrimages are also practiced, without regard for religion but rather of importance to a particular society. A large number of people have been making pilgrimages to sacred religious places or holy places. This practice is widespread in many parts of the world.

A pilgrimage is a journey to a sacred place or shrine of importance to a person's beliefs and faith. Peoples of every religion participate in pilgrimages.

British people often make pilgrimages to London to witness the public appearances of the monarch of the United Kingdom. A large number of people have been making pilgrimages to sacred religious places or holy places. This practice is widespread in many parts of the world. In the Christian world, for instance, a visit to Jerusalem or the Vatican is considered auspicious. Among Muslims, a pilgrimage to Mecca is considered a great act of faith.

In India, there are many pilgrimage centres and holy places belonging to all major religions of the world. India is among the richest countries in the world as far as the field of art and craft is concerned. Tourists like to visit and see the creative and artistic treasures of various countries.

Every country has certain traditional arts like soap sculptures and batik of Thailand; gems and jewellery, tie and dye works, wood and marble carving in Indonesia. Ivory, glasswork, hand block printing, sandalwood, inlay work are some of the examples of traditional art that attract tourists.

Music can be either traditional or modern. Traditional music like folk music and classical and country music is specific to every region and country.

Festivals like Christmas, Easter, Thanksgiving, Eid, Ramajan, Diwali and Holi and so on, also bring people to destinations where the celebration can be enjoyed. Some popular fairs which cater to fun and work are Pushkar Mela in Rajasthan, Prêt fair in Paris, Magic Fair in Vegas for garments, Hong Kong Fashion Week and various job fairs.

(C) Entertainment:

Tourist products that have entertainment as their main characteristic are many. Just to name a few there are amusement and recreational parks like Disneyworld in United States, Hong Kong, Paris, Singapore and theme parks in various countries and sites like Appu Ghar and Fun and Food Village in Delhi, Essel World in Mumbai, and so on.

Tourists may come to attend sports events and it is also an opportunity to explore the country.The fundamental concept is that all tourist activities have an influence on providing economic benefits and have a powerful influence in some definite locality.

There are many forms of dance in the world like classical and folk dances of India, Salsa, Hip-Hop, Jazz, Flamingo, Ballet and Traditional Dances. People who travel like to watch these dance performances and sometimes even take some introductory classes.

Many countries organise year round sports events like swimming meets, athletic meets, weight lifting events, cricket matches, baseball and Night Life, which are of prime attractions in a holiday. Tourists like to especially visit areas in cities where the night life activity is promoted. These areas are usually lit up with street stalls like flea markets and food areas. Bars, night clubs, casinos and very often open air bands attract and add to the psychological satisfaction and experience of tourists.

Cuisine is very often an understated but highly important part of any holiday. Now-a-days there is cuisine from all areas of the world which is found at most tourist destinations. Specialty restaurants serve Indian, Continental, Chinese, Italian, Japanese, Thai, Indonesian fast food, Mexican, Mediterranean, Arabic delicacies and so on. However, tourists usually like to eat the local food of the areas they visit.

(D) Business:

Business travel is also related to what is termed today as convention business, which is a rapidly growing industry in hospitality and tourism. A business traveller is important to the tourism industry as it involves the usage of all the components of tourism. He travels because of different business reasons – attending conventions and conferences, meetings, workshops, etc. Participants have a lot of leisure time at their disposal. The conference organizers make this leisure time very rewarding for participants by organising many activities for their pleasure and relaxation. The spouses and families accompanying the participants are also well looked after by the organisers. The organisers plan sight-seeing tours and shopping tours for the participants and their families. Conferences are events which require meticulous planning.

ADVENTURE TOURISM PRODUCTS

Adventure Toursims can also be explained as:

(a) Aerial Adventure Sports

- **Parachuting,** which involves jumping off from an aircraft or balloon and descending by means of a parachute. The infrastructure required, includes an aircraft, parachutes and large landing zones.
- **Sky Diving,** which involves a sky diver jumping off an aircraft or balloon at a much greater height without deploying his parachute initially and opening it after some interval at a pre-determined height.
- **Hand Gliding,** which involves running off a mountain or being towed by a winch and essentially flying like a glider where the directional control is achieved by a shift in his own weight by the pilot.
- **Para Gliding,** is the latest aero-sport which has taken the world by storm. A Para Glider is a specially designed square parachute, along with a harness attached by lines.

- **Para Sailing** is a simple sport that involves towing a parachutist to a height of a few hundred feet in the air and then descending by means of a parachute. As a year round activity, Para sailing can be done on land and water.
- **Bungee Jumping**, which requires no equipment except a 'bungee cord' made of nylon fibre of enough elasticity to be able to absorb the shock at the end of the jump. The jumper makes a headlong jump into empty space and the resultant rush of adrenalin makes the experience very exhilarating.
- **Ballooning**, where a balloon is attached to a basket by steel wire ropes. By regulating hot and cold air, the pilot can steer the balloon along any charted course.

(b) Water-Based Adventure Sports

- **White water rafting**, which is one of the most important and exciting water sports, which involves riding down water rapids in an inflatable raft which is used to negotiate fast flowing rivers.
- **Canoeing and Kayaking** are adventure sports which begin upstream where the water is wild and white. The gradient best suited for canoeing is the stage near the river's entry into the plains where the trip can be combined with a natural holiday in a forest. Kayaking is appealing as it enables innovation on the river by one or two oarsman seated in tandem.

Adventure sports in the waters of the sea like **wind surfing, scuba diving, snorkelling, yachting, water skiing**, etc. also offer thrilling activities to the tourist.

(c) Land Based Adventure Tourist Products

- Rock climbing, which originated as a means of practicing techniques for ascending high mountains. It was earlier provided as training to mountaineers but has now evolved into a highly developed sport. The climber moves up, using knowledge of rope handling, climbing, securing one to another, etc. Very sophisticated techniques and equipments are used nowadays to ascend or descend on very steep terrain.
- Mountaineering requires trained physical ability and suitable equipment.The higher peaks need better equipment which is also costly. The challenges which mountains like the Indian Himalayas pose attract mountaineers from various countries.
- Trekking the mighty Himalayas which spread across five Indian states

for a sweeping arc and comprise its expanse a wide geographical variety and contrasting cultures.

- Skiing is the practice of sliding over snow on runners, called skis, attached to each foot. There are three types of ski resorts, the first are large towns, second type are alpine villages and the third resorts built for skiing.
- Heli skiing is a type of alpine skiing where the skier is dropped to the top of a mountain by a helicopter and then he slides down on his own.
- Motor Rally is a sport that tests the navigational skills of man and his endurance with the machine. Motor rallies, grand prix racing, hill climbing rallies, vintage car rallies, sports car racing, etc. are some forms of this tourism product.
- Safaris were earlier taken on camel, horse and elephants as an excursion for/hunting or a journey. As a modern tourist product, now safaris are taken on jeeps and in the form of caravans. Viewing and enjoying nature, meeting the local villagers, seeing their traditions, customs and lifestyle, entertainment and camp fires are some of the characteristics of modern safaris. E.g., Egypt desert safaris. Horse and elephant safaris are arranged in most of the national parks and wildlife sanctuaries.

EVENTS-BASED TOURISM PRODUCTS

Events attract tourists as spectators and also as participants in the events, sometimes for both. The October festival organised in Germany, Dubai and Singapore shopping festivals, the camel polo at Jaisalmer, Kite flying in Ahmedabad attracts tourists, both as spectators and participants. Whereas Snake Boat race of Kerala can be enjoyed by witnessing it.

Event attractions are temporary, and are often mounted in order to increase the number of tourists to a particular destination. Some events have a short time scale, such as the Republic Day Parade, others may last for days together, for example, Khajuraho Dance Festival or even months like the Kumbh Mela.

SITE-BASED TOURISM PRODUCTS

A destination which may have little to commend it to the tourist can nevertheless succeed in drawing tourists by mounting an event such as an unusual exhibition. When an attraction is a place or site then it is called a site-based tourist product. Site attractions are permanent by nature, for example Taj Mahal, The Great Wall of China, The Grand Canyon in Arizona, Eiffel Tower, Statue of Liberty, Temples of Khajuraho, etc. A site destination can extend its season by mounting a off season event or festival.

A large number of tourists are attracted every year by the great drawing power of Stratford on Avon in England because of its association with Shakespeare, the city of Agra in India with its famous Taj Mahal, Pisa in Italy for its famous Leaning Tower.

Some new features have been added to the same product to keep the tourist interest alive in the products. For example, now visitors can see Taj by night, music shows have been organised with Taj as the backdrop so that there are repeat tourists.

OTHER TOURISM PRODUCTS

(A) Geotourism:

Geotourism is concerned with sustaining or enhancing a destination's geographic character – the entire combination of natural and human attributes that make one place distinct from another. Geotourism encompasses both cultural and environmental concerns regarding travel, as well as the local impact tourism has upon communities and their individual economies and lifestyles. Aesthetics, heritage and the well-being of residents are included as some of its concerns.

Geotourism has also been summarised as restorative and reconstructive form of tourism that enhances a destination's natural and cultural distinctiveness, as well as provide a high quality visitor experience. Geotourism is obviously closely related to sustainable tourism, even though it has its own refined concerns and focus.

Ecologically sustainable development relates to "Using, conserving and enhancing the community's resources so that ecological processes, on which life depends, are maintained and the total quality of life, now and in the future, can be increased."

(B) Ecotourism:

Ecotourism is ecologically sustainable tourism, with a primary focus on experiencing natural areas, that fosters environmental and cultural understanding, appreciation and conservation (Ecotourism Association of Australia).

Ecotourists, with their strong focus on learning about the natural environment, minimising negative impacts and contributing to its care, lie at one specialist end of the nature in tourism spectrum, albeit an important one. They are in effect ambassadors (or early adopters) for a set of personal values towards which it now appears many other market segments, potentially comprising much larger visitor numbers, are moving.

Conserved and protected areas (including Marine and National Parks), the Earth's biodiversity, and respect for local culture and those who have been traditional guardians of our natural environments, can be central to their interests.

Ecotourists are also characterised by knowing what they want and being strongly self-active in accessing it. They will often plan and book their experiences and travel needs themselves, leaving tourism operators with more time and the broader opportunity to pursue tourists with more mainstream nature-based interests, and those seeking adventure activity.

(C) Special Interest Tourism:

Most of these visitors are serviced and targeted by specialist tourism operators and suppliers who often provide highly expert guides as part of the service.

Examples include the 'not for profit' travel sector in the United States whose interests can range widely, encompassing anything from wildlife expeditions to scientific and cultural tours. The major non-profit institutions of North America, such as natural history museums, zoos, universities and botanical societies, commonly promote their own world-wide travel programs to membership.

(D) Nature Tourism:

'Nature Tourism' is not a term commonly used by visitors. It is not seen to be a holiday type in its own right – almost no one speaks of taking a "nature-based holiday" or trip, just as few people would describe themselves as cultural tourists! Instead it is a term of value to the tourism industry in the context of visits.

Nature in tourism, in its broadest sense, involves experiencing natural places, typically through outdoor activities that are sustainable in terms of their impact on the environment. These can range from active to passive and include everything from bushwalking and adventure tourism experiences to sightseeing, scenic driving, beach experiences and wildlife viewing. In many instances, a visitor may combine several of these in the one trip.

For keen outdoor enthusiasts, who are many, the great majority of adventure activities directly depend on nature and natural environments for their successful conduct. Fundamentally, the role of nature can vary from 'crucial to the visitor experience' to 'enhances the visitor experience' – particularly in relation to variables as active or passive measures of the activity involved.

For passive and active visitors alike, nature is also playing an increasingly important role in giving something back to people (relaxing, enrich in the spirit, getting back to basics). By doing so, it is able to enhance their broader experience of a destination. And for mainstream domestic visitors, these benefits tap more accurately into nature's deeper meaning. The deeper significance and role of 'nature' in tourism.

Nature-based experiences are intimately linked to all other aspects of the visitor's total experience of a destination, such as food, culture, relaxation, health, escape, family needs, accommodation, transport, etc. All serve to complement each other and together form the basis of a visitor's overall satisfaction with their holiday.

(E) Wildlife Tourism:

Wildlife tourism involves travel to observe wildlife in natural environments and preferably the native habitat. It is a further subset of nature tourism and one in which significantly high levels of domestic and international interest exist. Wildlife tourism involves wild and non-domesticated animals and can encompass free-ranging and captive circumstances.

Given the unique character and special appeal of most of Australia's wildlife, this suggests it may represent a tourism opportunity area for some destinations. The Blue Mountains, Barrington Tops, North and South Coast areas and Outback New South Wales possess great potential in this regard given their species diversity and relative convenience as destinations from major source markets and ports of entry.

Wildlife tourism encompasses the chance to encounter fauna (and flora) in terrestrial, aquatic/marine and aerial settings and to gain some further understanding of a wide variety of species (including viewing kangaroos, koalas, whales, dolphins, seals, fish and birds). Undertaking this activity in a manner that is environmentally responsible is important to ensure less disturbance. It may comprise:

- Wildlife and habitats and terms of major visitor trends, 'appreciative tourism' involving observation, photography and interaction with wild animals is large scale, prominent and growing.
- Consumptive tourism involving such activities as hunting and (non-catch and release) fishing is also large scale, but declining.

(F) Health Tourism:

Holidaying is generally considered as an investment in health, a subject that presents opportunities of cost-benefit analysis. The medical expertise of various countries has added a new product to the existing tourism products. People are travelling to various countries for treatment of various ailments and medical procedures like Cardio care, Bone Marrow Transplant, Dialysis and Kidney transplant, Neuro surgery, Joint Replacement Surgery, Urology, Osteoporosis, and numerous other diseases. Even cosmetic surgery, alternative system of medicines like homeopathy, acupressure, ayurvedic medicines and naturopathy are also becoming tourism products wherein travel companies are offering Yoga and Rejuvenation packages. Tourists travel for what is illegal in one's own country, e.g. abortion, euthanasia; for instance, euthanasia for non-citizens is provided by Dignitas in Switzerland. Tourists travel also for advanced care that is not available in one's own country, in the case that there are long waiting lists in one's own country or for use of free or cheap health care organisations.

(G) Rural Tourism:

Any form of tourism that showcases the rural life, art, culture and heritage at rural locations, thereby, benefiting the local community economically and socially as well as enabling interaction between the tourists and the locals for a more enriching tourism experience an be termed as rural tourism. It is multifaceted and may entail farm/agricultural tourism, cultural tourism, nature tourism, adventure tourism, and eco-tourism. The stresses of urban lifestyles have lead to this counterurbanisation approach to tourism. There are various factors that have lead to this changing trend towards rural tourism like increasing levels of awareness, growing interest in heritage and culture and improved accessibility and environmental consciousness. Tourists like to visit villages to experience and live a relaxed and healthy lifestyle.

(H) Ethnic Tourism:

Ethnic tourism is travelling for the purpose of observing the cultural expressions of lifestyles of truly exotic people. Such tourism is exemplified by travel to Panama to study the San Blas Indians or to India to observe the isolated hill tribes of Assam. Typical destination activities would include visits to native homes, attending traditional ceremonies and dances, and possibly participating in religious rituals.

(I) Senior Citizen Tourism:

A newly emerging trend in tourism, basically for senior citizens or old people who live in isolation, especially in the west, because of daily busy schedules of their children, and more importantly, the attitudes. The characteristic feature of this type of tourism is that the senior people are less demanding in the form of facilities and services, besides leaving minimum impact on the destination community and their main consideration is on personalised service.

(J) Spiritual Tourism:

Many people when living under conditions of stress turn to spirituality. The Eastern world is considered to be very spiritual with many of the new age Gurus and their hermitages. This takes the form of another tourism product, that is, spiritual tourism. Tourists visit places to attend spiritual discourses and meditation workshops. For example, The Osho Foundation, Art of Living Foundation which have centres all over the world, Buddhist Monasteries and Ashrams.

(K) Golf Tourism:

Golf has been enjoyed by many for a long time. Earlier it was enjoyed as a sport, but in recent times, it has developed into a hot tourism product. Many tourist organizations plan promotional packages to woo the golf tourist especially for Japan where the green fees are very high. These tourists take exclusive golfing holidays wherein their accommodation is also arranged near the course and they return after serious golf playing.

(L) Sustainable Tourism:

"A clear distinction should be made between the concepts of ecotourism and sustainable tourism: the term ecotourism itself refers to a segment within the tourism sector, while the sustainability principles should apply to all types of tourism activities, operations, establishments and projects, including conventional and alternative forms."

A major implication of the observation that tourism products require the active involvement of consumers in their production is illustrated by the Leiper (1993) and Smith (1993) debate. A question implicit in their debate was whether a business could belong to more than one industry.

5

Characteristics of Tourism Products

The tourism product includes all the experiences of a tourist from, when he leaves his home to, when he returns. An area's natural attractions, including climate, history and culture, can be seen as the raw materials of the tourism product. Other aspects that can help achieve tourist satisfaction include amenities such as water, electricity, transport and communication. The tourism product is the sum of all the factors in an area that can result in consumer satisfaction. A tourist or his travel agent combines the different components to get his own tourist product.

From the marketing perspective, product can be defined as 'anything – physical objects, services, persons, places, organization, and or ideas – that can be offered to a market for attention, acquisition, use, or consumption that might satisfy a want or need.'

The tourist products, from the industry perspective, can be comprehended at two levels – the total tourist product, consisting of a combination of all the services elements consumed by the tourist from the time of return. This product can be an idea, an expectation, or a frame of mind, at the point of scale. The explicit product such as attractions, accommodation, transport and other facilities, are elements of the total tourist product.

The structure of the tourism product is complex and it is the result of a complicated production process. Production of a tourism commodity begins with the physical plant, which is tangible and controlled to a high degree by the planning and management process. Then, in successive phases, the elements of service, hospitality, freedom of choice, and finally, personal involvement by the consumer are added to the emerging product.

In the final analysis, tourism product and process are inseparable. The tourism industry is the constellation of businesses, public agencies, and non-profit organizations that create products to facilitate travel and activity for people away from their home environment. The nature of these products, though, has not been well understood on a conceptual level. Without a clear statement of the nature of the tourism product and how it is produced, imaginative and successful development is hindered. The attempt is to make explicit the existence of a generic tourism product and production process. The production process and product may not be conventional, but they are real and of substantial economic importance to communities and nations worldwide.

Product in its generic sense can be thing, a place, a person, an event or an organization, which satisfies the need of a person. The product which is offered should have an intrinsic value for the customer in terms of satisfying his needs. Therefore, a product is an offering having some need-satisfying capabilities. This product can be exchanged with some other value, so that there accrues a mutual satisfaction for both the suppliers as well as the receiver of the product.

Products can be divided into two categories: Tangible Products and Intangible Products. Tourism products are intangible products or services having the following distinct characteristics: Intangibility, Inseparability, Perishability, Variability Absence of Ownership, and Customer Participation. Similarly, restaurants, flight catering, pack and carry establishments offer tangible products like Food and Beverages (F&B). Food is therefore a tangible product, storable, but perishable after a span of time. In the production of the product, some standardization is possible. Beverages like cold drinks or mineral water are products since they are tangible, separable and storable; they require the involvement of the customer only at the buying and consumption stage, and not at the stage of production.

A product could therefore be defined by its three characteristics. The product must be offered. It should satisfy the needs of the buyer. It should be exchanged for some value, either through barter or through money exchange.

Thus, tourism products can be divided into two categories: Service Products and Physical Products. All tourism products except shopping, souvenirs and cuisine fall under the category of service products while the exceptions fall, under physical products category. Tourism Product in the sphere of travel-trade has been confused with the products of non-tourism industries rather perceived imperfectly. The nature of tourism products is deemed to have much more delicate, tender or fragile – the experience the tourist has of his travel, of being at his destination, at the attractions, the human interactions, the resource-based nature of experience and so on.

Therefore, it is not merely a simple collection or putting together of product elements e.g. transport, hotels, attractions, services, etc., but the becoming of genuine experience to bring up expectation of the tourist. As tourists lay out high expectations in the magnetism of their tourism experiences, tourism product have to treat product integrity, i.e., the delivered has to match with marketed, and so expected.

Thus, tourism products incorporate quality elements of experience, product fabrication and integrity, at least at par with quantitative aspects, if not more. A convivial or big fun resort experience demands a hierarchy, diversity and exuberance of equipping at a tourist destination while an isolative tourist looks for wildness uninterrupted by the presence of other visitors.

The need of a tourist is to get comfort and pleasure in travel, food arrangements and to visit spots of interest and attraction. Hence, a tourist hopes that she or he will:

- Be looked after and cared for;
- Be able to visit places of interest,
- Spend adequate time at such places and engage in the activities that interest them;

- Not face wastage of time in waiting for transport or at places of no interest because of bad weather or other reasons;
- Be offered palatable and suitable food to one's taste and health;
- Get good company of others if in a group;
- Be able to experience in new places, the local life styles, culture, food etc. as per one's own choice, and
- Be facing no risk to one's person or belongings, etc.

TOURISM PRODUCT CHARACTERISTICS

Intangible:

Unlike a tangible product, say, a motor car or refrigerator, no transfer of ownership of goods is involved in tourism. The product here cannot be seen or inspected before its purchase. Instead, certain facilities, installations, items of equipment are made available for a specified time and for a specified use. For example, a seat in an aeroplane is provided only for a specified time.

Travel products cannot be touched as they include flight experience on an airplane, cruise on an ocean liner, a night's rest in a hotel, view of the mountains, a visit to a museum, a good time in a night club and much more. These products are experiences. Once they have taken place, they can only be recalled and relished.

Psychological:

A large component of tourism product is the satisfaction, the consumer derives from its use. A tourist acquires experiences while interacting with the new environment and his experiences help to attract and motivate potential customers.

Highly Perishable:

It is related to the fact that travel products are intended to be consumed as they are produced. For example, an airline has seats to sell on each flight; a hotel has rooms to sell for each night. If the airline is not able to sell all its seats on its flight, or a hotel is not able to sell its rooms for the night, then the opportunity to sell the product is lost forever. Service sector cannot keep inventory like products.

To overcome this problem, the travel industry has come up with various marketing strategies. One is to overbook. An airline overbooks its seats to a certain extent in anticipation that even though certain customers do not turn up but the flight will be fully seated.

Another strategy is multiple distributions. For example, a customer can buy an airline ticket from an airline, tour operator or from a travel agent. The chances of perishability are reduced if the tourist cannot visit the place, and thus, the opportunity is lost. Hence, this becomes one of its important characteristics.

A travel agent or tour operator who sells a tourism product cannot store it. Production can only take place if the customer is actually present. And once consumption begins, it cannot be stopped, interrupted or modified. If the product remains unused, the chances are lost, i.e., if tourists do not visit a particular place, the opportunity at that time is lost. It is due to this reason that heavy discount is offered by hotels and transport generating organization during off season.

Composite Product:

The tourist product cannot be provided by a single enterprise unlike manufactured product. The tourist product covers the complete experience of visit to a particular place and many providers contribute to this experience. For instance, airline supplies seats, a hotel provides rooms and restaurants, travel agents make bookings for stay and sightseeing, etc.

Unstable Demand:

Tourism demand is influenced by seasonal, economic political and others such factors. There are certain times of the year which see a greater demand than others. At these times, there is a greater strain on services like hotel bookings employment, the transport system, etc.

Fixed Supply in the Short Run:

The tourism product unlike a manufactured product cannot be brought to the consumer; the consumer must go to the product. This requires an in-depth study of users' behaviour, taste preferences, likes and dislikes so that expectations and realities coincide for the maximum satisfaction of the consumer. The supply of a tourism product is fixed in the short run and can only be increased in the long run following increased demand patterns.

Absence of Ownership:

When you buy a car, the ownership of the car is transferred to you, but when you hire a taxi you buy the right to be transported to a predetermined destination at a predetermined price (fare). You neither own the automobile nor the driver of the vehicle. Similarly, hotel rooms, airline tickets, etc. can be used but not owned. These services can be bought for consumption but ownership remains with the provider of the service. So, a dance can be enjoyed by viewing it, but the dancer cannot be owned.

Heterogeneous:

Tourism is multi dimensional industry with a heterogeneous group. It is a heterogeneous group embracing large variety of trades and industries, which have supply of tourism needs as their common function. Tourism supply is the combination of natural and man made attraction, services and goods that are likely to induce people to visit a particular country.

Tourism is not a homogeneous product since it tends to vary in standard and quality over time, unlike a T.V set or any other manufactured product. A package tour or even a flight or an aircraft can't be consistent at all times. The reason is that this product is a service and services are people-based. Due to this, there is variability in this product. All individuals vary and even the same individual may not perform the same every time. For instance, all air hostesses cannot provide the same quality of service and even the same air hostess may not perform uniformly in the morning and evening. Thus, services cannot be standardised.

Risky:

The risk involved in the use of a tourism product is heightened since it has to be purchased before its consumption. An element of chance is always present in its consumption. Like, a show might not be as entertaining as it promises to be or a beach holiday might be disappointing due to heavy rain.

Marketable:

Tourism product is marketed at two levels. At the first level, national and regional organisations engage in persuading potential tourists to visit the country or a certain region. These official tourist organisations first create knowledge of its country in tourist-generating markets and persuade visitors in these markets to visit the country. At the second level, the various individual firms providing tourist services, market their own components of the total tourist product to persuade potential tourists to visit that region for which they are responsible.

Inflexibility:

The tourism industry is highly inflexible in terms of capacity. The number of beds in a hotel or seats on a flight is fixed; so it is not possible to meet sudden upsurges in demand. Similarly, restaurants tables, hotels beds and flights seats remain empty and unused in periods of low demand.

Inconsistency:

A general norm is that, in Travel and Tourism industry, the product or the package of the tourism can be standardized, i.e., for example, of 2 days 3 night in a certain hotel, but the actual experience of consuming this package is highly inconsistent. There is high level of inconsistency prevailing.

Conclusion

The concept of tourism product is focal to understanding the connotation and practice of management in all sectors of the travel and tourism industry as tourism has generated analytical exploration of the various dimensions and details perceived as an economic activity having a consumption, or demand, aspect and a production, or supply aspect. The tourism products from the industry stance can be comprehended at two levels: The total tourism product, consisting of a combination of all the service elements consumed by the tourist, from the time he/she sets off home, to the time of return. This product can be an idea, an expectation, or a frame of mind, at the point of sale. The explicit products such as attractions, accommodation, transport and other facilities, are elements of the total tourism product. Common features of the Tourism product include – Attractions, Accessibility, Facilities/Amenities, Images, Price, Cultural Evaluations, Inseparability, Perishability, Seasonality, and Complementarity.

UNIT–II:

THE CONSTRUCT OF TOURISM

6

Tourism Make-Up: Objects of Tourism

A goal is a broad description of a desired end result. State it vividly and clearly, in detail. Your goal should motivate the whole team. One tourism team's goal might be to develop an annual art festival promoting local artistes. Another may be a set of a goal for increasing the recreational use of a local take.

A failed goal is a fantasy, entertaining but unproductive. Don't set a goal of a three day art festival with thousand of visitors when the area is actually able to support a one-day show for a couple of hundred in the local fire station. The best way to achieve a goal is to break it down into objectives – do able tasks to achieve the goal and then devise a plan of action to accomplish them. It may take several steps or projects to complete an objective.

Although there are many ways to achieve an objective, it is important to choose the action plan that is feasible, technically possible, and at a price you are willing to pay. Why not set a goal and have everyone work on it? Most commissioners are involved in lots of projects, and their tourism efforts are often made while doing other business.

Try to define each member by the description below and analyze the objective and the action plan to match particular personalities with certain types of tasks. By using these characteristics in your individual team members, your objective will be more easily accomplished. Bringing these individual strengths to the table, your team together will devise each objective's action plan by diagnosing the existing situation in relation to your goal. The diagnosis defines problems and needs that become objectives. Each time you achieve an objective, you will diagnose the situation again, and go on to other objective and set new ones.

During planning, the team decided upon a separate set of actions for each objective, then noticed duplication. The same action could bring results to more than one objective. You may then see ways to combine effort however, that in both cases, the team made the list of objectives which could all contribute to achievement of the goal.

Remember that the team is made up of a wide range of people. It's impossible for everyone to do a perfect job every time. Remind yourselves often that you are volunteers and that you are a team. This means that each of you has made a commitment to donate time, energy, and expertise towards achieving common goals. Uphold your commitment to the team and to the project.

The aims and objectives are mentioned below:

- To promote responsible and community-based tourism so that locals can enjoy increased socio-economic benefits and improved environment.
- To develop tourism with dignity, respect and nurture local cultures so that they enrich the tourism experience and build pride and confidence among local communities.
- To minimize negative social, economical and environmental impacts of mass tourism and promote tourism which is sustainable.
- To foster the development of community-based tourism products by providing marketing, training, financial and mentoring support.
- To preserve and enhance local culture, art, handicrafts, monuments and other natural and man-made tourist resources and protect them from over-commercialisation and over-exploitation.
- To promote and ensure the respect and dignity of people in tourism, marketing and promotion of tourism.
- To create and promote forms of tourism that provide healthy interaction opportunities for tourists and locals and increase better understanding of different cultures, customs, lifestyles, traditional knowledge and believes.

- To provide tourists with authentic, educational and quality experiences, e.g., by creating opportunities for them to interact with locals in an unstructured, spontaneous manner (e.g. through sports activities, visit to local schools/institutions/organizations and participation in local festivals and events etc.).
- To involve local communities in all stages of responsible tourism development, i.e., planning, decision-making and implementation of tourism development activities in their region so that the tourism is in harmony with the priorities of local communities.
- To encourage proactive participation and involvement by all stakeholders including government bodies, private sector, tourism organizations, local communities, NGOs, youth clubs etc. at all stages of tourism life cycle.
- To conduct research on different aspects of responsible and community-based tourism, make suitable plans and strategies and implement responsible tourism projects.
- To conduct market research and identify places and activities of touristic interest e.g. local music, dance, cuisine, art and craft, specialty agriculture, festivals and events etc. and use them in sustainable manner for tourism development.
- To generate employment and self-employment opportunities for the poor and disadvantaged section of the community by involving them directly in tourism services.
- To provide training and consultancy to local communities, government bodies, tourism organizations, and private sector and enable them to develop and promote responsible and community-based tourism in their areas so that positive impacts of tourism are maximized and negative one minimized.
- To organize and promote responsible and community-based tours, cultural exchange programs, student exchange programs, internships/training abroad and other such tourist activities at national and international level.
- To promote environmental awareness, conservation and sustainable use of natural resources.
- To seek help and assistance from the government and public sources for the promotion of responsible tourism.
- To raise funds and to receive donations, subscription, gifts and consideration to make provision for the implementation of the above objectives.

- To take on lease, purchase or to accept as gifts any land, building or to construct structure there on which may be necessary or convenient for carrying out the above objectives.

7

Motivations

Introduction

Tourist motivation is the reason why a tourist will make the decision to choose one destination over another and the attributes that governs that behavior. This is important to the tourist professional for a number of reasons. The tourist professional must have an understanding of what drives the tourist to initiate the vacation and then match a destination that fits with the tourist's travel motives. A good fit may ensure that the guest will enjoy the vacation and either come back year after year or book another trip with that professional.

The individual ought to be aware of the means (product or service) and must be able to make out that investing in the same is going to help in satisfying the need. Then, and only then, will the individual be persuaded to purchase it.

What is Motivation?

It is a person's desire to do the best possible job or to exert the maximum effort to perform assigned tasks. A person has many needs at any given time. Some needs are biogenic. They arise from physiological states of tension such as hunger, thirst, discomfort. Other needs are psychogenic. They arise from psychological states of tension such as the need for recognition, esteem, or belonging.

Most psychogenic needs are not intense enough to motivate the person to act on them immediately. A need becomes a motive when it is aroused to a sufficient level of intensity. A motive (or drive) is a need that is sufficiently pressing to drive the person to act. Satisfying the need reduces the felt tension.

Psychological theory holds that needs, wants and goals generate uncomfortable states of tension within individuals' minds and bodies, tension that cannot be released until the needs are satisfied. States of tension, including hunger, fatigue and loneliness as well as the drive for self-development, are thus the motivators that produce actions to release tension states. Motivations, therefore, are the dynamic process in buyer behaviour, bridging the gap between the felt need and the decision to act or purchase. Most readers will recognize in themselves many less important needs, which are not satisfied primarily because the felt motivation is not strong enough to overcome the inertia against decision choices.

A powerful motivator is one that triggers urgent action. In marketing sense, motivation bridges the gap between a general interest in a product, and a decision to go out and buy it. It is in this sense that products can be designed and marketed as *solution* to customers' needs (tension states). A marketing manager who has taken the trouble to understand customers' needs and attitudes will clearly be more able to trigger their decisions by targeting communication on their motivating influences.

The decision concerning the problem whether to travel or not to travel is not that simplistic an issue as it might seem to connote. It is a very vital, subjective but complex decision depending upon several local and alien factors in addition to various types of constraints and deterrents. The majority of people fail to express their travel motivations for setting forth holidaying.

Motivation and Tourism

Tourism is believed to be a satisfier of needs and wants. Some scholars/professionals hypothesize that people travel if they learn and perceive that travel on account of specific reason is going to facilitate the satisfaction of their needs and wants of priority, at least partially if not wholly, within the given constraints of time, money and social pressure.

Tourist motivations from this perspective become critical in the sense that it is just like the difference between looking on the tourist destination as merely a cluster of hotel rooms and landscapes/coastal area (beaches) or considering it as a satisfier of tourists' needs and wants.

Thus, it becomes all the more significant to understand the prime needs and wants of the tourists so as to be able to market potential tourists i.e. to convert the 'potential' tourists into 'actual' tourists. Drawing on the tourism psychology and motivation, it is a simple tourism that an individual normally travels for multiple reasons.

For instance, if one travels to an area for business reasons, the occurrence of a cricket world cup, or some music concert, or an international trade fair in the same area or nearby can prove to be an added attraction and reinforcement of the resolve to visit it.

Travel Propensity: Travel propensity is an effective index of tourism involvement. It explains that proportion of a population who actually practice tourism in terms of the penetration of tourism trips. Travel propensity is broadly of two types – Gross Travel Propensity, and Net Travel Propensity.

Travel Purpose: Because of quick and efficient transportation, people are spurred to travel for various reasons as destinations have become more accessible. Some of these reasons to travel are:

Sightseeing – historical, cultural, social and technological sights;

Relaxation – beach and mountain resorts;

Sport – mountain climbing, skiing, surfing, scuba diving, etc;

Special interest – study tours on art, history, religion, culture and science;

Shopping – personal and professional, business, governmental – political.

Travel reasons: People travel for two reasons: By obligation: Having to go somewhere on business, or feeling an obligation for religious reasons, or for reasons of family or friendship, or for medical reasons.

By motivation: The purpose here is to increase job satisfaction.

Travel Motivation: What motivates people to travel? In this regard, eighteen factors can be considered significant:

- To see how people in other countries live, work and play;
- To see particular sights;
- To gain a better understanding of what goes on in the news;
- To attend special events;
- To get away from the everyday routine;
- To have a good time;
- To achieve some short sexual or romantic experience;
- To visit places your family came from;
- To visit places your family or friends have gone.
- Weather (for instance, to avoid cold of winter or heat of summer);
- Health;
- Sports;
- Economy (inexpensive living);
- Adventure;
- One-upmanship;
- Conformity;
- To participate in the history;
- Sociological motives (get to know the world).

Prof. Donald E. Lundburg has developed sixteen reasons why people travel:

- Business;
- Pleasure;
- Health;
- The need for a change;
- Rest and relaxation;
- To search for the exotic;
- To learn;
- To experience natural power, beauty and wonder;
- Ego enhancement;
- For sports;
- To shop;
- Travel for travel sake;

- To gamble;
- Travel as a change;
- For acceptance;
- For spiritual values.

Tourism Needs and Motivations – The tourist needs can primarily be categorized into two categories.

- One, the needs relating to day-to-day requirements (products and services) that even exist at the normal place of habitation such as food and lodging, clothing, means of communication, newspapers, banking etc. that basically differ in terms of the place from where these must be satisfied and may be even in intensity from those of non-tourists.
- Two, the needs that hardly exist at the place of residence, e.g., special transport needs of the tourist, going in for purchase of souvenirs, or visiting places of interest.

Of course, pleasure travel has rarely been an elemental need of mankind as earlier journeys meant hassle and hardship. It was mainly the fancy and longing for biological or economic reasons that persuaded men to travel while geographical and climatic causes also forced the movement of people like the caravans of the nomads.

To travel independently and freely for adventure and pleasure, rest or recreation, culture or other reasons was quite rare and generally a prerogative of Emperors and Kings. However, modern tourism is deeply rooted in English, French and German Romanticism. The main trends – discovering nature, virgin landscape, and history are until date the impelling dynamism of tourist movement. While analyzing travel motivations of present day modern tourists, one comes across not only a pallet of tourism needs, but also vast discrepancies as to the origin and social stratum, for tourism needs. That is, tourist travel stipulations hold neither general nor permanent validity.

They are, rather inserted in the historical, geographical, political, economic and technological environment of the time and can only be understood by making allowance for these. To redress the several types of deficits, namely, social deficits, climatic deficits, deficits in movement and activity, deficits in the closeness to nature, deficits in experiences and change, deficit in enjoyment, luxury and prestige, and lack of freedom – that day-to-day life in a working performance society inevitably effectuates.

Physical and psychological recovery from stress, the pressure of performance and the monotony of everyday life, revitalizing or supporting physical and mental well-being, widening horizons, satisfying curiosity, self-realization, increase of the feeling of one's own value, self-reward, self-indulgence, one's own identity, honour, and pride.

Travel Patterns Choice: Once the selection of the destination is done, then comes the choice of Travel Patterns. An analytically critical look at the four-grid model under 'Typology of Pleasure Travel Patterns' does provide a strong base to understand the relationship between motivation and selection. Basically, they have taken 'Benefits-Sought Criteria' (Single or Multiple) on one scale and 'Number of Destinations Visited' (Single or Multiple) on the other.

Travel for Business: A sizeable measure of business travel is, however, mixed with pleasure. It is, in fact, difficult to come out with where business begins or pleasure ends when the business traveller is attending a convention in some metropolis where as much as half of his or her time may be spent gambling or devil-may-care gamboling i.e., skipping, jumping playfully or wandering. A Pan-American Airline study reveals that the business-pleasure mix varies widely according to nature of destination area. Although, most of business travel is undertaken by air, but most of business travel is hard work irrespective of the mode of transportation used.

Travel for Health: Holidaying is generally considered as an investment in health, a subject that presents opportunities of cost–benefit analysis. One needs to schedule one's health, say the health counselors, just as one needs to schedule work activities. It is suggested by many medical specialists that it is relatively more beneficial to go for a number of vacations at regular intervals for recouping energies both psychologically and physically, interest and passion than one all-out vacation per year. Moreover spacing holidays over different seasons is not only more satisfying to the holidayer but to the tourism industry as well, for the peaks and valleys of the business are leveled out.

Travel for Pleasure: Pleasure is primarily a state of mind where one's meat may be another's venom. It depends partly upon prior conditions or the anticipation of good things to come. Pleasure may be symbolized with the feelings that come with sensuous gratification – be it eating, drinking, basking in the sun, a warm bath, relief of pain, respite from boredom, or escape from the routine of life, sex or even the thought of it. That is, change, in itself may bring pleasure. Probably, the strongest of all individual travel motivations is that of satisfying a need for pleasure, and travel has the unique and unparalleled quality of being able to satisfy the need, that too, to a great extent. Practicing pleasure travel is, in itself, learned behaviour. Travel gives rise to satisfaction gained only by such experiences, and satisfaction many a time include a relaxation of tension.

The pleasure trip thus becomes a highly complex and primarily learned form of reducing tension. The planning and anticipation period in the pre-travel phase can be as gratifying as the trip-itself.

Discussing prospects of the trip with friends and colleagues, pursuing research, educational and shopping activities relating to the trip and the area to be visited is the most important part of the total pleasure travel experience. The romance of the trip is also an overpowering motivation for those galvanized with the romantic aspects of seeing, experiencing and enjoying strange and attractive places.

This is particularly true in case of honeymoon travel. The romance and pleasure of the trip are, indeed, the primary characteristics and qualities of the travel experience. What is pleasurable is a subjective phenomenon liable to changes with time and culture. For instance, the present older generation has been so programmed to believe that work is worship, i.e., it, in itself, is one of the highest goods. For this generation, pleasurable delight has never been of compelling concern.

But over time, keeping to the ostensible strait – laced ethic is melting away and sensuous gratification is back in favour. Work has become synthesized or interwoven with pleasure. That is, life can be fun. Similarly, holidaying for pleasure has changed and will continue to do so. In the last quarter of the nineteenth century, travel to the mountain resort or hill station in the summer was viewed as extremely pleasing as it extended an escape from the heat, kick and redressal for the stomach, rest and relaxation, and a chance to be with one's peer, or sanguinely one's betters.

Moreover, in the first half of the twentieth century, the only mode of transportation for travel abroad was ship. The shipboard activities turned out to be thrilling for some, inexorably prosaic to others. Wrapped in woolens, sitting in deck chairs and shivering against the cold winds was hardly pleasurable for a very few. Travel today, however, has become more comfortable and convenient especially with the advent of aviation technology in 1960s and 1970s. In addition, the criteria for what are pleasurable in travel and vacation for an individual even within a family is variable with time.

Travel for Seeking Knowledge: Man's urge to learn in all likelihood is intrinsic and can flourish into an incessant search for knowledge, truth and understanding. Travel and holidaying offer an opportunity to satisfy the urge to learn. Once an interest becomes deep-seated in a person, he/she is likely to enjoy pursuing it as interest.

The interest can be in almost anything – people, language, history, geography, culture, architecture and travel itself. The urge to meld oneself with the past, to understand it, to relive it runs strong in a sizable class of people. Historic buildings, monuments, battlefields, and shrines are a means of communicating with the past, of feeling at one with those who came before.

In the context of tourism, once an interest gets developed in a destination region, it keeps growing with every additional information. A well chalked out marketing mix, no doubt triggers off interest in a destination, but much more eloquent and persuasive is the effect created by a good reading, media, or above all, the word of mouth communication. Nevertheless, the effects of the elements of a marketing mix are difficult to compute individually; they may operate on a subliminal level of awareness for the potential holidaymaker. It is also a fact that travel is an enriching experience for many. Humans learn from an environment only to the extent that they respond to it. Moreover, it cannot be assumed that every traveller learns, many are mere spectators.

Travel and Tourism Consumption: It represents the value of products and services that have been consumed by visitors. It is the basic demand-side aggregate used to construct an explicitly defined production-side "industry" equivalent for comparison with all other industries. Travel and Tourism consumption includes Personal Travel and Tourism, more formally known as consumer expenditure, which captures spending by residents of an economy on traditional travel and tourism service (lodging, transportation, entertainment, meals, financial service, etc.) and goods (durable and non-durable) used for travel and tourism activities.

Business Travel by government and industry, which mirrors Personal Travel and Tourism spending on goods and services (transportation, accommodation, meals, entertainment, etc.) are intermediate inputs used in the course of business or government work. Government Expenditure (individual) by agencies and departments, which provide visitor, services such as cultural (art museums), recreational (national parks) or clearance (immigration/customs) to individual visitors.

Visitor Exports – which include spending by international visitor on goods and services.

Motivation (Travel) and Age: Age can be factor that can be critically instrumental in influencing the nature of experiences having a magnetic pull for an individual. For instance, in the early stage of life cycle, i.e., the adolescence or youth stage, the youth especially being receptive to new ideas, having interest in newer places, and possibly leas prone to humiliation and self-consciousness in differing social situations, may have a great endurance for all types of new experiences.

For the people belonging to middle age group, having achieved a certain position and status, this group seeks comforts in keeping with his/her position, in life, i.e., comfort factor carries relatively more weight. Besides, another consideration for the many is the desire to travel jointly or in company.

The forces governing such a desire may be the heightened inherent need for social comparison and camaraderie, and the reduced need for exploration emerging mainly from the feeling of the later years of life, i.e., old age. Such a person usually develops an extended forbearance for steadiness and an inward tendency. However, it is equally true that there is no particular age for being so and this stage may never occur.

Motivation (Travel) and Gender: Differences on account of sex crop up owing, in principle, to two distinct factors, namely, role conflict and training differences. The males particularly may have a dissension between professional/business and family positions and roles resulting in conflicts relating to appropriation of time and energy.

In order to avoid frictions, it is possible that they may do their best to keep the two spheres of their lives independent and separate. Conversely, in case of such a conflict, home and family usually comes first. Nevertheless, the fact is that, in the modern times, the roles are changing radically and thereby the differences between the males and the females in training, motivations, and interests perspectives are losing their sharpness that existed in the past.

However, when the kids and little ones are involved, their needs are likely to influence the motivations and choices of both the parents as a whole.

Motivation and interests – Travel motivation and interests were discussed earlier in the chapter. They can be summarized as: leisure, recreation motives and holidaying; visiting friends and relatives; business and professional motives; health treatment; religion pilgrimages; and others.

Linked to motivations and interests are peoples' needs and preferences. What do they like and what they do not? What particular product features are they looking for?s

Motivation for Travelling/Tourism – Motivation pinpoints, firstly, the purpose of the visit or travel. Although there are number of identified heads of purpose, but they differ in characteristics. The most accepted of these are: Holiday – rest and relaxation including visits to friends and relatives, generally referred to as V. F. R; Business – including meetings, conferences and conventions, etc. Others – including health, study, sports, religious pilgrimages, etc. Taking from the differing characteristics of each category of purpose, it becomes not only significant but also relevant to distinguish between each category of purpose. For example, the business travel is likely to be different from holiday travel in the sense that in the former, the person has little discretion as to the choice of destination, duration of stay and the timing of the trip, i.e., season.

These, rather have to be, often fixed up at short notice and for relatively brief period of time. However, this class of people, in the absence of economic constraints to undermine the travel plans as the travel bill is to be funded by the company, demands much in terms of tourism plant such as availability of customary regular transport, efficient service and good facilities at the destination.

That is, business travel is relatively price elastic. On the contrary, for the majority, holiday travel is highly price elastic. In this case, low travel costs are generally instrumental in two ways; one, in buoying up an increase in the number of holiday travelers; two, in stimulating other vacationers to redirect their destinations.

Such travellers are willing to put off their travel or make reservations well in advance for their travel requirements if it implies a sizable reduction in travel costs. Hence, the need for identifying the rationale behind choosing a particular type of holiday or destination. Though it is advocated that there should be different destinations for different markets/people, yet most of the times different markets instead of being in search of different destinations, seek different attributes in the same destination. For instance, a ski resort may be opted because of its cracking slopes and sporting facilities, owing to its climate, curative qualities, or healthy mountain air, or on account of the social life it holds out to skiers and non-skiers alike.

Motivation and Education: The difference in educational level also influences the nature and extent of new experiences acceptable to a person. While considering such differences, it must be taken into account that these are interwoven with elements like socio-economic standing and economy level.

It has been observed that individuals with higher level of education largely earn more money and are of higher status in comparison to those with lower educational level. The people belonging to the former category, comprising mainly business executives and management personnel are progressively mobile and initiator of most of social change, and are more inclined to appreciate change in their environment, as they are ever willing to take a chance and go to an unfamiliar place. They themselves are interested in travel and need not have to be told of about any specific travel concept.

Most of the times, they pose a challenge to people specializing in tourist services in case the latter are unable to provide a genuinely innovative experience. In contrast, a person with lower level of education is usually static and may not travel at all as he is extremely conscious of familiarity and social appearance, feels himself less cultured than even the average traveller, even though is nothing of the sort. Such an attitude is not because the person feels like holding on to the pattern, but because of the inherent fear of insecurity in trying something new.

Theories about Motivation:

Some of these theories are as follows:

Maslow's Theory of Motivation - Hierarchy of Needs

In 1943, Dr. Abraham Maslow's article "*A Theory of Human Motivation*" appeared in Psychological Review, which were further expanded upon in his book: *Toward a Psychology of Being.* In this article, Abraham H. Maslow attempted to formulate a needs-based framework of human motivation based upon his clinical experiences with people. From this theory of motivation, modern leaders and executive managers find means of motivation for the purposes of employees and workforce management. Abraham Maslow's book, formally introduced the Hierarchy of Needs.

The basis of Maslow's motivation theory is that human beings are motivated by unsatisfied needs, and that certain lower factors need to be satisfied before higher needs can be satisfied. As long as we are motivated to satisfy these cravings, we are moving towards growth, toward self-actualization.

As per 'Maslow's Needs Pyramid' or 'Maslow's Needs Triangle', after a need is satisfied, it stops acting as a motivator and the next need, one rank higher, starts to motivate as it attains psychological precedence.

A key aspect of the model is the hierarchical nature of the needs. The lower the needs in the hierarchy, the more fundamental they are and the more a person will tend to abandon the higher needs in order to pay attention to sufficiently meeting the lower needs. For example, when we are ill, we care little for what others think about us: all we want is to get better.

Maslow called the first four needs 'D-need' as they are triggered when we have a deficit. Only self-actualization is a need that we seek for solely positive reasons. Maslow also called them 'instinctoid' as they are genetically programmed into us as essential for evolutionary survival. Loss of these during childhood can lead to trauma and lifelong fixation.

'Maslow's Needs Pyramid' is depicted as under;

In practice, this hierarchy is only approximate and one does not have to have one's physiological needs fully satisfied before going on to seeking higher needs. In their global survey, for example, Tay and Diener found that people can be living in hazardous poverty and yet still derive much satisfaction from having social needs (belonging and esteem) fulfilled.

The Five Needs:

- Physiological needs have to do with the maintenance of the human body. If we are unwell, then little else matters until we recover.
- Safety needs are about putting a roof over our heads and keeping us away from harm. If we are rich, strong and powerful, or have good friends, we can make ourselves safe.
- Belonging needs introduce our tribal nature. If we are helpful and kind to others, they will want us as friends.
- Esteem needs are for a higher position within a group. If people respect us, we have greater power.
- Self-actualization needs are to 'become what we are capable of becoming', which would be our greatest achievement.

Three More Needs:

These are the needs that are most commonly discussed and used. In fact Maslow later added three more needs by splitting two of the above five needs.

Between esteem and self-actualization needs was added:

- Need to know and understand, which explains the cognitive need of the academic.
- The need for aesthetic beauty, which is the emotional need of the artist.

Self-actualization was divided into:

- Self-actualization, which is realizing one's own potential, as above.\
- Transcendence, which is helping others to achieve their potential.

This has the following effect/potential:

- Ability to distract people from higher needs, threaten their lower needs. It is no surprise that poison has been effectively used to bring down kings and princes without necessarily killing them.
- Capacity to perceive and help people to meet the needs on which they are currently focused. Their attention is here and they will express gratitude for assistance in meeting their present needs.
- Encouraging them in reaching up to higher needs. Let them see and

reach up to the greater things in life. Create a tension which you can use for own benefits.

Defending:

Seek only needs at your current level. Neither retreat too rapidly to lower needs nor reach too quickly for higher needs. When you are ready, only then reach in your own time for higher needs. If other people seek to help you, you may accept their help but are not obliged to repay in any way they demand.

(a) Self-Actualization:

Self-actualization is the summit of Maslow's motivation theory. It is about the quest of reaching one's full potential as a person. Unlike lower level needs, this need is never fully satisfied; as one grows psychologically there are always new opportunities to continue to grow.

Self-actualized people tend to have motivators such as:

- Truth
- Justice
- Wisdom
- Meaning

Self-actualized persons have frequent occurrences of peak experiences, which are energized moments of profound happiness and harmony.

According to Maslow, only a small percentage of the population reaches the level of self-actualization.

(b) Esteem Needs:

Esteem needs can be categorized as external motivators and internal motivators. External esteem needs are those such as reputation and recognition.

Some examples of esteem needs are:

- Recognition (external motivator)
- Attention (external motivator)
- Social Status (external motivator)

- Accomplishment (internal motivator)
- Self-respect (internal motivator)

Maslow later improved his model to add a layer in between self-actualization and esteem needs: the need for aesthetics and knowledge.

(c) Social Needs:

The first level of higher level needs are social needs. Social needs are those related to interaction with others and may include:

- Friendship
- Belonging to a group
- Giving and receiving love
- Safety Needs

(d) Once physiological needs are met, one's attention turns to safety and security. Such needs might be fulfilled by:

- Living in a safe area
- Medical insuranc
- Job security
- Financial reserves

According to the Maslow hierarchy, if a person feels threatened, needs further up the pyramid will not receive attention until that need has been resolved.

Physiological Needs:

Physiological needs are those required to sustain life, such as:

- Food
- Sleep

According to this theory, Higher needs such as social needs and esteem are not recognized until one satisfies the needs basic to existence. If Maslow's theory is true, there are some very important leadership implications to enhance workplace motivation, and one would not need a masters in applied psychology, for it to be evident.

Maslow's Theory – Limitations and Criticism:

Though Maslow's hierarchy makes sense intuitively, little evidence supports its strict hierarchy. Actually, recent research challenges the order that the needs are imposed by Maslow's pyramid. As an example, in some cultures, social needs are placed more fundamentally than any others.

While scientific support fails to reinforce Maslow's hierarchy, his theory is very popular, being the introductory motivation theory for many students and managers, worldwide.

Frederick Herzberg Motivational Theory:

Frederick Herzberg's book *'The Motivation to Work'* (1959) is an attempt to explain the factors that motivate individuals through identifying and satisfying their individual needs, desires and the aims pursued to satisfy these desires.

A list of motivation factors which will motivate when present is given below. Job dissatisfaction isn't usually blamed on Motivation Factors, but they are cited as the cause of job satisfaction. The list includes:

- Achievement
- Advancement
- Recognition
- responsibility

These two separate 'needs' are the needs to avoid unpleasantness and discomfort and, at the other end of the motivational scale, the need for personal development exists. A shortage of the factors that positively encourage employees (the motivating factors) will cause employees to focus on other, non-job related 'hygiene' factors.

Herzberg vs Maslow

1. Meaning

Maslow's theory is based on the concept of human needs and their satisfaction.

Hertzberg's theory is based on the use of motivators which include achievement, recognition and opportunity for growth.

2. Basis of Theory

Maslow's theory is based on the hierarchy of human needs. He identified five sets of human needs (on priority basis) and their satisfaction in motivating employees.

Hertzberg refers to hygiene factors and motivating factors in his theory. Hygiene factors are dissatisfiers while motivating factors encourage subordinates. Hierarchical arrangement of needs is not given.

3. Nature of Theory

Maslow's theory is rather simple and descriptive. The theory is based on long experience about human needs.

Hertzberg's theory is more prescriptive. It suggests the motivating factors which can be used effectively. This theory is based on actual information collected by Hertzberg by interviewing 200 engineers and accountants.

4. Applicability of Theory

Maslow's theory is most popular and widely cited theory of motivation and has wide applicability. It is mostly applicable to poor and developing countries where money is still a big motivating factor.

Herzberg's theory is an extension of Maslow's theory of motivation. Its applicability is narrow. It is applicable to rich and developed countries where money is less important motivating factor.

5. Descriptive or Prescriptive

- Maslow's theory or model is descriptive in nature.
- Herzberg's theory or model is prescriptive in nature.

6. Motivators

According to Maslow's model, any need can act as motivator provided it is not satisfied or relatively less satisfied.

In the dual factor model of Hertzberg, hygiene factors (lower level needs) do not act as motivators. Only the higher order needs (achievement, recognition, challenging work) act as motivators.

Motivation-Hygiene Theory:

The motivation theory propounds that intrinsic factors are related to job satisfaction and motivation, whereas extrinsic factors are associated with job dissatisfaction.

Motivation Research: It attempts to study the consumer's desires, emotions, intentions and reactions behind a purchase. Motivation research attempts to describe and forecast the motives of the population under investigation, by use of techniques originally used in psychology.

Motivation-McIntosh's Categorization: In McIntosh's view (1972), the basic travel motivators can be broadly categorized under following four heads:

- **Physical motivators** are mainly concerned with physical condition and mental health of the potential visitors with a characteristic feature in the sense that these facilitate release of stress and strains through physical activities. That is, such motivators are related to the individual's bodily, physical, rest and relaxation, and sporting activities. These include leisure, recreation and entertainment; rest and relaxation; sports participation; use of health spas and curative baths, etc.
- **Cultural motivators** imply motivations like inquisitiveness, anxiety and curiosity to learn about social classes, habits and customs, and lifestyles of other areas. Alternatively these are mainly concerned with informative and cultural factors such as the desire to learn and know about people of other countries, their artistic and cultural heritage. These mostly include knowledge of living patterns, fairs and festivals, music and art, architecture, cuisine, and religion.
- **Interpersonal motivators** are identified with the individual's ethnic and family ties or simply to escape from the routine of customary life and its compulsions and pressures. These are basically subjective in nature and imply an escape from routine activities and/or usual environment, visiting friends and relatives, a lust to meet new people, or making new friendships.
- **Status-cum-prestige** motivators are related to egocentric needs and

individual development. These involve the desire and longing of the individual for seeking knowledge, personal development, pursuit of pastime, and/or development of professional interests. For instance, the longing for recognition, appreciation, attention, good reputation, and knowledge can be satisfied through tourism activities related to business, conventions, pursuit of hobbies and education.

Motivation-Robinson's Classification: According to Robinson, the main purposes of people undertaking travel or tourism are:

- **Relaxation and Refreshment of Body and Mind:** This category of tourism motivations is the aftermath of increasing industrialization, growing urbanization, pressures, pushes and pulls of modern life. To overcome these, one necessitates rest and relaxation and undergoing enlivenment of mind and body every so often. The nature and the design in which relaxation, recreation or pleasure is sought vary with the individual. Relaxation and refreshment to some degree, whatever the form of holiday, are the predominant motivations of the holiday maker looking for escape from the pressures of every day life. Tourism, thus, becomes instrumental in breathing new life or rejuvenating an individual's moral, ethical health along with re-establishing the passionate poise.
- **Health:** Health is one of the critical objects for most of the people to practice travel or tourism (Health Tourism). Since primeval times, people have been visiting spas and other watering places to take and bathe in medicinal waters or undergo specialized medical treatments. Several spas and climes the world over are sought after for their curative aspects and entice many visitors. This has, indeed, contributed a lot in the development of 'Health Resorts' in many parts of the world. Lively involvement in a range of sporting activities as a means of recreation has evolved into one of the key motivations of modern tourism. Sports involving physical activities such as skiing, sailing, underwater swimming, surfing, mountaineering and trekking, etc., which offset and provide relief from the inertia and tedium of the daily working life, are for large number of people the *raison d' etre* of holiday.
- **Pleasure:** Robinson reiterates McIntosh's interpretation that the motivation for satisfying an individual's need for pleasure, good time and enthusiasm is "perhaps, the most predominant of all individual travel motivations" (Pleasure Tourism). A person's need for pleasure

of the kind mentioned is very deep-rooted and "travel has the unique quality of being able to satisfy this desire. While pleasure and romance (associated with the holiday) are primary attributes of the holiday travel experience, they are also very strong motivators".

- **Curiosity and Culture:** People are motivated by curiosity about other people, countries and their culture, i.e., an urge to seek new experiences (Cultural Tourism). "The increased interest shown by many in art, architecture, music, literature, dance, folklore, sports and pastimes of other people's culture or in archeological or historical remains and monuments is but another aspect of curiosity. This has been stimulated by more education".

For this class of people, international sports or mega events, special festivals and celebrations make up an outstanding pull.

- **Interpersonal Reasons:** The category of interpersonal motivations is linked to people's desire to visit their relatives, friends, families and ancestral homelands (Ethnic Tourism) or to meet new people and seek new alliances and intimacies. The motivation also finds manifestation in the individual's desire associated with an escape from his normal environment and surroundings.
- **Spiritual Purposes:** Large sections of people in different parts of the world are also motivated to travel as a result of spiritual motives, that is, visiting shrines, holy places and making pilgrimages to the sacred religious sites (Pilgrimage Tourism and Spiritual Tourism). The motivation is indicative of a way to discover oneself and may represent an irresistible act of faith, or an interest in the holy places.
- **Professional or Business Reasons:** Professional and business concerns also prove to be a strong motivation for many to travel (Business Tourism), often combining both the business activities and pleasure. On the whole, the basic motive for such a travel is personal development, enhancement of standing and status, and setting up and strengthening of contacts. Conventions, conferences and professional/business meetings allure people from their respective lines of work and walk of life at one forum to interact and/or transact with each other.

Motivations for Tourist Travel – According to Iso-Ahols's two-dimensional theory of leisure motivation, two motivational forces simultaneously influence the individual's leisure behavior. This theory says that, the psychological benefits of recreation emanate from the interplay of two forces: escaping from routine and stressful environment, and seeking of recreational opportunity for certain psychological rewards.

The two forces are one of seeking and one of escaping. As a consequence, people learn to desire vacations, especially shorter ones, for escape purposes and come to think of such vacations as essential for their psychological well being. The construct 'optimal arousal' is important for understanding travel and tourism motivation.

It was found that vacation preferences depend on the difference between the individual's optimal or ideal level of stimulation (a personality trait) and actual lifestyle stimulation experiences. It is hypothesized that those who take vacations to escape over-stimulation, participate in fewer leisure activities and are less likely to seek personal or interpersonal rewards from leisure participation during the vacation, than those who use vacations to increase the level of stimulation in their lives. This is also corroborated by this research.

The rich and the big, the famous and the busy seek the serenity of the Himalayas and the quiet of hill stations. They prefer to laze, stroll and gaze. But the not-so-busy and not-so-rich seek action and more stimulation. Children cutting across backgrounds look at travel as stimulation and get most bored if there is 'nothing to do'!

Maslow's notion of peak experience and Csikszentmihaliyis' concept of flow have been particularly attractive conceptualizations of leisure researchers, since they itemize a variety of characteristics of phenomenological experience derived from a wide range of engagements.

Leiper pointed out that all leisure involves a temporary escape of some kind but tourism's unique in that it involves physical escape reflected in travelling to one or more destination regions where the leisure experiences transpire. He says: 'A holiday trip allows changes that are multi-dimensional – place, pace, faces, lifestyles, behaviour, attitude. It allows a person temporary withdrawal from many of the environments affecting day-to-day existence.'

As such, Leiper argues, tourism changes leisure opportunities, particularly for rest and relaxation. Having established a 'break from routine' as the basic motivation for tourist travel, Crompton suggests that it is possible to identity more specific directive motives which serve to 'guide the tourist' towards the selection of particular type of vacation or destination in preference to all the alternatives of which the tourist is aware.

Conclusion

In their extensive review of research based on Maslow's theory, Wahba and Bridwell found little evidence for the ranking of needs that Maslow described or for the existence of a definite hierarchy at all. The order in which the hierarchy is arranged (with self-actualization described as the highest need) has been criticized as being ethnocentric by Geert Hofstede. Maslow's hierarchy of needs fails to illustrate and expand upon the difference between the social and intellectual needs of those raised in individualistic societies and those raised in collectivist societies.

Recent research appears to validate the existence of universal human needs, although the hierarchy proposed by Maslow is called into question. Other research indicates that Maslow's explanations of the hierarchy of human motivation reflect a binary pattern of growth as seen in mathematics.

Originally dealing primarily with maternal deprivation and concordant losses of essential and primal needs, attachment theory has since been extended to provide explanations of nearly all the human needs in Maslow's hierarchy, from sustenance and mating to group membership and justice. While Maslow's hierarchy remains a very popular framework in sociology research and secondary and post-secondary psychology instruction, it has largely been supplanted by attachment theory in graduate and clinical psychology and psychiatry.

The needs and drives of those in individualistic societies tend to be more self-centered than those in collectivist societies, focusing on improvement of the self, with self-actualization being the apex of self-improvement. In collectivist societies, the needs of acceptance and community will outweigh the needs for freedom and individuality. The term "Self-actualization" may not universally convey Maslow's observations; this motivation refers to focusing on becoming the best person that one can possibly strive for in the service of both the self and others. Maslow's term of self-actualization might not properly portray the full extent of this level; quite often, when a person is at the level of self-actualization, much of what they accomplish in general may benefit others or, "the greater self".

The position and value of sex on the pyramid has also been a source of criticism regarding Maslow's hierarchy. Maslow's hierarchy places sex in the physiological needs category along with food and breathing; it lists sex solely from an individualistic perspective. For example, sex is placed with other physiological needs which must be satisfied before a person considers "higher" levels of motivation. Some critics feel this placement of sex neglects the emotional, familial, and evolutionary implications of sex within the community, although others point out that this is true of all the basic needs.

In most decisions, more than one motive is operative. The different motives can be conceptualized as being located along a 'cultural socio-psychological disequilibrium continuum'. Seven of these, says Crompton, are identifiable as follows: Escape from a perceived mundane environment, Exploration and evaluation of self, Relaxation, Prestige, Regression (less constrained behaviour), Enhancement of kinship relationship, and Facilitation of social interaction. Two primary cultural motives expressed in Crompton's study were 'education' and 'novelty'.

UNIT–III:

TOURISM DEVELOPMENT: ISSUES AND PROBLEMS

8

Tourism Development: Issues and Problems in India

Twentieth centrury and early years of tweny first century witnessed a phenomenal growth in the volume of Tourism traffic and lead it from an incidental industry at the start of the century practically to world's largest industry. It was realized that opening of borders to the global community would improve economic conditions and widen horizons. The countries in Asia also took the advantage of the dynamic impact of the Tourism industry in terms of jobs creation, foreign exchange acquisition and as a catalyst for general economic development. India also did not lag behind and took steps to increase the potential economic role of the industry on the country, as she also wanted to derive some of the benefits originated by overall positive trend in tourist flow. It was presumed that the development of Tourism would turn out to be a panacea for India through its multiplier effect and would create both economic and social benefits. "The travel and Tourism industry is labour intensive, creating jobs of both skilled and unskilled variety. Approximately 200 million jobs were created in 1999; the forecast, according to a FICCI report, is that approximately 5.5 million new jobs would be generated per year till 2010. In the Indian context, it is estimated that every one million additional visitors could translate into Rs. 4,300 crores of revenue for the industry. Every additional investment of Rs. 1 million has a potential to generate 47.7 jobs. Every job created leads to creation of 11 indirect jobs."

There are certain specific problems, which have generally been constantly ignored by the government as well as providers of Tourism related services. For instance:

(a) Tourism firms offer services that depend on the presence of guests, so accurate correspondence between services offered and customers need is imperative.

(b) Tourist services are truly complementary, as tourists ask for a service package including transport, accommodation, catering, etc.

(c) A fixed offer is confronted with an elastic demand, which leads to a particularly high sales risk.

(d) Tourist trade is relatively capital intensive (it requires the provision of means of transport, accommodation, catering, and equipment for sports and leisure facilities, etc.). Fierce competition exists from both investment goods and especially from other touristic offers.

(e) The tourist market has changed from a seller's to a buyer's market. This mandates particular care in assessing demand for any decision about the activities of the company. As all these demands/problems are becoming more and more pronounced and serious day by day; these were supposed to be given a systematic and holistic view.

The factors/problems that impede the growth of Tourism sector can be broadly listed as follows:

- Tourism has been treated as an 'elitist' sector and a luxury for developing country like India.
- Lack of adequate infrastructure in the form of air services and airports, poor rail and road services, accommodation and poor sanitation services.
- Levy of tax on tourism and tourists that are not only high but also unscrupulous such as irrational taxes, high visa fee and lack of landing permits.
- There are policy hurdles, as plethora of clearances have to be obtained from numerous agencies of the central and state governments. There are difficulties in obtaining land for hotel projects. There are numerous restrictions on the movements of tourists and tourist vehicles.
- Lack of adequate security to foreign tourists to go around without fear of bodily harm or loss of belongings.
- There is poor human resource development. The visitor is treated as an intruder than as an honouring guest.

- Lack of innovativeness in marketing efforts to promote diverse Tourism products offered by the country.
- Considerable amount of revenue earned returns back to the tourist-generating countries in the form of leakages. This is on account of – (i) payment of loans and dividends on foreign investment; (ii) the importation of goods and services to supply the tourists; and (iii) salaries of senior personnels who are often temporary residents.
- Tourism industry carries within it the seeds of its own destruction if its development is undertaken in haste without proper planning.
- Climate of terrorism has proved to be a big hurdle for Tourism.
- Beggars on the streets, poor connectivity, pesky touts, unhygienic conditions, extremely prohibitive entry fees at many monuments and streets full of potholes are the limiting factors in attracting international tourists to India.
- India is high cost and highly taxed destination.
- Visas on entry for people from 16 countries – an excellent idea but merely on paper.
- Appalling inefficiency in clearing normal passenger traffic.
- Diktats for forcing of dress codes and restrictions on eating by some orthodox elements.
- Government policies keep changing overnight.
- Rupee-Dollar parity has become unfavourable and, as such, actual remittances have gone down greatly.
- Lack of a brand equity based on the country's civilization and culture.
- Greatly mismanaged overseas offices and funds merrily misused.
- Lack of coordinated efforts between the ministries of external affairs, commerce, industry, civil aviation and Tourism.
- Lack of vision.
- Marketing India as a whole.
- Lack of centre-state coordination.

To maximize the advantageous development of Tourism, it is necessary to formulate clear planning and management strategy. Making a strategy is an activity that all tourism organizations should engage in, irrespective of size or sector. Like many other acts of management, it calls for coordination and control through planning. The competitive pressure forces travel companies to tread new paths. In such a setup, no manager can assume that 'tomorrow will be an extension of today'. The nature of strategy and planning may be different in a small Tourism business and a large multi-product and multi-market business. However, if the staff is also involved in making of strategy and bringing their ideas and insight into the process, team building and coordination occur as a result.

This would require establishing a network of well-trained people catering to the tourists with care and proper guidance to create trusts in the minds of the tourists. A number of new management approaches have appeared ready to confront such challenges. Managing human resources is one such approach. Human resource management relates to the total set of knowledge, skills, and attitudes that firms needs to conform. The development of human resources requires identifying the existing workforce characteristics and future needs, and also tackling the planning and implementation of a programme to respond to these needs. In this regard, a comprehensive strategy would have to be evolved that should have following possible components.

- Survey the existing education and training institutions and evaluate their contribution to HRD; the quality of programmes and the capacity and output of trainees and students.
- Assess the capacity and quality of the existing education and training system and identify any training gaps.
- Prepare proposals for the improvements, expansion and development of the network of educational and training institutions and centres to meet future needs
- Review in-service training programmes, and other post-employment trainings, in relation to the identified needs.
- Identify future needs for specialized teachers and training staff, and formulate proposals for the teacher training programmes.
- Formulate programmes for all specialized trainings, including, for example, government Tourism officials, tourist guides, and planning and marketing specialists.
- Outline the proposals for the development of a comprehensive set of occupational skill standards for the sector.
- Consult with the universities on the development of their role in relation to both Tourism studies and research.

- Review with the educational authorities the introduction of Tourism-related education and training in existing educational institutions.
- Government, in close collaboration with the private sector, should encourage private enterprises to take appropriate training initiatives.
- Draft, review and finalize, or update and finalize, as the case may be, the Tourism HRD strategy.
- Consult extensively with any national, or council, or similar body, on all aspects of the strategy.
- Training opportunities must be provided within the destination and local skills must be raised, to secure the future of the industry in the country and its long-term self-sufficiency.
- Make a regular use of SWOT analysis of the strategies.

The globalization of the economy, and resulting global threats and opportunities have made it necessary to enter into strategic alliances on a worldwide basis. With the increase of the needs of the traveller, there is growing need to have strategic alliances and links between the travel industry, hotels, banking, and telecommunications. To meet the needs, till now being considered 'futuristic', strategic alliances may have to be formed between former competitors. As a result, rather than the traditional hierarchical organizational chart, the company will resemble an integrated network, with core competence in the centre and other supporting activities through out the system.

It may be pointed out here that due to the failure of globalization to redress the economic imbalance, the questions are being raised whether global economy will, at all, bring balanced, responsible and profitable tourism development to the emerging destinations in the years to come.

INFRASTRUCTURE AND SUPER-STRUCTURE

Tourism supply could be classified into four basic components – natural resources and environment; the built environment; transportation; and hospitality and cultural resources. All these components would definitely include air and climate, different land forms, terrain, flora and fauna, beaches, natural beauty and water supply.

To enjoy all this, a tourist requires at least a basic infrastructure – water supply systems, roads, communication networks and as well as the basic superstructures including airports, parks, marinas, hotels and motels. Transportation required would be of two types – one to reach the destination and other to reach the attractions. These could include hospitality and recrecational resources.

Hospitality and cultural resources include the nature of the people and the culture of the area that make tourism successful such as the history, literature, friendliness, courtesy and welcoming spirit. Keeping in mind all these we should not forget the segmentation based on geographical aspects of the tourist. The locational characteristics associated with the supply of different recreational resources; the patterns of demand and usage; and the spatial interactions demand for an supply of the recreational resource.

The research analysis shows the supply of recreational resources on the urban fringe and the concept and spatial analysis of the supply of tourism facilities.

This chapter deals with challenging subject of defining the tourism "industry" and the tension between a supply-side versus demand side definitions. No other industry uses demand-side definitions and the author argues for tourism definitions that begin to use supply-side concepts. While it is recognized that the tourism industry is unlike any other industry – it does not produce goods in an industry-wise standard manner – it posits that the tourism industry's primary product can be conceptualized as an experience involving all aspects of a trip.

A hypothetical structure of the tourism product is discussed and it includes five elements: a physical element; a service; hospitality; personal choice; and involvement by the visitor. The chapter also discusses Tourism Satellite Accounts (TSAs) that are an important standardized method for measuring the impact of the tourism industry. However, TSAs still define tourism using demand-side definitions.

The demand of infrastructure and superstrstructue would always depend upon the length of stay, type of traveller, type of trip, type of expenditure, transport mode or accommodation type. The Standard International Classification of Tourism Activities (SICTA) is also presented which is a globalized system for classifying and measuring tourism activity. It combines supply-side concepts – the basic structure is based on establishments, and demand-side concepts – establishments are selected according to the nature of their customers (e.g. the percentage of tourists)

Infrastructure: These are the basic public services needed for the successful operation of tourism enterprises for optimising the comfort of the visitors. It includes such services as roads, electricity, water, security, sanitation and health services, telephone and postal communication, railways and airports.

Superstructure: Superstructure includes hotels, accommodation units, restaurants and the whole range of tourist installations and services; hotels and other accommodation, restaurants, shopping facilities, entertainment services and structures (cinemas, theatres, museums, art galleries, concert halls) and traffic terminals. Dividing line between this and infrastructure is not distinct but is fundamental to planning of new resorts, etc.

Infrastructural Development: Development and improvement of infrastructure is another important benefit. The benefits from infrastructure investments, justified primarily for tourism – airports, roads, water supply and other public amenities – may be widely shared by the other sectors of the economy. In addition to development of new infrastructure, the improvements in the existing infrastructure which are undertaken in order to attract tourists is also of crucial importance. These improvements may confer benefits upon the resident population by providing them with amenities which, hitherto, they had not enjoyed. Furthermore, the provision of infrastructure may provide the basis or serve as an encouragement for greater economic diversification.

A variety of secondary industries may be promoted which may not serve the needs of tourism. Thus, indirectly, tourism expenditure may be responsible for stimulating other economic activities. One of the characteristics of underdevelopment is that of the deficiencies in the basic infrastructures, which lie at the root of a series of serious problems related to the development of tourism. Construction of primary infrastructures represents the foundation of any future economic growth, even though they are not directly productive.

The tourist industry illustrates the elementary need for basic infrastructures. It has today the important benefit of being able to profit from the existing infrastructures and thus to make a decisive contribution to the growth of the national economy. The traffic arising from international and national tourism, moreover, represents a reward for the capital invested and can now contribute to the financial efforts required for maintenance. The satisfactory degree of development achieved in this specific sector now permits major tourist progress, while giving further proof to the complementary character of tourism in relation to other economic sectors. Creation of basic infrastructure for tourist usage will also be of service to the other sectors of the economy like industry and agriculture. The outcome of this is better equilibrium of general economic growth.

The complex of economic sectors service material production and the non-productive sphere; the basic public services needed for the successful operation of tourism enterprises and optimize the comfort of the visitors. Infrastructure includes such services as the construction of road network, airports, railway lines, airport runways, the supply of water, electricity and other power supply, drainage and sewerage system, parking areas, security, sanitation and health services, telephone and postal communication, canals, bridges, ports, reservoirs, and warehouses, power supply, transport, communication, trade, the information processing system, etc. All these are necessary for intensive human living activity within an area. Moreover it must be adequate to serve tourists and local residents. It further provides the base for superstructure.

Attractions and facilities are not accessible to tourists' use until basic infrastructural and superstructure need of the destination have been met. These include:

- Water – Sufficient quantities of pure water are essential. It is estimated that a typical resort requires 1300 to 1500 liters of water per room per day.

- Power – The important considerations are that adequate supplies of power be available to meet peak-load requirements, that continuity of service be assured. The type of power supplied should be compatible with that used by the target markets of the destination.
- Communication – Despite the fact that many tourists may wish to get away from it altogether, it is necessary for most that proper communication services be available. The lack of these facilities in the hotel rooms will often discourage visitors from staying at a particular property because of the security aspects.
- Sewage/drainage – Water-storage reservoirs and sewage treatment plants must be designed on the basis of maximum average demand, and transmission lines must be designed on the basis of maximum peak demand.
- Health Care – The type of health-care facilities provided will depend upon the number of visitors expected, their age, the type of activities in which they will engage, and local geographical factors.
- Streets/Highways – The availability of first-class roads adds greatly to the accessibility of a region. Roads should be engineered for safety, by taking appropriate measures designed to safeguard the highway user.
- Transportation Terminals – There should be a degree of coordination between the three modes of air, road, and rail to facilitate passenger transfer between modes. A security system should be in place to prevent theft of luggage and/or mis-claiming of checked baggage at terminals. Complete information should be provided on the location, fares, schedules, and routes of local transportation services.
- Security – While on vacation tourists are in an unfamiliar environment. Because of this, the need for assurances regarding their safety is important. In the absence of this, when travelling long distances and foreign countries, the image gained of the destination gets distorted. It is necessary that the basic needs for security and safety be considered and assured to make the potential tourist feel secure prior to and during the vacation.

Influence of Infrastructure and Superstructure on Tourist Flows:

Infrastructural and superstructure development is a prerequisite for the development of tourism. The destination with proper infrastructure attracts more tourists. Besides, the infrastructure of a destination is shared both by tourists and residents. An upgradation of the elements of the infrastructure primarily for the purpose of attracting tourists will benefit the host population and help in the economic and the overall development of the destination.

Hospitality Resources:

Hospitality resources refer to the general feeling of welcome that visitors receive while visiting a destination area.

It is the way that tourist services are delivered by service providers, as well as general feeling of warmth from the general resident population.

The way in which services are delivered is particularly important because tourism is consumed on the spot.

Tourists will have a much more rewarding vacation if they feel welcomed by the host population.

Hospitality Training – A programme of hospitality training is generally aimed at motivating service providers to be hospitable in their dealings with tourists.

Traditionally, the tourism industries have lacked prestige. If service providers can be made to believe that their work and they themselves are important, the hope is that their work and specifically their actions toward tourists will reflect this new feeling. Moreover, visitors often bring demands with them that are difficult to satisfy.

As such, the ability to create a satisfied guest is a very demanding task. Those people who can do this have skills that should be highly regarded by themselves as well by others.

The key to the development of positive attitude towards visitors is being able to develop the ability to put oneself in the visitor's place.

At the same time, a positive attitude on the part of service providers toward tourists can come about only when employees are made aware of how important tourism is to their state, country, city, and property. This could be achieved by raising the knowledge level of the individual. This may be done in group sessions or through a variety of audio-visual means.

If people can be trained in specific desired behaviour and act them out, the positive feedback they receive will result in positive attitude.

Employees are often unaware of the negative messages their facial expressions or postures give. As such, they have to be taught to exhibit positive hospitable behaviour.

Food and Beverage:

It has been noticed that the states highest in per capita eatables sales are also top tourist states.

The type of food service provided will be related to tourist needs. At the same time, many areas have successfully developed menus consisting of indigenous items as a Unique Selling Point (USP).

Support Industries:

Beverage: These may include souvenir or duty-free shops (for goods), laundries and guides (for services), and festival areas and recreational facilities (for activities).

Influence of Facilities on Tourist Flows:

The number and types of facilities provided are normally determined relative to tourist needs.

If a sufficient number and mix of services are provided, the supply may actually stimulate demand. It may also increase the length of stay of visitors. The offering of a number of attractive alternatives may mean that the tourists will have enough things to buy and encourage them to stay longer.

Influence of Hospitality Resources on Tourist Flows:

The assumption is that providing more hospitable service will result in a more satisfied tourist who will be inclined to return and/or spread positive reactions through word-of-mouth advertising to other potential tourists.

The hope is that more hospital behaviour will come from a better self-image, and positive attitude about tourism's role in the community.

NATIONAL AND INTERNATIONAL CONCERNS AND PROBLEMS

Tourism is a complex and composite phenomena, which embraces the "incidence" of mobile population of travellers, who are stranger to the place they visit. It is composed of heterogeneous units and has directly or indirectly wide spread influences on almost every section and activity of the society. The tourism industry thus involves environmental, geographical, ecological, sociological and economic consideration with all the manifestations. However, its basic components are transport, locale and accommodation.

Tourism is a multi-dimensional concept and implies many things to many people. For the tourist it is travel, relaxation, a holiday, an expose to other cultures and traditions. Those who "sell" tourism naturally see things differently. To them, it is an industry, a source of income, especially of foreign exchange. Thus, conceptually it is an amalgam of phenomena and relationships arising from the movement of people "to" and their "stay" in the different destinations. The "journey" (a dynamic element) and "stay" (a static element) are the two necessary constituents of the mass phenomenon called tourism.

The Tourism Essence includes:

(A) *Travel*: To a location, that is not the tourist's home. The simplest spatial model of the tourist system consist of three spatial elements:

- The tourist's home (the tourist-generating region).
- The places people travel to reach *the Destination regions.*
- The *routes* people follow between the generating and destination regions.

(B) *Travel geography* is concerned with the study of all three elements of the system, *all spatial scales* from the study of domestic tourism with the city or region, through to world of intentional travel.

- It is concerned with the economic and physical charters of the tourist-generating region and the motivation of the tourists. That add up to the "PUSH" factors that make people wish to travel.

(C) *The nature of the destination areas* means The "PULL" factors that attract travellers to particular places. The route and organization of transport systems and services that enable the tourist to get from home to the tourist destination.

However, whole concept of tourism has been transformed from the Mass, Rigid and Packaged tourism (MSRP) to the present neo-tourism, which is Flexible, Segmented and Diagonally Integrated (FSDI). Moreover, in the wake of enforcing economic liberalization and globalization, the development policies of no sector can be independent and/or operative in isolation, remains static and unrelated to the broad national perspectives. This proposition is equally relevant to tourism involving the activities of humans travelling to and staying in places outside their usual habitat and environment for different motives and purposes – be it education, experiences, enrichment, or enjoyment.

Tourism Concern's campaigning efforts and programme activities have led to major positive change over the years.Tourism generates positive benefits as well as negative effects. Communities who have greater control within tourism development are able to direct development according to their priorities. Strategies must be prioritised to empower people to be better enabled to have a say in the development of their communities and country and the capacity to shape tourism development for equitable benefit. Tourism is our livelihood and the livelihood of the people, it is our joint responsibility to promote sustainable development in tourism. We travel extensively and try to influence good practice wherever possible.

Growth of Mass Tourism:

Mass tourism developed over the last few decades, due to market trend, tourists' higher levels of disposable income, greater leisure time, being better-educated and having more sophisticated tastes. There is now a demand for better quality products, which has resulted in a fragmentation of the mass market for beach vacations; people want more specialised versions, such as 'Club 18-30', quieter resorts, family-oriented holidays, or niche market-targeted destination hotels. As well, people are taking second short break holidays.

The developments in technology and transport infrastructure such as jumbo jets and low-budget airlines have made many types of tourism more affordable. There have also been changes in lifestyle, such as retiree-age people who live as a tourist all the year round. This is facilitated by internet-purchase of tourism products. Some sites have now started to offer dynamic packaging, in which an inclusive price is quoted for a tailor-made package requested by the customer, upon impulse.

There have been a few setbacks in tourism, such as the September 11, 2001 attacks and terrorist threats to tourist destinations such as Bali and European cities. Some of the tourist destinations, including the beach resorts of Cancún have lost popularity due to shifting tastes. In this context, the excessive building and environmental destruction is often associated with traditional "sun and beach" tourism.

These developments coincided with a significant contribution of post-war affordable air travel in combination with the package tour the bilateral agreements that enabled international mass tourism to develop. The terms Tourism and Travel are sometimes used interchangeably. In this context travel has a similar definition to tourism, but implies a more purposeful journey. The terms Tourism and Tourist are sometimes used pejoratively, to imply a shallow interest in the cultures or locations visited by tourists.

Other miscellaneous types of niche tourism include:

- *Armchair tourism* and *virtual tourism*: not traveling physically, but exploring the world through internet, books, or TV.
- *Dark tourism* includes travel to sites associated with death and suffering, such as the scene of the Hindenburg airship disaster, or to the sites of disasters (Disaster tourism).
- *Drug tourism*, (e.g., to use drugs in Amsterdam).
- *Free Independent Traveler*: a sector of the market in which the tourists select their own accommodation and transport, rather than using the established tourism booking system.
- *Pop-culture tourism*: tourism by those that visit a particular location after reading about it or seeing it used as a location in a film (e.g., the Lord of the Rings film sets in New Zealand).

- *Perpetual tourism*: individuals always on vacation; some of them, for tax purposes, to avoid being resident in any country.
- *Pilgrimage* Tourism: pilgrimages to ancient holy places (Rome and Santiago de Compostela for Catholics, temples and stupas of Nepal for the Hindus and Buddhist, Mount Athos or Painted churches of northern Moldavia for the Orthodox), religious sites such as mosques and shrines.
- *Sacred travel* or metaphysical tourism is a form of New Age travel where believers travel to and perform rituals at religious sites.
- *Sex tourism* (e.g., to have sex with prostitutes).
- Shopping Tourism: promoting shopping festivals such as the Dubai Shopping Festival.
- *Space tourism*: traveling in outer space or on spaceships.
- *Vacilando* is a special kind of wanderer for whom the process of traveling and discovery is more important than the destination.
- Visiting Family and Relatives (VFR) Tourism: traveling to visit persons related by close family ties and combining this with vacation-type activities; distinct from ancestry tourism, which involves genealogical research.

Tourism and Crime: One of the most significant and least desirable by product of tourism is its effect on the moral standards of the host population. The growth of prostitution, crime and gambling has been mentioned frequently as evil of the tourism development. Tourists are often targeted as victims of two types of crime.

Common crime: tourists are at risk with regard to certain types of common crimes, particularly assault, mugging and highway robbery. It is certain that tourists will be found carrying cash, travellers cheques, and credit cards. Tourists themselves are usually conspicuous. Hire cars and tourist cars are usually easy to identify.

Politically motivated crime: tourists are made the targets of political movements – usually through kidnapping and sometimes assassination. By committing crimes against tourists, revolutionary groups hope to gain publicity for their cause. Many countries have decided to set up a tourist police unit. The objectives of this unit can be summarized as supporting tourism by providing tourists with security and assistance, and by preventing crimes against tourists or crimes committed by tourists.

Tourism and Cultural Change: Cultural change is induced both by factors which are internal and external to culture. Cultures would change in the absence of tourism. Cultural change may occur as a result of: Modifications of the ecological niche occupied by a society. Changes to the habitat of a society often induce changes, which may involve cultural adaptation, and change. Contact between two societies with different cultures may bring about changes to both groups.

Evolutionary changes occurring within a society. This refers to the process of adaptation where societies change in response to internal, biological and social needs to ensure satisfaction from their environment. Tourism could conceivably influence all three of these modes of change, but the literature on tourism documents the effects in the second category. Any tourist analyst faces severe difficulties in separating the effects of tourism on host cultures from those changes induced by other causes. Tourism represents only one form of exposure of hosts to elements of societies with a different culture. It appears that tourism is able to accelerate cultural change, but the effects are not endemic to tourism and some of the modifications mentioned in the literature may reflect a series of changes, not all of which are the results of tourism alone.

Tourism and Environment: Tourism is called smokeless industry, which can be synonymous with the protection and conservation of the environment. The improvement, conservation of natural, and man made tourist resources, contribute to tourist product and has no danger to the nation's resources. The scenic beauty, local culture, life styles, valleys, mountains are of great interest to visitors or tourists. The growth of tourism both domestic and international does less harm to the environment as compared to other industrial development. However, tourism specifically international tourism has negative impact on the environment, but this impact is negligible. Tourism can become an instrument for beautification and improvement of the environment, if it is planned in a systematic manner.

Environment, today has acquired a broad definition. It not only includes land, air, water, flora and fauna, but also encompasses people, their creations, and social, economic and cultural conditions that affect their lives. Environment, whether natural or man-made, is an essential resource for tourism. Changes are unavoidable if we have to develop tourism, but these changes can be done aesthetically without damaging it in anyway. Conservation really means wise use of resources. It implies safeguarding the visual beauty of the countryside. Conservation of wildlife means survival of all living things – flora and fauna, providing them ample space to live, grow and breathe fresh air. The protection given by the governments, especially in India has given a new lease of life to endangered species of animals, but the present danger is in the of form poachers.

Tourism Issues Needs Attention

Currently, with the tremendous boost in travel world over, it has been realized, not only by the individual governments, particularly of the developing nations but also by the International organisations that "World belongs to man and everyone has a right to know and enjoy the world not just around him but also beyond him".

To emphasise the significance of the above statement, it will be appropriate here to quote the extract from the United Nations' Conference on International Travel and Tourism held in 1963, which underlined the need for a National Tourism Administrative (NTA) using the following words:

"The Conference considers that it is incumbent on governments to stimulate and coordinate national tourism activities and is convinced that this task can, in the main, be carried out through the medium of National Tourist Organisations".

Therefore, the planning process in tourism should outline the optimum objectives to be attained in a given period of time. This planning should be treated as an integral part of the country's general economic and social planning. The key phases in tourism planning are as follows:

- Assessment of tourism demand and a scientific planned approach to the supply of such demands.
- Tourism objectives should cover the overall development of a nation.
- Tourism site planning should be done by totally avoiding damage to natural and cultural assets.
- Focus should be on development of basic infrastructure which would be needed by any tourist.
- Financial planning should be done involving public, private agencies and foreign investment.
- Appropriate man-power planning must be done, especially because tourism is a service industry.
- There is also a need for efficient Administrative planning.
- Focus to be placed also on tourism marketing, promotional strategies within & outside the country.
- Lastly, monitoring and evaluation must be done on a consistent basis.

Attitude of Tourists

The immediate challenge to nations in this era of global travel is to retain their own identity and yet adopt modernism. Environmental issue is probably the most burning issue in this context today. The likely long-term environmental losses due to tourism need to be weighed against its short-term gains. In fact, we find ourselves in the midst of a business paradigm transition where the traditional/conventional norms for profitability and sustainable success are becoming obsolete.

Understanding international consumers and their needs, motivations and different travel styles, will enable you to see where your product fits internationally and select the right markets. To be successful in the export tourism industry, it is important to understand the roles of Tour Operators, International Wholesalers, Retail Travel Agents and other partners in the international travel distribution system. You will need to identify key partners and establish and maintain relationships with them. Your product price structure should also support the commission levels required by your partners in the distribution system. It takes time to establish a successful level of international sales and position your product in the international market. Your marketing strategies should be well-planned and incorporate a variety of activities that target both the international consumer and the travel trade.

And a new paradigm, primarily characterized by the focus on achieving profitability through system economies (quality tourism per se that destroys the environment), it is poor tourism planning and ineffective management that does it. Managed efficiently and effectively, tourism can definitely be far less destructive than the non-tourism industries while being no less earning.

Youth tourism is considered one of the largest and fastest growing segments of the global tourism industry, accounting for approximately 20 per cent of international tourist arrivals. The majority of youth travellers are students under the age of 25, but there is a category of older "youth" travellers in their early thirties, and the number of these may be expected to grow in coming years.The UNWTO has even coined the term "flashbackers" for these older youths. In a 2008 study, UNWTO wrote that, "a new generation of "flashpackers" (older backpackers with bigger budgets) is emerging, extending the 'youth travel' market to 30+ years.

The youth market is one of the fastest growing tourism segments, with numbers increasing at 3-5%, and sometimes as high as 8% annually. Youth overnight stays are expected to rise to 500 million by 2020 from the current 300 million overnight annual stays.

The Internet has fuelled the growth of the travel industry by providing online booking facilities. It has also provided people with the power to explore destinations and cultures from their home personal computers and make informed choices before finalizing travel plans. With its immense information resources, the Internet allows tourists to scrutinise hotels, check weather casts, read up on local food and even talk to other tourists around the world about their travel experiences for a chosen destination.

This new trend has made the tourism job very challenging. The holiday makers want a good rate of return on their investment.

They are to be with value additions and improved customer service. This also put emphasis on the regular flow of manpower with specific skills at the appropriate levels to match and cater to global standards. The success of the hospitality industry comes from provision of quality rooms, food, service and ambience. There is no doubt that fitness has increasingly become a larger part of everyone's life.

Tourism Ethic: It is up to the residents to plan for the type of tourism that best suits the community. Tourism rarely occurs by accident; people want it, foster it or tolerate it. Communities need to take control and shape the type of tourism that fits their lifestyle, their community, and does not destroy their surroundings.

Residents need to adopt and use a tourism ethic. This means that when planning for tourism, residents must consider the social, cultural and environmental consequences of tourism. The sheer fact that alternative tourism is being discussed within the industry is an acknowledgement that mass tourism has contributed to the destruction of resources around the world and is becoming a cause for concern.

Change is required and the change has to begin from within the host community. Tourists too must adopt a tourism ethic– they must consider the social cultural and environmental consequences of their actions. This requires knowledge and tourism education. Most tourists do not realize what it means when they litter, even if just a little bit. They also might not understand what it means to purchase banned products while they may be contributing to the destruction of wild life (e.g. ivory from elephant trunks) or a special environment (e.g. destroying coral in the ocean).

Tourism education is necessary for the tourists and residents alike. Both need to become more sensitive to each other's need and culture and to the consequences of being insensitive and unaware. Tourism professionals and educators have a stake in developing a tourism ethic. The long-term future of tourism is more secure to the extent that such an ethic conserves resources, smoothens relations between hosts and guests, and assists with the management of tourism.

Like environmental ethics, it will take a long time to develop a tourism ethic. The task although large and time-consuming should not be shunned. In the end, tourism may not be able to absorb the costs of doing otherwise.

Tourism Expected Trends: The World Tourism Organization (UNWTO) forecasts that international tourism will continue growing at the average annual rate of 4%. By 2020, Europe will remain the most popular destination, but its share will drop from 60% in 1995 to 46%. Long-haul will grow slightly faster than intraregional travel and by 2020, its share will increase from 18% in 1995 to 24%.

Awareness should be created about the environment and education. A collective effort and co-operation with powerful networking are the need of the hour. People should be acting as the watchdogs of the society as far as environmental issues are concerned. Eco-tourists are a growing community and tourism promotions have to adopt such eco-practices which could fit this growing community.

Recently, environmentalists have become quite vocal in voicing their protests against the unregulated growth of tourism at the cost of the environment. The WTO and PATA have laid down guidelines to protect the environment and some countries have enacted laws for its conservation and preservation. India is one of the countries to have set up a separate Ministry of Environment and Forests to monitor the use of land from the environment point of view. The ministry is very vigilant about the land, which is under the forest department, and prior clearance from the central government is essential before any tourist project can be set up in such areas. The world now has become very environment-conscious and this approach can harmonize tourism and nature.

A brilliant article, '*Who is a tourist? A critical review*' by Scott McCabe, is very useful to understand psychology of the tourists.

This article discusses the concept of the 'tourist' within tourist studies. It critiques the conceptual category of tourist in recent literature on typologies of tourists and tourist experiences. Although greater understanding of the tourist has been identified as one of the principal research issues for tourism research, the focus is on types and forms of touristic experience rather than uses of the concept of 'tourist' as a lay category, thereby taking for granted its function within a wide cultural discourse of holidaymaking and travelling.

The article raises questions concerning the construct 'tourist' and discusses the implications of such ambiguities for theory and empirical analysis of interview data on tourist experiences. This discussion reviews the literature on tourist experience and typologies, a discussion on the use of the concept of 'tourist'.

Being a tourist is supposed to be a pretty miserable existence. In a whole range of contexts, tourists are portrayed as second-class citizens. As the quote above ably demonstrates, local residents at destinations appear to think that the activities of tourists are fatuous, lazy and plain 'dumb'. A tourist has become a central theme in tourist studies. However, conventional notions of touristic behaviour and attitudes are beginning to be challenged. The most recent developments in these elaborations have noted a shift to more post-modern conceptualizations of tourist experience.

However, in all the recent developments in theorizing about tourist experience, a surprising omission has been a reflection on the use of the term 'tourist' as an everyday, lay concept constructed and deployed purposely to convey meanings about social activities and social actors.

In direct consequence, empirical interpretations of tourists' talk have tended to make truth claims which cast doubt on the claims made about the nature of tourist experiences. This article argues that 'tourist studies' has emerged without an appropriate level of reflective attention given to the use of the term 'tourist' by interview subjects in research studies. It is argued that recent research has focused on disaggregating types and forms of touristic behaviour, or on understanding ideographic meanings behind touristic consumption, derived largely from interview data thereby disregarding the discursive functions of practical language used by tourists in their accounts; the contextual settings of such language use; and the value and validity of data derived in such discursive setting as a mechanism to interpret 'real', underlying, subjective meanings, thus disregarding fundamental cartesian arguments.

Researchers of tourists tend to treat culturally embedded, flexibly deployed and ideological language (of interviews specifically) in a largely unproblematic and disinterested way as a means to gain access to underlying meanings and identities of the speakers. Such realist accounts conflate constructivist interpretations of touristic experience with the cultural and interactional context in which all interaction is situated thereby disregarding the fundamental debate ongoing in the social sciences on such interpretations of empirical data.

CONCERNS AND SOLUTIONS

Geographical Elements – Leiper describes three main geographical elements in his system's model. These are: Traveller-generating region; Tourist destination region and; Transit route region. The traveler-generating region (TGR) exemplifies the area breeding markets for tourism and practically acts as the 'push force to motivate and stimulate, i.e., set off and encourage travel. It is this region where the tourist tries to seek information, goes for reservations and makes the departure. This region is basically related to the demand aspect of travel and tourism. The tourist destination region (TDR) symbolizes the 'sharp end of tourism' and is, indeed, the raison d'etre for tourism. The pull force of the destinations activates the whole tourism system besides begetting demand for travel in the traveller generating region

We and Our Environment

The race for becoming the most advanced and most developed state in the world, has led man to destruct the natural resource in our stock and our biosphere. Today, most of the underground and surface ground resources are on the verge of collapse, resulting in abrupt climate, natural disaster and more. Now, man is facing two very extremely dangerous conditions – 'Global Warming' & 'Greenhouse Effect', both of which will lead to the total destruction of the Planet Earth. It is now high time that the entire human community contributes its bit to job of saving our Earth from complete destruction. It is now every man's duty to do as much as possible to save our Planet Earth.

In 1992, the 'Earth Summit' in Rio established the triple principles of environmental, economic and social sustainability. Since then, the principles of sustainable tourism have been adopted by the tourism industry worldwide. In India, the tourism sector is based on exploiting its unique endowments of biodiversity, forests, rivers, and its rich culture and heritage. The challenges in this sector lie in successfully preserving these in their original form, and making them accessible to domestic and international travellers. Tourism in India has the potential to create economic interest of local communities in the protection of its natural and cultural endowments leading to a more sustainable growth.

The realization of the country's huge, barely tapped, tourism potential is contingent upon simultaneously addressing the multiple challenges thrown up by capacity constraints and inadequate policies. These constraints include inadequate transportation infrastructure; accommodation; land; multiple taxes and an overall high tax burden; inadequate financial resources for enterprises; skills; safety and hygiene conditions around tourist attractions; and convergence of actions by multiple agencies. The challenges are further magnified in the context of a federal structure where the responsibilities for policy making and implementation is fragmented across levels of government and co-ordination between them is often lacking.

Tourism should be concerned with campaigns for better tourism. A world free from exploitation in which all parties involved in tourism benefit equally and in which relationships between industry, tourists and host communities are based on trust and respect.

In a Rights-based Approach

- Local communities must have the right to participate in the decision making about tourism development where they live.
- Tourism industry operators and governments must be accountable to the people whose land and cultures are being utilised for the benefit of the tourists and tourism industry operators.
- Tourism Concern campaigns for better tourism.
- We work with partners in destination countries and work to influence the industry to ensure that tourism always benefits local people.
- Explore how tourism can have a negative impact on holiday destinations.

What can concerned travellers do to help fight exploitation in tourism? In addition to supporting Tourism Concern, travellers should understand the issues, know the many solutions that already exist which they can implement in the planning stage of their holiday, while at their destination or after they've come home. Tourism concern entails:

- An ethical holiday which is enjoyable and enriching for both you and for the host communities you visit.
- Whether soaking up sun in the tropics, there are simple steps we can all take to lessen the water impact of our holiday.

Tourism concern works with tour operators, travel agents and volunteering organisations that are committed to fairly traded and ethical tourism. We have developed guidelines and principles for the industry, explain what fair trade tourism is all about, and offer practical advice on how to make your business more ethical.

Taking the fair trade and human rights approach to tourism actually makes economic sense as well as making sure tourism activities do not have adverse impacts on local people. There is need to demonstrate that they have attained a recognised level of responsibility in the way they recruit volunteers, find placements and manage the volunteering process.

Tour operators should strive to improve their Ethical and Responsible Tourism practices. A package of activities designed to facilitate dialogue, provide essential information and skills to support operators is the challenge of running a socially responsible tourism business. There should be a campaign on social or environmental issues relevant to the travel industry.

Mission should achieve this through the way in which we behave in business. We aim to influence our supply chain to create long term dividend. Our responsibility lies in ensuring that our relations with our suppliers and clients are beneficial, sustainable and equal.

How you can make your business more prosperous while ensuring local communities benefit from tourism. Taking the fairtrade and human rights approach to tourism actually makes economic sense as well as making sure tourism activities do not have adverse impacts on local people.

A process that enables fairly traded tourism products developed within a transparent decision making process that involves the producers, service providers and communities, and based upon clear development principles, can create an alternative trade in tourism which will enable long-term, sustainable benefits for local economies and communities.

Most organisations working in tourism would acknowledge that their activities are not yet fairly traded nor sustainable. Tourism Concern welcomes the opportunity to work with any organisation willing and capable of change so long as this reflects our mission and does not compromise our values.

Tourism Concern seeks to strengthen the bargaining position of local destination interest groups, facilitate equitable market access for small stakeholders, raise awareness amongst consumers and influence international trade policy.

As a hotel or travel company, taking steps to conserve water and understand your business impacts on the surrounding community makes business sense on several levels.

A social enterprise established by the environmental NGO is Agent Green that is focusing on conservation of naturally protected areas in Romania. Golden eagles, lynx, grey wolves, brown bears, marmots, otters, red deer and chamois are still common in these mountains.

In responsible eco-tourism that emphasizes respect for wildlife, the environment, indigenous cultures, and the wilderness communities, we visit. Our aim is to operate a company that not only provides unforgettable wildlife experiences for our clients, but also directly contributes to the effective conservation of wildlife and natural habitats, and rewards responsible eco-tourism initiatives in small (often remote) communities with much needed income.

Tourism has proven to be one of the world's leading job creators. Numerous specialized training courses have been given by the UNWTO. Themis Foundation is the body responsible for UNWTO's work in the field of education and training, improving the quality and efficiency of tourism programmes worldwide.

But it is also one of the most complex, impacting on and impacted by countless actors and actions. As the UN specialized agency for tourism, UNWTO offers a common platform from which the different stakeholders involved both directly and indirectly in the sector – governments, the private sector, academia, international organizations and the UN family – can coordinate and move the tourism agenda forward.

UNWTO set goals in 2010 to maximize and raise awareness of tourism's important role in the global economic and development agenda and to make of tourism work as a true force to attain our common goals of development and growth.

The idea of focal points in this context appeared in the aftermath of the first World Congress against Commercial Sexual Exploitation of Children, held in Stockholm, Sweden, from 27 to 31 August 1996, which, in its Agenda for Action, asked all the concerned stake-holders to "mobilize the business sector, including the tourism industry, against the use of its networks and establishments for the commercial sexual exploitation of children".

It defined "organized sex tourism" as "trips organized from within the tourism sector, or from outside this sector but using its structures and networks, with the primary purpose of effecting a commercial sexual relationship by the tourists with residents at the destinations".

"The exploitation of human beings in any form, particularly sexual, especially when applied to children, conflicts with the fundamental aims of tourism and is the negation of tourism; as such, in accordance with international law, it should be energetically combated with the cooperation of all the States concerned and penalized without concession by the national legislation of both the countries visited and the countries to which of the perpetrators of these acts belong, even when they are carried out abroad".

Could there be a way of alliance between the conflicting 'target groups' and policy enforcement organization where community and consensus of interests may lead to some kind of righteous tourism package that fits in the philosophy of Sustainable Tourism Development (Gunn, 1988) suggest four perspectives in this context, viz., those of the tourist, the developers, the providers of services, and the local resident community. Also, alternative forms of tourism have been experimented with fair measure of success in some of the countries, under different titles, such as Green Tourism, Soft Tourism, Rural Tourism, Heritage Tourism, Cultural Tourism, Appropriate Tourism etc., but the spirit behind them all is most humanizing and development of tourism sum up its basis (shades of Green 1990) – Conserving the natural resources; Deepening the visitors experiences and; evaluating the social and economic well-being of the community.

Global economists forecast continuing international tourism growth, ranging between three and six percent annually, depending on the location. As one of the world's largest and fastest growing industries, this continuous growth will place great stress on remaining biodiverse habitats, often used to support mass tourism. Sustainable tourists are aware of these dangers and seek to protect their favorite destinations, and to protect tourism as an industry.

Large conventions, meetings and other major organized events drive the travel, tourism and hospitality industry. Cities and convention centers compete to attract such commerce, commerce which has heavy impacts on resource use and the environment. Major sporting events, such as the Olympic Games, present special problems regarding environmental burdens and degradation. But burdens imposed by the regular convention industry can be vastly more significant.

Green conventions and events are a new but growing sector and marketing point within the convention and hospitality industry. More environmentally aware organizations, corporations and government agencies are now seeking more sustainable event practices, greener hotels, restaurants and convention venues, and more energy-efficient or climate-neutral travel and ground transportation.

Additionally, some convention centers have begun to take direct action in reducing the impact of the conventions they host. One example is the Moscone Center in San Francisco, California, which has a very aggressive recycling program, a large solar power system, and other programs aimed at reducing impact and increasing efficiency.

With the advent of the internet, some traditional conventions are being replaced with virtual conventions, where the attendees remain in their home physical location and "attend" the convention by use of a web-based interface programmed for the task. This sort of "virtual" meeting eliminates all the impacts associated with travel, accommodation, food wastage, and other necessary impacts of traditional, physical conventions.

For passive and active visitors alike, nature is also playing an increasingly important role in giving something back to people (relaxing, enriching the spirit, getting back to basics). By doing so, it is able to enhance their broader experience of a destination. And for mainstream domestic visitors, these benefits tap more accurately into nature's deeper meaning.

Deeper Significance and Role of 'Nature' in Tourism

Nature-based experiences are intimately linked to all other aspects of the visitor's total experience of a destination, such as food, culture, relaxation, health, escape, family needs, accommodation, transport, etc. All serve to complement each other and together form the basis of a visitor's overall satisfaction with their holiday.

Ecotourism

Ecotourism is ecologically sustainable tourism, with a primary focus on experiencing natural areas, that fosters environmental and cultural understanding, appreciation and conservation (Ecotourism Association of Australia).

Ecotourists, with their strong focus on learning about the natural environment, minimising negative impacts and contributing to its care, lie at one specialist end of the nature in tourism spectrum, albeit an important one. They are in effect ambassadors (or early adopters) for a set of personal values towards which it now appears many other market segments, potentially comprising much larger visitor numbers, are moving.

Earth's biodiversity, and respect for local culture and those who have been traditional guardians of our natural environments, can be central to their interests.

Ecotourists are also characterised by knowing what they want and being strongly self-active in accessing it. They will often plan and book their experiences and travel needs themselves, leaving tourism operators with more time and the broader opportunity to pursue tourists with more mainstream nature-based interests, and those seeking adventure activity.

Nature-based tourism and its various subsets can also encompass some particularly challenging, but potentially high spending, special interest market segments. These often comprise socially and environmentally aware, highly educated and potentially demanding visitors who travel both to learn and to achieve personal and social goals.

Most of these visitors are serviced and targeted by specialist tourism operators and suppliers who often provide highly expert guides as part of the service.

To Achieve this, following steps are proposed:

Strategic control: It is the task of evaluating whether the company's marketing strategy is still appropriate to the market conditions. Because of the rapid changes in the marketing environment, each company needs to reassess periodically its marketing effectiveness through a control instrument known as the marketing audit.

Strategic HR choice: The options available to a firm in designing its human resources system. A firm's strategic HR choices are the options it has available in designing its human resources system. Choices are strategic to the extent that they help in making firm's performance either favorably or unfavorably in the long run.

Strategic human resource (HR) planning: The process of formulating HR strategies and establishing programs or tactics to implement.

Strategic Management: A multi-step process that encompasses strategic planning, implementation, and evaluating. The field of strategic management has emerged from being a pre-theoretic case study based capstone integrative course into a reasonably distinct sub-discipline in management studies. A substantial body of knowledge has accumulated especially over the last three decades of twentieth century which directly or indirectly addresses issues related to strategy formulation and implementation in organizations. Gluck et. al. (1980) identify that the modern origins of 'strategic management' can be traced back to the 1960s and has come through four discernible stages of its evolution up to 1980s. Each stage has been underpinned by a distinctive value system (e.g. meet the budget, predict the future, think strategically, and create the future) while reflecting in contemporary views as to the primary role of forward planning in organizations.

Strategic Plans: Plans that apply to the entire organization, establish the organization's overall goals and seek to position the organization in terms of its environment.

Strategies: The term strategy has a military origin. A strategy may be designed to win a particular battle with a minimum loss of men and materials. It sets out the series of actions chosen to try and do this.

Strategies consist of the specific courses of action needed to meet the policy. Strategy establishes the basis for identifying objectives and results, and listing activities needed to achieve them. The strategy should outline the actual shape which tourism will take. In doing so, it should concentrate principally on marketing opportunities. These point to the tourism possibilities offered, and the likely scale and volume of tourism and its expected contribution to the economy. It can also help to formulate what types of tourism should be developed and where, how many new hotels and other facilities and services should be added – of what types and where, and how many cultural and other attraction – of what types and where. It can also indicate the various improvements in facilities and services that need to be undertaken.

Whilst for some, the word 'strategy' is accredited to have its origin from Greek word 'stratos', meaning something exhaustive, of the first order, and of higher importance; others believe that it is derived from the Greek world 'agein', suggesting to act or guide. Therefore, strategy means thinking, decision making and actions towards superior long-term goals, without being deflected by short-term advantages, disadvantages or variations. Although strategy is undoubtedly an important variable of corporate and market analysis, it is difficult to measure or even confirm its existence within many organizations. The notion of strategy is often misinterpreted, considered to be the same as normal processes, leading to various types of misconceptions, fallacies and error. Strategy is generally viewed as a pattern of important decisions that –

(i) guides the organization in its relationships with it environment,
(ii) affects the organization structure, and
(iii) centrally affects the organization's performance.

Strategy checklist: Is the marketing mix of the tour operators, selling incoming inclusive tours, compatible with the marketing mix of the destination? In particular: What is the difference (distinctiveness) and positioning of destination in relation to the other destinations offered in the operator's catalogue? What image of the destination does the operator project in the catalogue and other printed material? Does this reflect the desired appeal? What is the positioning of the price/value relationship in comparison to the other destinations offered? Does it appear to make sense? What is the promotional impact of the tour operator's material? Is it suitable in terms of layout, copy, graphics, quality, etc? How much material and how many catalogues are distributed? How and where? What is the coverage in terms of retailers and geographical areas? What promotional programmes support retail sales?

Currently, with the tremendous boost in travel, world over, it has been realized, not only by the individual governments, particularly of the developing nations but also by the International organisations that "World belongs to man and everyone has a right to know and enjoy the world not just around him but also beyond him".

To emphasise the significance of the above statement, it will be appropriate here to quote the extract from the United Nation's Conference on International Travel and Tourism held in 1963, which underlined the need for a National Tourism Administration (NTA) using the following words:

"The Conference considers that it is incumbent on governments to stimulate and coordinate national tourism activities and is convinced that this task can, in the main, be carried out through the medium of National Tourist Organisations".

Therefore, the planning process in tourism should outline the optimum objectives to be attained in a given period of time. This planning should be treated as an integral part of the country's general economic and social planning. The key phases in tourism planning are as follows:

Assessment of tourism demand and a scientific planned approach to the supply of such demand.

- Tourism objectives should cover the overall development of a nation.
- Tourism site planning should be done by totally avoiding damage to natural and cultural assets.

- Focus should be on development of basic infrastructure which would be needed by any tourist.
- Financial planning should be done involving public, private agencies and foreign investment.
- Appropriate man-power planning must be done, especially because tourism is a service industry.
- There is also a need for efficient administrative planning.
- Focus to be placed also on tourism marketing, promotional strategies within & outside the country.
- Lastly, monitoring and evaluation must be done on a consistent basis.

Conclusion

The elements of tourist destination have their own specific and collective influence on tourist flows. However, the best of the elements would not have the positive influence if the host population is not friendly. Deficiency in the elements of destination can be compensated by the use of the friendly attitude of the local community, but there is no compensation for the lack of positiveness on their part.

Although the tourist is most directly affected by the degree of the excellence of destination's elements and hospitality shown by service providers, the overall feeling of welcome within a community will enhance or detract from the vacation experience.

It is true that while residents of a destination cannot be trained to act in a hospitable way toward tourists, but a community awareness programme can help develop a more positive attitude toward the tourist. This programme will have twofold effects – build acceptance of tourism and build an understanding of the tourist.

9

National and International Organizations

An organization is a deliberate arrangement of people to accomplish some specific purpose; or an organized body, system, or society; or way of arranging something so that it works efficiently; or group/institution which is arranged for efficient work.

Organization relates to the mobilization and deployment of resources and technology. It provides the foundation for working towards the objectives and results.

An organization is made up of individuals whose sole aim is the fulfilment of the objectives for which it has been set up. The aim of an organization is to arrange people in to groups in order to obtain the defined result from their combined efforts. An organization is in fact the framework within which an industry works.

Organization in the Tourism Industry is connected with associations, groups, and official or semi-official bodies involved in this field. In terms of Structure they take, two categories are possible:

- *Official or Semi-official bodies,* e.g. National, Regional and Local tourist organizations and Public Sector Undertakings;
- *Private voluntary organizations,* e.g. Hotels or a Travel Agents Associations.

In terms of scope and function, they fall under two categories:

- *Organizations based on a particular tourist service* – Like an association of tourist guides or restaurant waiters, etc. These are described as sectorial organizations, since their scope and functions are limited to a particular sector of the Tourism Industry.

- *Organizations based on a geographical area serving global interests,* e.g. National Tourist Organization or a Regional Tourist Authority or local tourist authority.

Due to rapidly growing awareness of economic, financial and social advantages of tourism development, many countries have set up organizations to deal specially and manage tourism on scientific lines.

However the nature of these organizations differs from country to country. Most Governments are involved in activities relating to travel and tourism – either at the planning and development stage, or later.

Governments get involved in tourism promotion and marketing, because it is in their interest to ensure that this industry expands domestically and internationally.

In India, the Department of Tourism has been entrusted with the responsibility of looking after the affairs of tourism in India and abroad.

Tourism Organization: Very often, sound tourism development plan and scientific marketing tourism plans have writhed at the altering of bad organization and inefficient management. Thus, rational organization structure and efficient management are fundamental to the success of any industry including tourism.

The empirical evidence suggests that the success of tourism industry depends upon –

(i) the nature and variety of tourist attractions,

(ii) the magnitude and quality of tourist facilities,

(iii) socio-economic, political and geographical distance from prime tourist generating markets,

(iv) the quality of organizational and management structure.

There is no uniform structural framework of national tourist organization, which can be commended for adoption in all the countries of the world. However, any form of tourist organization with built in capacity and flexibility to harness the advantages of actual and potential tourist inflow, is suitable.

Broadly speaking, the tourist organization is particularly concerned with the development and promotion of tourism product. It this context, the National Tourist Organization is inherently poised to perform the following functions:

Development: It covers formulation and implementation of tourism development programmes including creation and expansion of correct type of accommodation, environmental planning and protection, simplification of customs and immigration formalities, creation of tourism consciousness in the country, training of tourism personnel, promotion of research and regulation of the activities of travel agents and allied problems.

Marketing: It includes all measures to promote tourism.

Coordination: Owing to the involvement of various Government/Departments/Agencies and different private agencies in the travel trade, the need for coordination becomes self-evident. The organization set-up must promote the convergence of the activities of all these agencies and blunt the programmes and policies of various agencies that are likely to cause their functioning at cross-purposes.

Finance: Financial management entails the procurement of government loans and seeking of adequate incentives for the promotion of tourism industries. The objective is not only to seek expansion of the financial base but also to manage these finances in accordance with scientific principles.

Administration: Inculcation of discipline, formulation of work norms and enforcement of decisions are the prime constituents of sound administration. All told, organizational framework is to establish purposeful links with international tourist organizations and to provide appropriate direction to the growth of tourism.

Patterns of Tourist Organization:

The National Tourist Organization can be under the form of a ministry, commissariat, commission, board, council or even corporation. All that matters is that such body be afforded the necessary opportunities and resources to enable it to take effective action, as desired by the Government, for the development of tourism industry.

The structure of official tourism body will vary from one country to another according to its constitutional form unitary or federal. In some countries having even federal political system, National Tourist Organization is a central body with state level organization being subservient to itself being subordinate to Central Government, examples are Mexico and India. Some countries have two parallel systems, one central system and several state organizations, examples are Japan and Egypt.

INTERNATIONAL AIR TRANSPORT ASSOCIATION (I A T A)

IATA i.e. International Air Transport Association, the governing body for world airlines establishes fares or fare levels, rules and regulations concerning carriage by air, and an approved and legitimate trade association maintained by international and overseas airlines.

IATA: Role and Aims

For the Airlines: IATA provides machinery for finding joint solutions to problems beyond the resources of any single company. It has become the means by which they knit their individual networks into a worldwide public services system, despite differences in languages, currencies, laws and measurements.

For Governments: IATA furnishes a forum for developing industry working standards and coordinating international fares and rates. It helps to carry out fast and economical transport of international airmail and to ensure that the needs of commerce, and the safety and convenience of the public are served.

For the general public: IATA simplifies the travelling process. Thanks to the co-operation extended by airlines through IATA, any individual passenger can by one telephone call and payment in a single currency, arrange journeys covering many countries and make use of the several scheduled airlines.

The basic Trade Association activities of IATA include such aspects as Technical, Medical, Legal, Security procedures and administrative matters, Management information, Staff training, Automation, Projects and Finance services for airlines. Tariff co-ordination activities include the negotiation of fares, rates and charges and levels of commission on agents' sales. IATA has two main offices, one in Montreal and the other in Geneva. Regional Directors are based in Singapore, Geneva, Buenos Aires, Beirut and Washington and Regional Technical Directors in Bangkok, Dakar, Geneva, London, Nairobi and Rio de Janeiro. IATA's operational task is to ensure that the aircrafts utilized to carry the passengers are able to operate with maximum safety and efficiency, under clearly defined and universally understood regulations. IATA's commercial objective is to ensure that people, cargo and mail can move on this vast global network as easily as if they were on a single airline within a single country.

IATA has played and continues to play an important part in the drafting of the ICAO Standards, and Recommended Practices which comprise the technical regulation of Civil Aviation and Cooperates closely with ICAO to encourage governments to implement them fully and keep them up-to-date. IATA works with other organizations also the same way such as International Telecommunication Union, the World Meteorological Organization and the International Standards Organization. Current activities can be grouped under seven broad headings.

Avionics and Telecommunication: dealing with air to ground to air communications, radio navigation and landing aids, all of which contribute to cost-efficient, on-time journeys.

Engineering and Environment: covering latest technology, both on board aircraft and on ground, developing airline policy on important environment issues including aircraft noise, aviation fuel standards and emissions from aircraft engines.

Airports: defining IATA policy on airline requirement for airport terminals, expansion of existing airports and development of new ones.

Flight operations: dealing with safe operations of aircraft such as A/C systems, procedures for operational equipment to be provided at airports and flight crews training.

Medical: monitoring of health standards for flight crews, hygiene and sanitation in aircraft catering making travel easier for disabled passengers.

Facilitation: simplifying bureaucratic procedures i.e. reduce to the minimum, time consuming Government formalities such as customs and immigration.

Security: takes anti-hijacking measures, efforts to counteract fraud and theft in a variety of forms including working in close contact with Interpol, local police forces, airport and airline staff.

Air Law: Legal committee concerned with all legal matters having a bearing on international air transport. Main activities are formulation of conventions related to liability of air carriers, the commission of offences on board the aircraft, carriage of potentially hazardous material and airmail. Another important work is the legal aspect of airline documents.

Financial: deals with all aspects of accounting and settlements between airlines in respect of business they do with one another or one another's behalf. Also concerned with data collection, common problems with regard to currency and exchange, taxation, charges, insurance and statistics.

An example of IATA's financial work is the IATA clearinghouse, through which the airlines settles monthly accounts for interline revenue transactions. Clearing House operations began in January 1947 and today its participation has crossed 300 airlines carrying out 12 billion dollars worth of transactions annually.

IATA, the governing body for world airlines, establishes fares or fare levels rules and regulations concerning carriage by air including that for approved and legitimate trade association maintained by international and overseas airlines.

The IATA conference promotes a consolidated system of air transportation on international routes, decides upon fares, rates, safety standards, and conditions of service. In addition, it appoints and oversees travel agents to deal in international tickets.

IATA is the world organization of scheduled airlines. Its members carry the bulk of the world's scheduled air traffic under the flags of over 100 nations. Originally IATA was founded in the Hague in August 1919 with the primary objective of making a transport more convenient and acceptable to customers. Following the Chicago Conference of 1944, the airlines re-established IATA as the International Air Transport Association. Thus, IATA was founded by airlines in April, 1945 to help to meet the problems anticipated in the expansion of civil air services after the Second World War.

During World War II, the air transport industry had been affected very badly at the world level, in general and, in the USA, UK, Germany, India, France and Canada, in particular. The International Air Transport Association, a successor to the International Air Transport Association formed at Hague in 1919, is nodal organization, founded in 1945 by the airlines of certain countries with the prime objective of overcoming the complexities and problems arising from the rapid expansion of civil air services and World War II. As a non-governmental organization, it derived its legal existence from a special Act passed by the Canadian Parliament in December, 1945. The IATA closely resembles with the International Civil Aviation Organization in terms of its activities and organizational structure. The IATA is voluntary, non-exclusive, non-political and democratic organization, whose membership is open to any operating airline, which has been licensed to run scheduled air services by the government. Thus, the members of IATA are scheduled international airlines while scheduled airlines in domestic services can join IATA only as associate members.

IATA-UFTAA Dialogue: In the marketing of air transportation as defined by the IATA agency conferences, the IATA-UFTAA Consultative council, composed of both IATA and UFTAA members regularly examines the role and function of travel agent.

IATA and Geography: IATA Traffic Conference Area:

IATA has divided the world into 3 "Areas", known as Area-

1, Area-2, Area-3 or "Tariff conference 1, 2 and 3" abbreviated TC1, TC2, and TC3.

Area-1: It includes all of the North and South American Continents and the adjacent islands; Central America, Greenland, Bermuda, the West Indies and the Islands of the Caribbean Sea, the Hawaiian Islands (including Midway and Palmyra).

Area-2: It includes all of Europe (including all countries west of the Ural Mountains) and the islands adjacent thereto, all of Africa, Ascension Island, that part of Asia lying west of and including Iran.

Area-3: All of Asia and the adjacent islands except that portion included in Area-2; all of the East Indies, Australia, New Zealand, and the adjacent islands; the islands of the Pacific Ocean except those included in Area-1.

Note: IATA has further sub-divided the above 3 areas into a number of sub areas. You can refer these sub-areas which appear in certain Tariffs and other publications.

There are two more terms which you will also come across frequently in the context of fare calculations. They are defined as below: "Western Hemisphere" means all of Area-1, i.e., North, central and south America. "Eastern Hemisphere" means all of Area-2 and Area-3, i.e., Europe, Africa, Asia and Australia.

IATA Rate of Exchange (IROE): means the rates of exchange notified by IATA to convert local currency fare to NUC and to convert total NUC amounts to the currency of the country of commencement of transportation.

IATA Recognition – The most important recognition a travel agent should posses is the IATA recognition. This enables an agent to make reservations and issue tickets on IATA members' airlines. It also enables the agent to claim his commission of 9% from the respective airlines, for issuing such tickets. There are about 132 airlines which are members of IATA. The agency seeking IATA recognition has to meet stringent requirements and qualification. Before a travel agency applies for IATA recognition, it should be functioning as a full fledged travel agency for a minimum period

9-12 months. An application has to be submitted to the area headquarters of IATA (in our case the local co-ordinator is Air India, called AIP 9-Agency Investigation Panel), with detailed information regarding the company such as: Background of partners or directors or proprietor and their staff; Financial standing/Capital investments, etc; Location and area; Security measures; Present turnover; Balance sheet; profit and loss account, names of Bankers; Sales figures. The application is screened by a panel of airlines. If the panel is satisfied with all the requirements and conditions, the agency qualifies for recognition. The processing of the application could take anything between 3-9 months. After approval has been granted, there is an annual review and the agent has to keep up the minimum level of productivity as stated by the panel. In the event of its inability to meet this level continuously for three years, the agency could run the risk of losing its recognition.

IATA Tariff Coordination activities – Its main aim is the negotiation of international fares and rates for submission to governments. Worldwide Tariff Co-ordination meetings (Tariff Conferences) are held usually once a year. Meetings to review fares for passenger tariffs are normally held in the autumn and those involving air cargos in the spring, special meetings may be held interim if required.

IATA Traffic Services – IATA Traffic Services, significant area for the worldwide system, is the whole series of standardization measures – ticket format, airway bills and other documents, plus uniform procedures for passengers, baggage and cargo handling. These activities are grouped – under the heading "Traffic Services" and falls into 3 main areas: Passenger services; Cargo services; Airport handling. The most significant accomplishment has been the creation of the Multilateral Interline Traffic Agreements (MITA). More than 200 airlines belong to the agreement and accept each others passenger and cargo traffic, tickets and airways bills on a routine basis.

MINISTRY OF TOURISM, GOVT. OF INDIA

The Organisation

The Ministry of Tourism, is the nodal agency for the formulation of national policies and programmes and for the co-ordination of activities of various Central Government Agencies, State Governments/UTs and the Private Sector for the development and promotion of tourism in the country. This Ministry is headed by the Union Minister of State for Tourism (Independent Charge).

The administrative head of the Ministry is the Secretary (Tourism). The Secretary also acts as the Director General (DG) Tourism. The office of the Director General of Tourism, now merged with the office of Secretary (Tourism), provides executive directions for the implementation of various policies and programmes.

Directorate General of Tourism has a field formation of 20 offices within the country and 14 offices abroad and one sub-ordinate office/project i.e. Indian Institute of Skiing and Mountaineering (IISM)/Gulmarg Winter Sports Project. The overseas offices are primarily responsible for tourism promotion and marketing in their respective areas and the field offices in India are responsible for providing information service to tourists and to monitor the progress of field projects.The activities of IISM/ GWSP have now been revived and various Ski and other courses are being conducted in the J&K valley.

The Ministry of Tourism has under its charge a public sector undertaking, the India Tourism Development Corporation and the following autonomous institutions:

- Indian Institute of Tourism and Travel Management (IITTM)
- National Institute of Water Sports (NIWS)
- National Council for Hotel Management and Catering Technology (NCHMCT)
- Institutes of Hotel Management.

Role and Functions of the Ministry of Tourism

The Ministry of Tourism functions as the nodal agency for

the development of tourism in the country. It plays a crucial role in coordinating and supplementing the efforts of the State/Union Territory Governments, catalyzing private investment, strengthening promotional and marketing efforts and in providing trained manpower resources.

The Functions of Attached Office, viz. Directorate General of Tourism are as under [The office of DG (T) has now been merged with the office of Secretary (Tourism)]:

- Assistance in the formulation of policies by providing feedback from the field offices.
- Monitoring of Plan Projects and assisting in the Plan formulation
- Coordinating the activities of field offices and their supervision.

Regulations:

- Approval and classification of hotels and restaurants.
- Approval of travel agents, Inbound tour operators and tourist transport operators, etc.
- Inspection & Quality Control
- Guide service
- Complaints and redressal

Infrastructure Development:

- Release of incentives.
- Tourist facilitation and information.
- Field publicity, promotion & marketing.
- Hospitality programmes.
- Conventions & conferences.
- Assistance for Parliamentary work.

Travel Trade:

The Ministry of Tourism has a scheme for granting approval to hotel projects from the point of view of this suitability for international tourists. A classification committee set up by the Ministry classifies the functioning hotels under the star system into six categories from star one to five star deluxe. Similarly, the Ministry has a scheme of approving Travel Agents, Tour Operators,

Adventure Tour Operators and Tourist Transport Operators, the idea being to encourage quality, standard and service in these categories so as to promote Tourism in India. This is a voluntary scheme open to all bonafide agencies.

Travel Agents:

A Travel Agent is one who makes arrangements of tickets for travel by air, rail, ship, passport, visa, etc. It may also arrange accommodation, tours, entertainment and other tourism related services.

Inbound Tour Operators:

An Inbound tour operator is one who makes arrangements for transport, accommodation, sightseeing, entertainment and other tourism related services for foreign tourists.

Tourist Transport Operators:

A Tourist Transport Operator Organization is one, who provides tourist transport like cars, coaches, boats etc. to tourists for transfers, sightseeing and journeys to tourist places, etc.

Adventure Tour Operators:

An Adventure Tour Operator is one who is engaged in activities related to Adventure Tourism in India namely, water sports, aero sports, mountaineering, trekking and safaries of various kinds, etc. In addition to that, he may also make arrangements for transport, accommodation, etc.

Domestic Tour Operator:

A domestic tour operator is one who makes arrangements for transport, accommodation, sight seeing, entertainment and other tourism related services for domestic tourists.

It has been the endeavour of the Ministry of Tourism to put in place a system of training and professional education with necessary infrastructural support capable of generating manpower sufficient to meet the needs of the tourism and hospitality industry, both quantitatively and qualitatively. As of now, there are 29 Institutes of Hotel Management (IHMs), comprising 21

Central IHMs and 8 State IHMs, and 5 Food Craft Institutes (FCIs), which have come up with the support of the Ministry. These institutes were set up as autonomous societies with specific mandate to impart/conduct hospitality education/training in hospitality skills.

Training Programmes:

Training programmes in the field of Hotel Management, Catering and Nutrition were initiated by Government of India in the year 1962 under the Department of Food, Ministry of Agriculture. To begin with, four Institutes of Hotel Management, Catering Technology and Applied Nutrition were set up at New Delhi, Mumbai, Chennai and Kolkata. For imparting training in hospitality related craft disciplines, 12 Food Craft Institutes were also set up at different places in the country. Consequent to transfer of the programme to the Ministry of Tourism in October 1982, format of the various training programmes was reoriented and remodeled keeping in view the professional workforce requirements of the country's fast expanding accommodation and catering industry. In order to harness the resources and also to provide a central thrust to the programme, Ministry of Tourism also established the National Council for Hotel Management and Catering Technology (NCHMCT) in the year 1982. Main objectives for setting up the Council at the apex level were:

- To advise the Government on coordinated development of hotel management and catering education.
- To collect, collate and implement international development in the area of human resource development for the hospitality sector.
- To affiliate institutes and prescribe courses of study and instructions leading to examinations conducted by it.
- To standardize courses and infrastructure requirements for institutes imparting education and training in hospitality management.
- To prescribe educational and other qualifications, experience, etc. for members of staff in the affiliated institutes and organize faculty development programs.
- To award Certificates and Diplomas in Hospitality and Hotel Administration.

- As a result of vast expansion and modernization of the country's hospitality industry, hotel management and catering education programmes gained tremendous popularity and the profile of students seeking admission to these courses also underwent transformation. As a result, courses offered by the National Council are of international standard which have been recognized by the hospitality industry. At present, there are 41 Institutes of Hotel Management comprising of 21 Central IHMs, 8 State IHMs and 12 Private IHMs and 5 Food Craft Institutes following National Council's course curriculum.

Publicity and Marketing:

As part of its marketing/publicity activities, the Ministry of Tourism brings out brochures, leaflets, maps, films, CDs, etc. on various topics. The leaflet/folder/brochure gives the information about the place or the destination with various facets of the facilities available, sight seeing around the place, important telephone numbers and the contact points of India tourism officers. Similarly, the films deal with the subject in its entirety covering all destinations of the country.

The Ministry of Tourism, Government of India, through its 14 overseas offices endeavors to position India in the tourism-generating markets as a preferred tourism destination, to promote various Indian tourism products vis-à-vis competition faced from various destinations and to increase India's share of the global tourism market.

The above objectives are met through an integrated marketing and promotional strategy and a synergised campaign in association with the Travel Trade, State Governments and Indian Missions. The specific elements of promotiona efforts undertaken overseas include advertising in the Print and Electronic Media, participation in Fairs and Exhibitions, organising Seminars, Workshops, Road Shows & India Evenings, Printing of Brochures and Collaterals, Brochure Support/Joint Advertising with Travel Agents/Tour Operators, inviting the Media and Travel Trade to visit the country under the Hospitality Programme, etc.

Incredible India International Campaigns

Ministry of Tourism commenced its International TV Campaign (2009-10) for Europe and American region, which finished in the first half of the 2010-11.

In December, 2010, the Ministry launched its International TV Campaign 2010-11 – Europe. Leading TV channels of pan-regional reach are part of the Media Plan of the Ministry.

International Accolades:

PATA Grand Award 2010: Heritage Category – Rural Tourism Project – A Case Study of Hodka Village.

PATA Gold Award 2010 : Marketing – Primary Government Destination – Eco Tourism Marketing Campaign.

PATA Gold Award 2010: Marketing Media – Travel Advertisement Print Media – Mahatma Gandhi Creative.

India has been voted as the 7th best destination in the world in the Conde Nast Readers' Travel Awards 2010.

World Travel Award 2010 for "World's Leading Destination Marketing Campaign 2010".

Asian Guild Award 2010 – recognizing the "contribution made by the Incredible India campaign in creating awareness about India among Britishers and British Asians living in UK".

Global Traveller Award 2010 : India has been voted as the "Best International Tourism in Travel Fairs and Exhibitions".

India Tourism offices overseas have participated in the major international Travel Fairs and Exhibitions in important tourist-generating markets the world over as well as in emerging and potential markets to showcase and promote the tourism products of the country. These include Arabian Travel Market (ATM) in Dubai, PATA Travel Mart in Macau, World Expo 2010 in Shanghai, China International Travel Mart in Shanghai, ITB – Asia in Singapore, World Travel Market (WTM) in London, IMEX in Frankfurt, FITUR in Madrid and ITB in Berlin.

India Tourism, Beijing was awarded the "Best Tourism Promotion Award" at the World Travel Fair in Shanghai. India tourism, Tokyo was awarded the "Best Booth Operation Award" at the Korea World Travel Fair and the "Best Tourism Promotion Award" at the Busan International Tourism Fair in South Korea.

Some major promotional activities undertaken for overseas promotion:

Ministry of Tourism, Govt. of India undertook a series of promotional initiatives to aggressively promote tourism to India. As part of the promotional initiatives undertaken, Road Shows were organized in important tourist-generating markets overseas with participation of different segments of the travel industry.

Road Shows, in collaboration with the Indian Association of Tour Operators were organized in CIS Countries, during the months of September-October 2010. Road Shows in collaboration with the PATA India Chapter were organised in May, 2010 in USA and Canada.

India Tourism Toronto undertook massive advertising and outdoor publicity during the Vancouver Winter Games, 2010 in Vancouver and also Paralympics Games, 2010 from February to March, 2010.

India Tourism Paris participated and supported the 3rd France-India Business Cup Golf Tournament held at St. Tropez, France during 13th–17th October, 2010. A high level delegation led by Hon'ble Minister for Tourism, Joint Secretary (T), Regional Director, India Tourism Frankfurt attended the event. Hon'ble Minister of Tourism inaugurated the France-India Business Cup Golf Tournament on 14th of October and there was a meeting held with various stakeholders for promotion of Golf Tourism.

India Tourism, Dubai organized the Golf Tournament at Ras-Al-Khaimah, United Arab Emirates. India Tourism, Johannesburg organised "Know India" seminar for the group of 12 people travelling to India and for the group of 6 ladies travelling to south India giving information about shopping, hotels, ayurveda and spas and safe travelling for women.

Market Research:

Statistical data is an important tool for the planners and policy makers not only for planning/policy formulation but also to monitor the progress of the schemes and evaluate their impact. The Ministry of Tourism brings out an Annual Publication called "India Tourism Statistics" every year giving details of international and domestic tourism, including details about the classified hotels, etc. In addition, a small brochure called "Tourism Statistics at a Glance" is also brought out, giving updated and latest key statistical data. The Ministry also estimates month-wise Foreign Tourist Arrivals (FTAs) figures and Foreign Exchange Earnings (FEE) from tourism, and this is brought out within a time lag of just 4-5 days.

International Co-operation Division is one of the important divisions of the Ministry of Tourism, which engages in various consultations and negotiations with the international organisations such as United Nations World Tourism Organization (UNWTO); Economic and Social Commission for Asia and the Pacific (ESCAP); Bay of Bengal Initiative for Multi Sectoral Technical and Economic Co-operation (BIMSTEC); Mekong-Ganga Co-operation (MGC); Association of South East Asian Nations (ASEAN) and South Asian Association for Regional Co-operation (SAARC) and South Asian Sub-regional Economic Co-operation (SASEC).

This Division holds consultations and negotiations with other countries for signing of Agreements/Memorandum of Understanding (MoU) for bilateral/multilateral cooperation in the field of tourism, organizes Joint Working Group Meetings with other countries and attends Joint Commission Meetings in coordination with the Ministries of Commerce, Culture, External Affairs, Civil Aviation, Finance, Petroleum, etc. for development and promotion of tourism.

WORLD TOURISM ORGANIZATION (WTO)

World Tourism Organization (WTO) was established on 2 Jan, 1975. It is inter-government body dealing with all aspects of tourism. It was originally known as IUOTO, i.e. , International Union of Official Travel Organization, a non-governmental body to promote tourism for economic, social and cultural advancement of the country. Thus, IUOTO was transformed to WTO, to deal with tourism-related problems at governmental level. The main aim and objective of World Tourism Organization is to promote and develop tourism at global level with a view to economic development, international understanding, peace and universal respect for human rights and fundamental freedom. Its head quarters are in Madrid, Spain.

WTO is an international organization that is concerned with the economic, social, and culture impact of tourism through the world. It is an inter-governmental technical body dealing with all aspects of tourism, came into legal existence as travel had created the need for a world body able to deal with tourism problems at the government level. The Headquarters of the organization was decided to be set up in Madrid (Spain) by the first General Assembly of the World Tourism Organization in May, 1975. The activities of the organization cover all sectors of tourism on a worldwide basis. WTO works in cooperation with all international organizations, the United Nations in particular, as well as with commercial and non-commercial bodies involved in tourism. The WTO has a very emphatic technical character. The establishment of WTO was to play a central and decisive role "in the field of tourism and to maintain effective collaboration with the appropriate organs of the United Nations and its specialized agencies". The WTO became an executing agency of the UNDP in May, 1976. The UNDP Resident Representatives throughout the world became WTO representatives for all matters concerning technical cooperation in the field of tourism.

World Tourism Organization (WTO) Aims:

The fundamental aim of the organization is the promotion and development of tourism with a view to contributing to economic development, international understanding, peace, prosperity and universal respect for and observance of human rights and fundamental freedoms for all without distinction to race, sex language or religion. The organization will take all appropriate action to attain this objective. In pursuing this aim, the organization will pay particular attention to the interests of the developing countries in the field of tourism. In order to establish its central role in the field of tourism, the organization will establish and maintain effective collaboration with the appropriate organs of the United Nations and its specialized agencies. In this connection, the organization strives for a cooperative relationship with and participation in the activities of the United Nations Development Programme as a participating and executing agency.

World Tourism Organization (WTO) Activities

The WTO performs a number of activities for its members in the area of promotions and development of tourism, which are:

- Constant review of tourism trends and development and exercising vigilance over changes in world economic and social conditions affecting tourism, market fluctuations and maintenance of standards within tourism sector.
- Clearing house for all available information on international and domestic including, statistical data legislation, regulation facilities and special events.
- Systematic collection analysis and dissemination of data on various aspect of tourism.
- Collecting legislative texts, regulations and documentation on all aspect of travel.
- Conducting research studies covering tourism markets plant and enterprises; physical planning and area development; promotion and marketing; and economic analysis and financing techniques, etc.
- Regular supply of studies as well as updated information on trends in the various fields of tourism to its members.
- Fostering the adoption of measures in cooperation with competent specialized bodies regarding simplifying frontier formalities and removing barrier to the free movement of tourists.
- Organizing and convening international conferences, seminars, workshops, round tables and technical meetings on all aspects of tourism.
- Preparation of draft international agreements on tourism.
- Examining vocational training programmes with a view to contributing to the establishment of suitable teaching programmes tailored especially for the developing countries.

World Tourism Organization (WTO) Functioning

WTO functions through its various organs. The responsibilities of these organs are well defined and within the framework of the organization. The three main organs through which the WTO functions are:

General Assembly – The General Assembly is the supreme organ of the organization. It is the sovereign body of the WTO. It is composed of delegates representing full members, associate members and representatives of Affiliate members. It meets every two years and makes recommendations on any matter within the competence of WTO. It provides general guidelines for the administration of the organization.

Executive Council – The Executive Council consists of full members elected by the assembly at a ratio of one member for every five full members of the WTO organization with a view to achieving fair and equitable geographical distribution. The Council's task is to take all necessary measures in consultation with the Secretary General, for implementing the resolutions of General Assembly. The Council meets at least twice a year.

The Secretariat – The Secretariat of the organization consists of the Secretary General and the staff members. The Secretary General is responsible for carrying out the general policy and work programme of the organization in accordance with the directions of the General Assembly and the Executive Council.

WTO Membership: The three categories of members of this organization are:

Full Members- They are all the sovereign states;

Associate members- They are the territories or groups of territories not responsible for their external relations but whose membership is approved by the state assuming responsibility for their external relations.

Affiliate Members- They are international bodies, both intergovernmental and non-governmental concerned with specialized interests in tourism as well as commercial and non-commercial bodies and associations whose activities related to the aims of WTO or fall within its competence.

INDIA TOURISM DEVELOPMENT CORPORATION (I T D C)

Travel and Tourism:

- Travel and tourism in India is an integral part of Indian tradition and culture.
- In the olden days, travel was primarily for pilgrimage – as the holy places dotting the countryside attracted the people from different parts of the vast sub-continent.
- People also travelled to participate in fairs and festivals in different parts of the country.
- The dimensions of tourism changed as trade and commerce developed.
- The spice trade brought India into contact with the world more than before.
- The silk route trade also opened India's immense cultural heritage and natural beauty to the world outside.
- The establishment of Indian railways, modernization of the ports, and development of hill stations – all these added to the growth of Indian tourism Industry in the 19th and the early part of the 20th century.
- Pandit Jawaharlal Nehru's oft-quoted remark: "Welcome a Tourist and send back him as a Friend" was the essence of India's tourism approach in the post-independence era.
- The tourism policy making bodies had their beginning in the report of the Sargent Committee in 1946.
- The Committee recommended that it would be in the interest of India to develop tourist traffic, both domestic and international.
- In 1962, there was a decline in tourist traffic to India.
- This prompted the government to appoint an ad-hoc committee on tourism in March 1963, under the Chairmanship

of L.K. Jha, the then Secretary, Department of Economic Affairs, Ministry of Finance. S.N. Chib, the then Director General of Tourism, was the Member Secretary.

- As a follow-up to the Jha Committee recommendations, a single **India Tourism Development Corporation** (ITDC) was set up on October 1, 1966.

India Tourism Development Corporation (ITDC)

- The purpose of setting up ITDC was to give the Department of Tourism an agency which could perform some functions on its behalf as an autonomous body.
- The idea was to provide western comforts to international visitors at the major tourist attractions in the country.

The ITDC was to play the role of a catalyst in developing a modern super structure for international tourists.

The government set up the infrastructure to promote tourism by establishing India International and Tourism Promotion Offices in London and Frankfurt.

The tourism sector was initiated to establish luxury facilities for the high spending tourist.

The first pioneer in this field was Mohan Singh Oberoi who began his career in Hoteliering with the Clarks Hotel in Shimla and the Grant Hotel in Kolkata.

Following the report of the ad hoc **Committee on Tourism** also known as the **Jha Committee (1963)**, which recommended that the public sector should assume a more active and positive role in promoting tourism, the Government of India set up in 1965, in the Department of Tourism three separate tourist corporations in the public sector to develop hotels, transport and entertainment.

These Corporations were set up under the provision of the Companies Act 1956.

The main function of these Corporations was to construct and manage hotels in the public sector, produce material for tourist publicity and to provide transport facilities to the tourists.

The Government later decided to merge these undertakings into one composite undertaking, for the purpose of securing coordination in the policy and efficient and economic working of the three corporations.

Accordingly, the Government set up in October 1966, a public sector undertaking namely, the **India Tourism Development Corporation Ltd** by amalgamating the erstwhile three separate corporations.

The unified Corporation started functioning with effect from October 1, 1966.

In pursuance of the recommendations of the Administrative Reforms Commission (ARC), the control of the Ashoka Hotels Ltd. and Janpath Hotels Ltd. was transferred from the then Ministry of Works, Housing and Supply to the Ministry of Tourism and Civil Aviation from July 2, 1968.

These two hotels were amalgamated with India Tourism Development Corporation from March 1970.

The amalgamated Company known as India Tourism Development Corporation Ltd. (ITDC) came into being with effect from March 28, 1970.

The amalgamated company known as ITDC Ltd. came into being with effect from March 28th 1970.

Objectives and Functions

Broadly, the objectives and functions of the unified India Tourism Development Corporation fall under the following categories:

- Construction and management of hotels, motels and restaurants, tourist bungalows, guesthouses and beach resorts at various places for accommodating tourists;
- Provision of transport facilities to tourists;
- Provision of entertainment facilities to tourists by way of organizing cultural shows, music concerts, sound and light shows, etc.;

- Provision of shopping facilities for tourists;
- Provision of publicity services to assist India's promotion overseas as a tourist destination and projecting the national importance of tourism at home.

With these objectives, ITDC has provided a wide range of services essential for the promotion of tourism.

Working in close cooperation with the Department of Tourism is the Central ministry of Commerce, which is primarily concerned with the establishment of a solid infrastructure for the tourist industry and the provision of commercial services essential for the growth of tourist traffic.

Conclusion

It is interesting to note that since its inception, ITDC is one of the few public sector corporations which has been profitable, though profit margins have been very small. It is perhaps the only undertaking of its kind in the world, offering almost complete package of tourist services – accommodation, transport, shopping, entertainment and publicity. It offers all this in a spirit of health competition with the private sector. It has emerged as a pioneer, opening up new tourist destinations, popularizing Indian cuisine and providing entertainment.

Presently, the Government is not funding ITDC. It has been asked to create its own resources to meet its expansion plans. There is also a move to sell some of its hotels – presently operated by ITDC. In the coming years, the ITDC will have to undergo several structural changes in the coming years to cater to the current environment. It is difficult to predict ITDC's future in current environments of globalization and liberalization. However, the travel industry of India cannot forget the debt it owes to ITDC for its pioneering efforts and dynamic approach to tourism development at a time when the private sector was not interested in tourism projects.

UNIT–IV:

IMPACTS OF TOURISM

10

Impacts of Tourism

Introduction

Tourism involves people who come from other countries for the pleasure of visiting the environment. Since tourists spend money on travel, hotels, food, entertainment and recreation, they can be an important source of income and thus for economic development for the destination with few other possible sources of revenue.

The tourists who come to the destination are attracted by its surroundings and environment: sun and sea, white sandy beaches and waving palm trees, lush vegetation and friendly natives. The reality is never quite the same as the tourist image, but while it can be different, it should not disappoint them, otherwise tourism will ultimately fail. People do not come several thousand kilometres to see the same dirt, pollution, industry and degraded environments that they have at home.

As an industry, the impact of tourism is manifold. Tourism industry nourishes a country's economy, stimulates development process and restores the cultural heritage. This industry enjoys a major advantage over other industries that of having a unique product, which might differ from, state to state.

About India:

As far as India is concerned, one can find:

- Poverty, greed, overpopulation and disease have been a hindrance to the development of tourism in India.

- India suffers from the problem of overpopulation. The population of India is very high at an estimated 1.2 billion.
- One-third of India's population lives below the poverty line and India is home to one-third of the world's poor people.
- Lack of proper sanitation is a major concern for India.
- Statistics conducted by UNICEF have shown that only 31% of India's population is able to utilise proper sanitation facilities as of 2008.
- It is estimated that one in every ten deaths in India is linked to poor sanitation and hygiene.
- Since the Indian Constitution was completed in 1949, education has remained one of the priorities of the Indian government.
- The first education minister Maulana Azad founded a system of education which aimed to provide free education at the primary level.
- Primary education was made free and compulsory for children from 6-14, and child labour was banned.
- The government introduced incentives for education and disincentives for not receiving education – for instance, the provision of mid-day meals in schools were introduced.
- While many schools were built, they had poor infrastructure and inadequate facilities. Schools in the rural areas were especially affected.
- According to District Information System for Education (DISE) in India in 2009, only about 51.5% of all schools in India have boundary walls, 16.65% have computers and 39% have electricity.
- Of which, only 6.47% of primary schools and 33.4% of upper primary schools have computers, and only 27.7% of primary schools have electricity.
- Learning in poorly furnished schools was not conducive, resulting in poor quality education.
- Economic and social disparities also plague the fundamentals of the education system.
- Rural children are less able to receive education because of greater opportunity costs, since rural children have to work to contribute to the family's income.
- According to the Annual Status of Education in 2009, the average attendance rate of students in the rural states is about 75%.
- Further impediments: Hindutva, Hindu nationalism, Islamic Extremism, Khalistan movement, Islamic terrorism, and Christian terrorism.

- Anti-Christian violence in India, Anti-Christian violence in Karnataka, and Religious violence in Orissa.
- Over the years, various incidents of violence against Dalits, such as Kherlanji Massacre, have been reported from many parts of India.

Tourism's effects on the social, cultural and physical environments in which it operates are well documented. Yet, it appears that little research has been conducted examining the underlying reasons why such impacts appear to be inevitable.

Tourism enjoys a love-hate relationship with its host community. It is both a much sought after and much reviled activity.

The factors determining the nature and extent of tourism-related impacts on a destination can usefully be divided into three groups:

- Factors relating to the characteristics of the destination.
- Factors relating to the characteristics of tourist.
- Factors relating to the type of tourism development.

Tourism Development:

Tourism depends on the quality of the environment for its success, and good tourist development requires the protection and even the improvement of the environment. The most important tourism resources are the natural beauty of the island, their distinctive or exotic character, their recreation possibilities, and the cultural interest of the people. The hotels, resorts, transportation networks, recreation facilities and other tourism infrastructure can complement but never completely replace the dependence on environmental resources.

Tourism development might be narrowly defined as the provision or enhancement of facilities and services to meet the needs of the tourists. To what extent do these impacts contribute to the development of countries, regions or communities? To what extent does tourist's contribution to the state of development in any area depend on the way tourism there has developed? It is argued that it is tourism itself, rather than the original attractions, which draw visitors to a particular area. A number of explicit questions are raised.

Visibility and Activities of Tourists

Visibility and Activities of touris influence impacts on the natural, social and cultural environments. The greater the differences of visitors in appearance, language, culture, the greater the potential for adverse social impacts such as resident hostility, mutual misunderstanding and social tensions to result.

The types of activities undertaken by tourists will be important in influencing the extent of contact with residents. Tourists often, out of ignorance or carelessness, fail to respect local customs and moral values.

As such, tourism depends on the quality of the environment for its success, and good tourist development requires the protection and even the improvement of the environment. The most important tourism resources are the natural beauty of the island, their distinctive or exotic character, their recreation possibilities, and the cultural interest of the people.

The basic problem with tourism development is that tourism facilities and the tourists themselves have impacts on the environment. If care is not taken, the tourism development itself can gradually destroy the environmental resources on which it depends.

CHARACTERISTICS OF DESTINATION

Environmental and Heritage Features of the Area

Tourists often opt for pleasing environments to which tourism is linked and are among the least resilient, including fragile natural areas and ecosystems, historic cities, heritage sites, and ancient monuments.

Carrying Capacity

Each destination and attraction has a carrying capacity. Carrying capacity, according to Archer and Cooper "–the point beyond which further levels of visitation and development would lead to an unacceptable deterioration in the physical, and social environment and of the visitor experience". Carrying capacity is a part of planning process which sets carrying capacity of a particular destination, or an attraction.

In this regard, only two types are taken in to consideration Physical Carrying Capacity and Social Carrying Capacity so that social and cultural integrity of destinations maintained.

Physical Carrying Capacity

The physical capacity of a destination or site is determined by availability of space. It also covers the form of the landscape and the carrying capacity of the land. It recognises the demands on the landscape, and requires tourism levels which do not damage the soil, plants or animals, reduced environmental quality.

Social Carrying Capacity

Social Carrying Capacity recognises that there is a limit based on the tolerance of visitors by the host population. It is important to decide 'How many visitors are wanted', rather than 'How many can be attracted'.

Carrying capacity is an important planning concept that can be prescriptive in assigning a preferred type and amount of use to a tourism site. Once the carrying capacity for an area has been established, management policies and control systems can be enacted to restrict unhampered growth. These can include the use of visitor management techniques such as user fees, management of visitor flows, traffic restrictions etc.

There are no satisfactory indicators of carrying capacity or the ability of environments to sustain tourism. Johnson and Thomas state that the Socially Optimal Visitor Flow will occur where marginal social benefits are equal to marginal social costs, i.e., where the net social gain from visitors is maximised. This optimal visitor flow is difficult to measure however.

CHARACTERISTICS OF TOURISTS

Number of Tourists and Length of Stay

The number of tourists and how long they stay are definitely to play an important role in determining the nature of impacts on the communities within the host destination. A concentration of large numbers relative to resident population can lead to overcrowding of attractions and place excessive demands on existing infrastructure such as roads, public transport systems, water and electricity supply, sewage disposal. Congestion leads to loss of amenity, loss of leisure time, increased accidents, fuel consumption, and pollution in all of its forms.

Increasing tourism numbers can magnify tensions between visitors and residents. Moreove, differences in economic status between tourists and residents can foster resentment by locals as well as raising their aspiration levels beyond that, which is realistically achievable.

A 'demonstration effect' can increase aspiration levels beyond the destination norm. This occurs where residents seek to copy tourist behaviour and spending patterns (REF). Differences in economic status can foster resentment in residents, as well as raising their aspiration levels. These differences are likely to be less noticeable in developed countries than in undeveloped countries where the 'demonstration effect' can act to increase resident's aspirations above what they can realistically attain.

The net benefits of tourism are normally significantly lower than the aggregate expenditure of the tourists, however, because it is necessary to give up real resources, goods and services to provide for these tourists.

Economic Impacts

The economic impacts of tourism is a big subject that cannot be covered thoroughly here. They should be examined in detail for any large tourism development project. This chapter seeks to introduce some of the important concepts and concerns associated with expanding the economic benefits of tourism through investment in infrastructure. It is adapted from previous work by the author and colleagues, and was presented in part in a World Tourism Organization publication.

Economic impact analyses provide tangible estimates of these economic interdependencies and a better understanding of the role and importance of tourism in a region's economy.

There is growing recognition that innovative approaches must be adopted in order to maintain the economic health of many countries, communities and regions. While conditions vary from region to region, tourism has been seen as an important form of economic development. It has also been promoted as a somewhat benign agent of economic and social change, a promulgator of peace through interaction and dialogue, and a service-based industry capable of creating employment and income.

The perception that tourism has only positive economic benefits has lessened in recent years, due to the growing awareness and knowledge of the more intangible and indirect economic costs of tourism. While it can be argued that tourism does offer an important alternative form of economic activity, it must be seen as only one component of a larger series of development initiatives within any economic system. That is not to say that tourism in selected circumstances cannot be the major source of income and jobs in a community or region, but rather that the impact and role of tourism will vary from region to region.

Tourism is travel based on desires to relax, sightsee, appease curiosity, satisfy a sense of adventure or an adventurous self-image, compete with one's peers or colleagues, re-create images of paradise or luxury or the exotic, and escape. Tourism affects the economies and cultures of destination sites in both positive and negative ways. Those locales may organize their production activities around the satisfaction of tourists' demands for leisure, fantasy, adventure, or knowledge-activities that may operate to the detriment of local cultures.

Economically, tourism can create jobs for local people and bring money into the country. However many tourists like their comforts from home, and it is often necessary to import a large part of their requirements, so that much of the money may leave the country again to pay for these imports. If the resorts and hotels have been financed by overseas investors, they will also want to export their profits. The developers may want the government to improve the airport, roads and other infrastructure, and possibly to provide tax breaks and other financial advantages, which cost the country money. The net benefit to an island country from some kinds of tourism development may thus be small indeed. Other kinds of tourist facilities provided by villages or financed locally may be economically more interesting.

As with any human relations involving production and consumption, even an activity centered on leisure, tourism thus calls for ethical and philosophical reflection. Only recently, however, has the phenomenon of tourism become a subject of ethical consideration, largely through its connection to other concerns, such as environmental degradation (to which "ecotourism" is one response), economic development, and cultural impacts.

The most important economic benefits of tourism is the earnings of foreign exchange. The receipts from international tourism provide a valuable source of earnings for many countries, both developed and developing; the importance of earnings for developing countries is, however, much more than that for developed countries. Although tourism is sensitive to the level of economic activity in the tourist generating countries, it provides more stable earnings than being provided by primary products. The income from tourism has tended to increase at a higher rate than merchandise export in a number of countries.

There is now almost an assured channel of financial flows from the richer countries to the not-so-richer, and developing ones, raising the latter's export earnings and the rate of economic growth. Although the amount contributed in foreign currency per tourist varies greatly from one place to another, the importance of receipts from tourism in the balance of payments, and of tourist activities in the national revenue, has became considerable for many countries.

Income from foreign tourism in the form of foreign exchange earnings adds to the national income and, as an invisible export, may offset a loss on the visible trading account and be of critical importance in the overall financial reckoning. This is more true in the case of developing countries.

While it can be argued that tourism does offer an important alternative form of economic activity, it must be seen as only one component of a larger series of development initiatives within any economic system. That is not to say that tourism in selected circumstances cannot be the major source of income and jobs in a community or region, but rather that the impact and role of tourism will vary from region to region. Experience has shown that tourism may take many forms and meet a number of tourist motivations. Experience has also shown that destinations can rise and in popularity, driven by various factors in the destination's internal and external environment (e.g., political unrest, natural catastrophes and demand or supply-side problems). A destination that is entirely dependent on tourism is much more vulnerable to these shifts than an economy that is well diversified and has tourism as just one of its industries.

Walter Jamieson and Tazim Jamal has shown that tourism may take many forms and meet a number of tourist motivations. Experience has also shown that destinations can rise and fall in popularity, driven by various factors in the destination's internal and external environment (e.g., political unrest, natural catastrophes and demand or supply-side problems). A destination that is entirely dependent on tourism is much more vulnerable to these shifts than an economy that is well diversified and has tourism as just one of its industries.

Possible Economic Impacts of Tourism Development

- Transport networks, all of which can improve the quality of life for residents as well as facilitate tourism.
- Increases governments' tax base.
- Expands an economy's export base.
- Catalyst for economic development.
- Assists in the development of remote or improves transport infrastructure.
- Diversifies and stabilizes economic activity, offering additional livelihood opportunities for local communities.
- Locally owned small enterprise development is an important mechanism for diversifying the local economy.
- Can provide self-financing mechanism for natural and heritage attractions and so serve as tool for environmental preservation.

- Can serve as vehicle providing economic support for preservation of local culture through sale of culturally inspired handicrafts produced by local community.
- Can be good employer of women and can upgrade their economic status.
- vulnerability of the area to decisions made elsewhere by consumers and investors.
- Decline of other industries as resources flow into tourism industry.·
- Higher levels of public indebtedness and/or higher taxes to pay for increased infrastructure and services and can lead to reduced public expenditure on essential community services.
- Many jobs for locals are low level or unskilled, seasonal, low wage, part time with low annual earnings and little opportunity for advancement.
- vulnerability of the area to decisions made elsewhere by consumers and investors.
- Decline of other industries as resources flow into tourism industry.
- Higher levels of public indebtedness and/or higher taxes to pay for increased infrastructure and services and can lead to reduced public expenditure on essential community services.
- Many jobs for locals are low level or unskilled, seasonal, low wage, part time with low annual earnings with little opportunity for advancement.

A variety of economic analyses are carried out to support tourism decisions. As these different kinds of economic analyses are frequently confused, let's begin by positioning economic impact studies within the broader set of economic problems and techniques relevant to tourism. A feasibility study determines the feasibility of undertaking a given action to include political, physical, social, and economic feasibility. The economic aspects of a feasibility study typically involve a financial analysis to determine financial feasibility and a market demand analysis to determine market feasibility. A feasibility study is the private sector analogue of benefit cost analysis.

On the basis of analysis what could possibally be the Direct, Indirect and Induced Effects.

A standard economic impact analysis traces flows of money from tourism spending, first to businesses and government agency.

Other Businesses — supplying goods and services to tourist businesses,

Households — earning income by working in tourism or supporting industries, and

Government — through various taxes and charges on tourists, businesses and households.

Formally, regional economists distinguish direct, indirect, and induced economic effects. Indirect and induced effects are sometimes collectively called secondary effects. The total economic impact of tourism is the sum of direct, indirect, and induced effects within a region. Any of these impacts may be measured as gross output or sales, income, employment, or value added.

Direct effects are production changes associated with the immediate effects of changes in tourism expenditures. For example, an increase in the number of tourists staying overnight in hotels would directly yield increased sales in the hotel sector. The additional hotel sales and associated changes in hotel payments for wages and salaries, taxes, and supplies and services are direct effects of the tourist spending.

Indirect effects are the production changes resulting from various rounds of re-spending of the hotel industry's receipts in other backward-linked industries (i.e., industries supplying products and services to hotels).

Changes in sales, jobs, and income in the linen supply industry, for example, represent indirect effects of change in hotel sales. Businesses supplying products and services to the linen supply industry represent another round of indirect effects, eventually linking hotels to varying degrees to many other economic sectors in the region.

Induced effects are the changes in economic activity resulting from household spending of income earned directly or indirectly as a result of tourism spending. For example, hotel and linen supply employees, supported directly or indirectly by tourism, spend their income in the local region for housing, food, transportation, and the usual array of household product and service needs. The sales, income, and jobs that result from household spending of added wage, salary, or proprietor's income are induced effects.

By means of indirect and induced effects, changes in tourist spending can impact virtually every sector of the economy in one way or another. The magnitude of secondary effects depends on the propensity of businesses, and households in the region to purchase goods and services from local suppliers. Induced effects are particularly noticed when a large employer in a region closes a plant. Not only are supporting industries (indirect effects) hurt, but the entire local economy suffers due to the reduction in household income within the region.

Retail stores close and leakages of money from the region increase as consumers go outside the region for more and more goods and services. Similar effects in the opposite direction are observed when there is a significant increase in jobs and household income.

What does an economic impact study cost?

Costs will depend largely on the size and scope of tourism activity to be covered, the size and complexity of the study region, how much primary data are to be gathered and the level of accuracy and details desired. Tourism economic impact studies require considerable technical judgement of specialists and a mix of corresponding skills, viz:

1. Knowledge of tourism.
2. Expertise in conducting tourism surveys, particularly spending studies.
3. Regional economic modeling skills, including knowledge and access to economic data bases, multipliers and input-output modeling systems.
4. Communication skills.

Each of the principal components of an economic impact estimate (visits, spending, and multipliers) involve different costs and somewhat different skills. The costs and needed skills will vary considerably depending on whether primary or existing data are to be used.

If levels and types of tourism activity are known and spending averages and multipliers are taken from secondary sources, a complete economic impact assessment can be conducted in less than a month and in many cases, for under $5,000. You are paying primarily for the time, judgement and skills of the analyst.

In many cases, the tourism activity and visitor spending data needed for an economic impact analysis can be gathered in a general visitor survey or market study. Spending averages for particular tourist segments can be estimated by having a portion of the general survey respondents complete an extra page of spending questions.

Armed with good estimates of the number and types of visitors and their spending patterns, one can complete an economic impact study at little additional cost.

Thus, the principal motivation for a business or region to serve tourists are generally economic. An individual business is interested primarily in its own revenues and costs, while a community or region is concerned with tourism's overall contribution to the economy, as well as its social, fiscal and environmental impacts. A good understanding of tourism's economic impacts is therefore important for the tourism industry, government officials, and the community as a whole.

Tourism economics is unfortunately a technical area, involving concepts, methods, and models that are unfamiliar to most non-economists. In this bulletin, attempt has been made to define the key concepts and explain the basic methods for estimating the economic impacts of tourism, without technical nuances to the extent possible.

Understanding the concepts and methods is critical to interpreting, evaluating, and applying economic impact results. This bulletin should be read along with one or more economic impact reports that can be used as examples and opportunities to test one's grasp of the issues.

For those who do not have a particular tourism economic impact report in mind, at the risk of oversimplifying a complex topic, five pieces of advice are mentioned below, tendered to people who ask about tourism economic impacts.

Most important information for estimating tourism impacts is a good estimate of the number of tourists. This requires clearly defining what one wishes to include as "tourism" and the region of interest.

It is recommend that tourists be divided into distinct subgroups (segments) with distinct spending patterns and likings reacting differently to various policy and marketing actions.

In particular, local customers should be distinguished from visitors outside the region and day users from overnight visitors.

Multiplier effects are not nearly as important in most cases, as their use in tourism would suggest and multipliers tend to introduce complexities that most users of the results do not fully understand. Even if multiplier effects are important for the purpose of study, it should be borne that any errors in estimates of the direct effects will also be multiplied by any multiplier.

Tourism sales multipliers are often close to one because the secondary effects of tourist spending are generally just large enough to offset the spending that is not captured by the local economy.

If you must include multiplier effects, be sure to report the direct effects separately, so readers can decide whether and when to include the secondary effects.

Finally, it is recommend income or value added as the best measures of economic impacts, to report. Sales and job impacts can be quite misleading, as sales may go largely to buy parts from outside the region and job estimates are distorted by part time and seasonal positions, not to mention quite different wage rates across industries. Income or value added are the best measures of the economic gain to the region from tourism

Environmental Impact:

Tourism has the potential to create beneficial effects on the environment by contributing to environmental protection and conservation. It is a way to raise awareness of environmental values and it can serve as a tool to finance protection of natural areas and increase their economic importance.

Particularly nature and ecotourism — help promote conservation of wildlife and natural resources such as rain forests, as these are now regarded as tourism assets. It also helps generate funding for maintaining animal preserves and marine parks through entrance charges and guide fees. By creating alternative sources of employment, tourism reduces problems such as over-fishing and deforestation in developing nations.

Tourism is called smokeless industry, which can be synonymous with the protection and conservation of the environment. The improvement, conservation of natural, and man made tourist resources, contribute to tourist product and has no danger to the nation's resources. The scenic beauty, local culture, life styles, valleys, mountains are of great interest to visitors or tourists. The growth of tourism, both domestic and international, does less harm to the environment as compared to other industrial development.

However, tourism – specifically international tourism – has negative impact on the environment, but this impact is negligible. Tourism can become an instrument for beautification and improvement of the environment, if it is planned in a systematic manner.

Environment, today has acquired a broad definition. It not only includes land, air, water, flora and fauna, but also encompasses people, their creations, and social, economic and cultural conditions that affect their lives. Environment, whether natural or man-made, is an essential resource for tourism. Changes-are unavoidable if we have to develop tourism, but these changes can be done aesthetically without damaging it in anyway.

Conservation really means wise use of resources. It implies safeguarding the visual beauty of the countryside. Conservation of wildlife means survival of all living things – flora and fauna – providing them ample space to live, grow and breathe fresh air. The protection given by the governments, especially in India has given a new lease of life to endangered species of animals, but the present danger is in the form of poachers.

Some critics of modern tourism have described tourists as "new barbarians" who ruin ancient monuments by petty vandalism who furtively chip away pieces of marble to take home as souvenirs. They steal artifacts from temples, churches and museums, gouge out mosaics from walls and top of all, they often carve their names into ancient walls of temples and forts.

With tourism developing at a rapid pace, many people are concerned about its impact on natural environment. Recently, many environmentalists have become quite vocal in voicing their protests against the unregulated growth of tourism at the cost of the environment.

The WTO and PATA have laid down guidelines to protect the environment and some countries have enacted laws for its conservation and preservation. India is one of the countries to have set up a separate Ministry of Environment and Forests to monitor the use of land from the environment point of view. The ministry is very vigilant about the land, which is under the forest department, and prior clearance from the central government is essential before any tourist project can be set up in such areas.

The world now has become very environment conscious and this approach can harmonize tourism and nature. Tourism and health are essentially linked in three ways: the betterment of health is a common motive for travel. Health of climate, mineral springs and other environmental conditions, the standards of public health in destination areas contribute to the quality of the tourist product. Disease may get contracted by tourists in one place and transferred to other destinations or their homes.

Tourism can contribute to the maintenance and improvement of public health facilities in destination areas because it provides additional sources of revenue, which can be invested in their upgradation. However, tourism also induces pollution, which may be conducive to the development of disease itself. Thus, paradoxically, tourism can aid the improvement of public health facilities in destination areas and at the same time, lead to a deterioration in the standards of health. It is not always the host who is affected by tourism. In some cases, it is the tourist who is influenced much more than the host.

This is especially the case with those seeking to reinforce or expand their political, ideological or religious beliefs by visit to such places as Israel, India, Cuba, Mecca and Lourdes. Information suggests that tourism has a positive effect in this domain, i.e., worldwide understanding resulting from international tourism.

The result of the research – does tourism help set the stage for improving international understanding – suggests a qualified yes. Perhaps, the strongest statement possible now is that very little evidence has been discovered to indicate that international tourism is obstructing international understanding.

Environmental Effects — Negative:

Tourism poses a threat to a region's natural and cultural resources, such as water supply, beaches, coral reefs and heritage sites, through overuse. It also causes increased pollution through traffic emissions, littering, increased sewage production and noise.

The quality of the environment, both natural and man-made, is essential to tourism. However, tourism's relationship with the environment is complex. It involves many activities that can have adverse environmental effects. Many of these impacts are linked with the construction of general infrastructure such as roads and airports, and of tourism facilities, including resorts, hotels, restaurants, shops, golf courses and marinas. The negative impacts of tourism development can gradually destroy the environmental resources on which it depends.

Negative impacts from tourism occur when the level of visitor use is greater than the environment's ability to cope with this use within the acceptable limits of change. Uncontrolled conventional tourism poses potential threats to many natural areas around the world. It can put enormous pressure on an area and lead to impacts such as soil erosion, increased pollution, discharges into the sea, natural habitat loss, increased pressure on endangered species and heightened vulnerability to forest fires. It often puts a strain on water resources, and it can force local populations to compete for the use of critical resources.

Depletion of Natural Resources:

Tourism development can put pressure on natural resources when it increases consumption in areas where resources are already scarce.

Water Resources:

Water, and especially fresh water, is one of the most critical natural resources. The tourism industry generally overuses water resources for hotels, swimming pools, golf courses and personal use of water by tourists. This can result in water shortages and degradation of water supplies, as well as generating a greater volume of waste water.

In dryer regions like the Mediterranean, the issue of water scarcity is of particular concern. Because of the hot climate and the tendency of tourists to consume more water when on holiday than they do at home, the amount used can run up to 440 liters a day. This is almost double what the inhabitants of an average Spanish city use.

Golf course maintenance can also deplete fresh water resources. In recent years golf tourism has increased in popularity and the number of golf courses has grown rapidly. Golf courses require an enormous amount of water every day and, as with other causes of excessive extraction of water, this can result in water scarcity. If the water comes from wells, overpumping can cause saline intrusion into groundwater. Golf resorts are more and more often situated in or near protected areas or areas where resources are limited, exacerbating their impacts. An average golf course in a tropical country such as Thailand needs 1500kg of chemical fertilizers, pesticides and herbicides per year and uses as much water as 60,000 rural villagers.

Local Resources:

Tourism can create great pressure on local resources like energy, food, and other raw materials that may already be in short supply.

Greater extraction and transport of these resources exacerbates the physical impacts associated with their exploitation. Because of the seasonal character of the industry, many destinations have ten times more inhabitants in the high season as in the low season. A high demand is placed upon these resources to meet the high expectations tourists often have (proper heating, hot water, etc.).

Land Degradation:

Important land resources include minerals, fossil fuels, fertile soil, forests, wetlands and wildlife. Increased construction of tourism and recreational facilities has increased the pressure on these resources and on scenic landscapes. Direct impact on natural resources, both renewable and nonrenewable, in the provision of tourist facilities can be caused by the use of land for accommodation and other infrastructure provision, and the use of building materials.

Forests often suffer negative impacts of tourism in the form of deforestation caused by fuel wood collection and land clearing. For example, one trekking tourist in Nepal - and area already suffering the effects of deforestation - can use four to five kilograms of wood a day.

Pollution:

Tourism can cause the same forms of pollution as any other industry: air emissions, noise, solid waste and littering, releases of sewage, oil and chemicals, even architectural/visual pollution.

Depletion of the Ozone Layer:

The ozone layer, which is situated in the upper atmosphere (or stratosphere) at an altitude of 12-50 kilometers, protects life on earth by absorbing the harmful wavelengths of the sun's ultraviolet (UV) radiation, which in high doses is dangerous to humans and animals. For instance, one of the reasons scientists have put forward for the global decrease of amphibian populations is increased exposure to UV radiation.

Ozone depleting substances (ODSs) such as CFCs (chlorofluorocarbons) and halons have contributed to the destruction of this layer. The tourism industry may be part of the problem; direct impacts start with the construction of new developments and continue during daily management and operations. Refrigerators, air conditioners and propellants in aerosol spray cans, amongst others, contain ODSs and are widely used in the hotel and tourism industry. Emissions from jet aircraft are also a significant source of ODSs. According to Tourism Concern, scientists predict that by 2015, half of the annual destruction of the ozone layer will be caused by air travel.

UNEP's Ozon Action Programme works with governments and industries, including the tourism industry, to phase out ODSs and find safer alternatives. UNEP has developed extensive information and guidance on how many types of businesses can eliminate ODSs and contribute to preservation of the ozone layer.

Global tourism is closely linked to climate change. Tourism involves the movement of people from their homes to other destinations and accounts for about 50% of traffic movements; rapidly expanding air traffic contributes about 2.5% of the production of CO_2. Tourism is thus, a significant contributor to the increasing concentrations of greenhouse gases in the atmosphere.

Air travel itself is a major contributor to the greenhouse effect. Passenger jets are the fastest growing source of greenhouse gas emissions. The number of international travellers is expected to increase from 594 million in 1996 to 1.6 billion by 2020, adding greatly to the problem unless steps are taken to reduce emissions.

Air and Noise Pollution :

Transport by air, road, and rail is continuously increasing in response to the rising number of tourists and their greater mobility. To give an indication, the ICAO reported that the number of international air passengers worldwide rose from 88 million in 1972 to 344 million in 1994. One consequence of this increase in air transport is that tourism now accounts for more than 60% of air travel and is therefore responsible for an important share of air emissions. One study estimated that a single transatlantic return flight emits almost half the CO_2 emissions produced by all other sources (lighting, heating, car use, etc.) consumed by an average person yearly.

Transport emissions and emissions from energy production and use are linked to acid rain, global warming and photochemical pollution. Air pollution from tourist transportation has impacts on the global level, especially from carbon dioxide (CO_2) emissions related to transportation energy use. And it can contribute to severe local air pollution. Some of these impacts are quite specific to tourist activities. For example, usually in very hot or cold countries, tour buses often leave their motors running for hours while the tourists go out for an excursion because they want to return to a comfortably air-conditioned bus.

Noise pollution from airplanes, cars, and buses, as well as recreational vehicles such as snowmobiles and jet skis, is an ever-growing problem of modern life. In addition to causing annoyance, stress, and even hearing loss in humans, it causes distress to wildlife, especially in sensitive areas. For instance, noise generated by snowmobiles can cause animals to alter their natural activity patterns.

Solid Waste and Littering:

In areas with high concentrations of tourist activities and appealing natural attractions, waste disposal is a serious problem and improper disposal can be a major despoiler of the natural environment – rivers, scenic areas, and roadsides. For example, cruise ships in the Caribbean are estimated to produce more than 70,000 tons of waste each year. Today, some cruise lines are actively working to reduce waste-related impacts. Solid waste and littering can degrade the physical appearance of the water and shoreline and cause the death of marine animals.

In mountain areas, trekking tourists generate a great deal of waste. Tourists on expedition leave behind their garbage, oxygen cylinders and even camping equipment. Such practices degrade the environment with all the detritus typical of the developed world, in remote areas that have few garbage collection or disposal facilities. Some trails in the Peruvian Andes and in Nepal frequently visited by tourists have been nicknamed "Coca-Cola trail" and "Toilet paper trail".

Sewage:

Construction of hotels, recreation and other facilities often leads to increased sewage pollution. Wastewater has polluted seas and lakes surrounding tourist attractions, damaging the flora and fauna. Sewage runoff causes serious damage to coral reefs because it stimulates the growth of algae, which cover the filter-feeding corals, hindering their ability to survive. Changes in salinity and siltation can have wide-ranging impacts on coastal environments. And sewage pollution can threaten the health of humans and animals.

Aesthetic Pollution:

Often tourism fails to integrate its structures with the natural features and indigenous architectural of the destination. Large, dominating resorts of disparate design can look out of place in any natural environment and may clash with the indigenous structural design.

A lack of land-use planning and building regulations in many destinations has facilitated sprawling developments along coastlines, valleys and scenic routes. The sprawl includes tourism facilities themselves and supporting infrastructure such as roads, employee housing, parking, service areas, and waste disposal.

Physical Impacts:

Attractive landscape sites, such as sandy beaches, lakes, riversides, and mountain tops and slopes, are often transitional zones, characterized by species-rich ecosystems. Typical physical impacts include the degradation of such ecosystems.

An ecosystem is a geographic area including all the living organisms (people, plants, animals, and microorganisms), their physical surroundings (such as soil, water, and air), and the natural cycles that sustain them. The ecosystems most threatened with degradation are ecologically fragile areas such as alpine regions, rain forests, wetlands, mangroves, coral reefs and sea grass beds. The threats to and pressures on these ecosystems are often severe because such places are very attractive to both tourists and developers.

In industrial countries, mass tourism and recreation are now fast overtaking the extractive industries as the largest threat to mountain communities and environments. Since 1945, visits to the 10 most popular mountainous national parks in the United States have increased twelve-fold. In the European Alps, tourism now exceeds 100 million visitor-days. Every year in the Indian Himalaya, more than 250,000 Hindu pilgrims, 25,000 trekkers, and 75 mountaineering expeditions climb to the sacred source of the Ganges River, the Gangotri Glacier. They deplete local forests for firewood, trample riparian vegetation, and strew litter. Even worse, this tourism frequently induces poorly planned, land-intensive development.

Physical impacts are caused not only by tourism-related land clearing and construction, but also by continuing tourist activities and long-term changes in local economies and ecologies.

Construction Activities and Infrastructure Development:

The development of tourism facilities such as accommodation, water supplies, restaurants and recreation facilities can involve sand mining, beach and sand dune erosion, soil erosion and extensive paving. In addition, road and airport construction can lead to land degradation and loss of wildlife habitats and deterioration of scenery.

In Yosemite National Park (US), for instance, the number of roads and facilities have been increased to keep pace with the growing visitor numbers and to supply amenities, infrastructure and parking lots for all these tourists. These actions have caused habitat loss in the park and are accompanied by various forms of pollution including air pollution from automobile emissions; the Sierra Club has reported "smog so thick that Yosemite Valley could not be seen from airplanes". This occasional smog is harmful to all species and vegetation inside the Park.

Deforestation and Intensified or Unsustainable Use of Land:

Construction of ski resort accommodation and facilities frequently requires clearing forested land. Coastal wetlands are often drained and filled due to lack of more suitable sites for construction of tourism facilities and infrastructure. These activities can cause severe disturbance and erosion of the local ecosystem, even destruction in the long term.

Effects of Development of Marina:

Development of marinas and breakwaters can cause changes in currents and coastlines. Furthermore, extraction of building materials such as sand, affects coral reefs, mangroves, and hinterland forests, leading to erosion and destruction of habitats. In the Philippines and the Maldives, dynamiting and mining of coral for resort building materials has damaged fragile coral reefs and depleted the fisheries that sustain local people and attract tourists.

Overbuilding and extensive paving of shorelines can result in destruction of habitats and disruption of land-sea connections (such as sea-turtle nesting spots). Coral reefs are especially fragile marine ecosystems and are suffering worldwide from reef-based tourism developments. Evidence suggests a variety of impacts to coral result from shoreline development, increased sediments in the water, trampling by tourists and divers, ship groundings, pollution from sewage, overfishing, and fishing with poisons and explosives that destroy coral habitat.

Trampling:

Tourists using the same trail over and over again trample the vegetation and soil, eventually causing damage that can lead to loss of biodiversity and other impacts. Such damage can be even more extensive when visitors frequently stray off established trails.

Loss of Biological Diversity:

Biological diversity is the term given to the variety of life on Earth and the natural patterns it forms.

The Effects of Loss of Biodiversity:

It threatens our food supplies, opportunities for recreation and tourism, and sources of wood, medicines and energy.

It interferes with essential ecological functions such as species balance, soil formation, and greenhouse gas absorption.

It reduces the productivity of ecosystems, thereby shrinking nature's basket of goods and services, from which we constantly draw.

It destabilizes ecosystems and weakens their ability to deal with natural disasters such as floods, droughts, and hurricanes, and with human-caused stresses, such as pollution and climate change.

Tourism, especially nature tourism, is closely linked to biodiversity and the attractions created by a rich and varied environment. It can also cause loss of biodiversity when land and resources are strained by excessive use, and when impacts on vegetation, wildlife, mountain, marine and coastal environments and water resources exceed the carrying capacity. This loss of biodiversity in fact means loss of tourism potential.

Introduction of Exotic Species:

Tourists and suppliers – often unwittingly – can bring in species (insects, wild and cultivated plants and diseases) that are not native to the local environment and that can cause enormous disruption and even destruction of ecosystems.

UNEP's Energy Programme provides, among other things, information and publications on energy efficiency and alternative energy sources to reduce the environmental impacts of energy use and of transportation.

HOW GLOBAL ENVIRONMENTAL AFFECTS TOURISM

Natural Disasters:

Catastrophes like floods, earthquakes, wildfires, volcanoes, avalanches, drought and diseases can have a serious effect on inbound and domestic tourism and thus on local tourism industries. The outbreak of the foot and mouth disease epidemic in England in 2001, for instance, had severely affected Great

Britain's inbound tourism market. A BHA/Barclays Hospitality Business Trends Survey found that 75% of hotels in England, 81% in Scotland and 85% in Wales continued to be affected by the foot and mouth outbreak, and over 60% forecast a decline in business in the June-September 2001 period.

Climate Change:

Climate scientists now generally agree that the Earth's surface temperatures have risen steadily in recent years because of an increase in the so-called greenhouse gases in the atmosphere, which trap heat from the sun. One of the most significant of these gases is carbon dioxide (CO_2), which is generated when fossil fuels, such as coal, oil and natural gas are burned (e.g. in industry, electricity generation, and automobiles) and when there are changes in land use, such as deforestation. In the long run, the accumulation of CO_2 and other greenhouse gases in the atmosphere can cause global climate change – a process that may already be occurring.

Tourism not only contributes to climate change, but is affected by it as well. Climate change is likely to increase the severity and frequency of storms and severe weather events, which can have disastrous effects on tourism in the affected regions. Some of the other impacts that the world risks as a result of global warming are drought, diseases and heat waves.

The quality of the environment, both natural and man-made, is essential to tourism. However, tourism's relationship with the environment is complex.

Many of these impacts are linked with the construction of general infrastructure such as roads and airports, and of tourism facilities, including resorts, hotels, restaurants, shops, golf courses, and marinas. The negative impacts of tourism development can gradually destroy the environmental resources on which it depends.

The OECD (1980) classifies the adverse environmental impacts of tourism under seven headings:

Effects of pollution (air, water, noise, littering)

Loss of natural habitat including agricultural and pastoral lands.

Destruction of flora and fauna, vandalism.

Degradation of landscape and of historic sites and monuments.

Effects of congestion including crowding.

Effects of conflicts over land use.

Possible Environmental Impacts of Tourism Development

Positive	Negative
Tourism development can:	**Tourism development can:**
be a relatively 'clean' industry, foster conservation and preservation of natural resources, encourage community revitalization and beautification, and raise revenues for establishing administrative and planning controls to maintain quality of environment.	degrade or destroy water quantity and quality. It can use air quality, waste production and recycling practices, efficiency of resource use, quality of natural sites and scenery species demographics habitats of local wildlife by the introduction of non-native species, toxics and pollutants.

Social Impacts:

The technique of assessing social impact of tourism fall into two broad categories: "top-down", aggregate or macro-level approaches; and "bottom-up", project or micro-level approaches. Tourism throughout the world is promoted as a means to achieving development, and India is no exception. But the question is: development for whom? Who are the winners and the losers? And at what cost? These are some of the questions that form the backdrop to exploring the relationship between tourism, peace, and conflict in India. If one were to approach development holistically, then it should contribute economically, environmentally, socially, and culturally to the people and the region in a balanced and sustained manner.

In order to the measure the social impact of tourism, one has to consider social aspects of tourism. In that respect, the main macro-level indicator is employment created by the tourism economy for sub-regions of India. Employment is one of the most readily available indicators to begin measuring the social impact of tourism, since job creation generally helps create the opportunities for better standards of living and related conditions of socio-economic progress. The importance of tourism becomes more significant when the work force amounts to 5.4 per cent in India.

It is then possible to improve the social situation of people, often through Government policies and programmes. In addition, revenue generated from tourism has enabled Governments to allocate financial resources for improving education and health conditions.

More up-to-date, systematic statistics and general descriptions of gender patterns in national tourism industry in India can help strengthen the analysis about the social impact of tourism from a gender perspective. This can help to improve the image of career opportunities for women and men in the tourism industry. In addition, it can help employers as well as government policy makers to have a more complete understanding about the gender dimensions of tourism industry employment.

Moreover, the moment a traveller/tourist sets foot in India and is greeted by a graceful namaste, a gesture that denotes both welcome and respect, they are on the way to one of the most rewarding experience of their life. India, always warm and inviting, is a place of infinite variety – one that favors the tourist with a different facet of its fascination every time he/she comes on a visit.

The improvements to infrastructure and new leisure amenities that result from tourism also benefit the local community. Tourism encourages the preservation of traditional customs, handicrafts and festivals that might otherwise have been allowed to wane, and it creates civic pride. Interchanges between hosts and guests create a better cultural understanding and can also help raise global awareness of issues such as poverty and human rights abuses.

For many countries, tourism is considered as an easy way of economic development, especially for developing and under developed countries. As the economic impacts are more really measurable, types of impacts tend to remain more hidden, particularly social effects. However social change may have more significant costs than economic benefits in the long term.

Tourism is a social event. It is all about people and how people as tourists interact with other locations and peoples, engaging in experiences that may influence their own or host community attitudes, expectations opinions and life styles. Thus, wide range of tourism social events for the traveller and host community. Social impact relate to change in societal values, systems, individual behaviour social relationship, life styles, modes of expression and community structure. The focus of social impact is centered on host, a community person who resides in tourist destinations.

It has been stated that from social perspective, the rapid expansion of tourism is important in two respects:

Firstly, development of tourism as a vehicle for modernisation and diversification leads to changes and development in the structure of society. This may be positive or negative. In positive sense, there may be society wide improvements on income, employment opportunities, education, local infrastructure and services. On the negative side, there may be a threat posed to traditional social values, creation of frictions and there are peoples fascinated with western culture in the society who may take advantages of others and adaptations or weakening of cultural values.

Secondly, all tourists to great extent inevitably carry their own beliefs, values and behavioural models what may be termed as cultural baggages.

Therefore, the scope for mixing of culture is great. This gives rise to two arguments about socio-cultural effect of tourism.

The interaction between host and guest could destroy traditional culture, i.e., tourism primary as a threat to culture and people.

The interaction between host and guest could create new opportunities for peace and greater understanding.

There is evidence to prove that both aspects are correct and a consensus is by no means easy to generate. The study of the impact on society is complicated by the nature of more general social change. The forces of change are many and varied, tourism being just one factor. Other aspects include the role of advertising and media, effect of multinational companies, the aspirations of government, education and immigration. Given the complexity of influencing factors, it is hard to extrapolate as one example of potential social impact due to tourism.

Factors Influencing Socio Cultural Impacts

The main factors influencing the nature and extent of social impacts are:

- Types and number of tourists.
- Importance of tourism industry in the economy.
- Size and development of tourism industry.
- Pace of tourism development.
- Nature of guest-host interaction.
- Nature of host destination and social simulates.
- Community tolerance capacity.

Experts comment that cultural similarity or dissimilarity is one of the major factors in shaping social impact.

UNESCO (1976) suggests that host-guest interactions in mass tourism are characterized by four properties:

- Transitory nature.
- Temporal and spatial constraints.
- Lack of spontaneity.
- Unequal and unbalanced experience.

These properties appear especially valid in the context of mass tourism to developing countries. The primary problems associated with tourism are the demonstrations effect; acculturation increase in crime, prostitution and health; displacement of community, general host irritation and; commercialisation of culture.

Demonstration Effect:

Demonstration effect is defined as changes in attitudes, values or behaviour which can result from merely observing and imitating tourists. This may be advantageous or disadvantageous to the host community. Tourists to developing countries, especially if they come from very different societies, introduce and display a very foreign way of life to the host population. This may be positive when it stimulates certain behaviours or inspires people to work for things they lack. More commonly, it is detrimental and causing discontent and resentment among local people especially in developing countries because of the lack of wealth to satisfy these desires.

The demonstration effect has also economic implication. Local people often tend to imitate rich persons that changes the pattern of consumption from local product to western products. Local people may take to illegal means to obtain the desired luxuries, thus crime rate may increase as a result of tourism in a destination.

The demonstration effect has the greatest influence on young people and may create generation gaps and class difference between the young generation and those who wish to retain the traditional way of life. The young, especially the educated, tend to migrate. The young people wish for material aspects of modern life but fail to see the negative effects – such as stress, unemployment, and environmental degradation. This type of changes may be a disruptive force to traditional kinship overtime.

Social Effects — Negative:

There is no doubt about the economic benefits brought by tourism, but these are not explained reliably. Visitor behavior can have a detrimental effect on the quality of life of the host community. For example, crowding and congestion, drugs and alcohol menance, prostitution and increased crime levels can occur. Tourism can even infringe on human rights, with locals being displaced from their land to make way for new hotels or barred from beaches. Interactions with tourists can also lead to an erosion of traditional cultures and values.

Tourism has often brought social problems including exploitation and trafficking of women and children for sex and/ or cheap labor, the spread of HIV/AIDS, and the sale and use of illegal drugs, all of which affects vulnerable populations in the developing countries.

The danger arises when saturation levels are reached, which is the point at which citizens no longer feel that the city, neighbourhood, or the area they have always used for leisure belongs to them. We must explain the direct, indirect and induced jobs provided by this activity. We must also explain how, year after year, revenue from tourism has helped and helps to reduce the deficit of the balance of payments in this country, a balance that is affected by a structural deficit. Thanks to tourism activity, a huge volume of revenue is created in the form of tax: social security contributions, income tax, VAT, corporate tax, etc.

In a country like India, we can certainly find direct responsibility on the part of business people in the sector (not everyone) who are making up the most of the higher spending power of tourists resulting in increase of prices, creating artificial inflation in the process that also affects the local population. And if we look at residential tourism, the economic effects worsen considerably, as the demand for homes increases above normal levels, and therefore, the prices do too, leaving local residents unable to access the housing market.

What options are available so that we do not squander an activity that has brought us so many social benefits? We must either implement a new model or take measures to reduce negative effects as much as possible.There must also be a call for social responsibility among tourism companies in terms of price fixing. But in addition to that, we must put an end to the increasing trivialisation of tourism, where anything goes.

The social impact of tourism refers to the manner in which tourism and travel effect changes in collective and individual value systems, behaviour patterns, community structures, lifestyle and quality of life.

Acculturation:

Many impacts of tourism appear relatively quickly while others tend to manifest themselves more gradually. The external influences and the evolution of society results into change, regardless of the existence tourism. The enhanced networks of communication, technology and emergency of global market are all part of this process. Nepal is a best example, which is becoming a mainstream tourist destination, and westernisation of Kathmandu is occurring as a result of tourism. This type of change, coca-colanization or McDonalisation, is acculturation through tourism. International tourism is thought to influence social change through the process of acculturation. A major concern is that when a culturally weak society comes into contact with a strong one, the process will be one way, that is the values and attitudes of the strong nation are transferred to the weak nation.

Possible Social Impacts of Tourism Development

Positive	Negative
Tourism development may:	**Tourism development may:**
contribute to the removal of social or national prejudices, the promotion of better understanding and social change encourage civic involvement and local pride in a destination and play a supportive force for peace, foster pride in cultural traditions and help avoid urban relocation by creating local jobs, improve quality of life of locals, increase availability of recreation facilities/opportunities, improve quality of police protection.	increase drug pedding and crime, create a hectic community, and life-style, introduce an immigrant workforce and attendant social problems, cause competition and conflict between tourists and residents for available services, facilities, and recreational opportunities.

Language:

Language is a key indicator of acculturation because it is a social vehicle of communication. Tourism can change the language of host community and make an aversion towards regional languages and dialects which take place in three ways:

- Economic changes through bringing of immigrant or expatriate labour.
- Demonstration effect where the local community aspires to achieve the status of visitors.

- Direct social contact and the need to converse to make commercial transactions.

Sometimes, the host is obliged to learn the main incoming tourist languages in order to deal with their requirements.

Religion:

In some tourist destinations, religion (churches, temples and mosques and monasteries) has been promoted as major tourism products and their sites attracts large number of visitors, who may or may not have belief in that particular religion Because of this, increasing conflicts exists between local worshippers, devout visitors and sight seers. The tourists do not always recognize traditional ceremonies, rites and practice. In Bhutan, tourists are not permitted to visit Monasteries. In India, temples are not opened to non-Hindus in order to prevent tourism from disrupting religious life. In many countries, particularly Islamic countries, tourists clothing can cause offence.

Displacement:

It is also important to understand the wider repercussions of tourist development where economies have been given priority before community concerns. The most widely discussed phenomenon is the displacement of local communities who have to move away from their residence to make way for tourism. Land is taken over by government or private investors for various reasons such as construction of hotels and other infrastructure.

The forceful displacement not only makes the local community homeless but also loss livelihood. In the name of development, all over the world, millions of poor tribal societies have been displaced and driven in to abject poverty. Universal declaration of human rights (1948), which states, "the basic standards that must underpin contemporary global society is clearly contravened by some of the examples of tourism development".

Tourism and Crime:

Tourism and crime is a new emerging area of study within tourism but there is no universal agreement on whether tourism development leads increased crime in a locality. Tourists are vulnerable because they are in unfamiliar surroundings possessing expensive consumer items, cash, credit cards and passports which are valuable commodities in the black market.

Tourists may engage in crime and illicit activities such as violent drunken behaviour, drug smuggling and sex tourism. It appears that, especially on seasonal basis, tourism raises the crime level as the tourist influx provides for more soft targets and possibly easier and wealthier targets. Some scholars have established certain relationship between crime and tourism.

Sex Tourism and Prostitution:

Prostitution undeniably existed before the onset of mass tourism to developing countries. However, in many countries tourism has undoubtedly contributed to an increase in prostitution, organized gambling and various types of crimes. Although, there exists casual connection between crimes and tourism, it is very difficult to find hard evidence about the role played by tourism. Given the fact that similar effects have been experienced in countries that witness low levels of tourism. It is thus wrong to make tourism the scapegoat for changes.

In relation to prostitution, it seems that different attitudes to sex in some third world countries were responsible for the growth prevalence of sex tourism which dates back to the accounts of early European adventures. This image has persisted in the marketing of some exotic destinations like Thailand and other South Eastern countries. The demand for such services now includes almost all places witnessing mass tourism. The tiny West African country of the Gambia has been successfully marketed in Scandinavian countries as the closest place to Europe guaranteeing a pleasant climate during the northern winter. It is also a place deeply affected by tourism impact on moral behaviour.

The scare of AIDS had a dramatic affect on prostitution. The threat of this disease as incurable sexually transmitted diseases will have important implications on the popularity of some tourist destinations. The tourists demanded more and more young prostitutes in the hope that there was a lower likelihood of contracting this disease. In recent years, however several industrialised countries have finally passed legislation, which prosecutes their residents for sex with minors overseas (e.g.,Germany, Sweden). It is hoped that this will serve as a disincentive.

With respect to crime and gambling, although there is plenty of evidence in the developed metropolitan countries of a positive relationship between tourism and increase in crime, there are few studies, which examine the situation from third world perspective. Matheson and Wall suggest that tourism and crime are influenced by population density during the peak seasons, the location of resort in relation to an international border and differences in per capita incomes between host society and the tourists.

Health:

Tourism has the dual effect of promoting the provisions of improved health care in third world destination, but in addition, it acts as a vehicle in spreading some forms of diseases. There is increasing concern about spreading of sexually transmitted diseases (STDs) at a variety of level from minor diseases to spread of HIV and AIDS, through sex tourism.

Standard health care may improve in tourism destination as better facilities are introduced to cope with increased seasonal population. In some destinations, cultural differences in safety standards can create unknown levels of risk. Western visitors occasionally regard the fact that a low standard of public hygiene in parts of third world exists with rare safe drinking water supply and hospitals resulting in difficulty in attracting or retaining the services of skilled personnel.

It appears that little research has been conducted examining the underlying reasons as to why such impacts appear to be inevitable. The reason may be:

1. As an industrial activity, tourism consumes resources, creates waste and has specific infrastructure needs.
2. As a consumer of resources, it has the ability to over consume

resources.

3. Tourism, as a resource-dependent industry must compete for scarce resources to ensure its survival.
4. Tourism is a private sector-dominated industry, with investment decisions being based predominantly on profit maximisation.
5. Tourism is a multi-faceted industry, and as such, it is almost impossible to control.
6. Tourists are consumers, not anthropologists.
7. Tourism is entertainment.
8. Unlike other industrial activities, tourism generates income by importing clients rather than exporting its product.

Tourism enjoys a love-hate relationship with its host community. It is both a much sought after and much reviled activity. As such, the social ramifications of tourism warrant careful consideration, as impacts can either become assets or detriments to communities. Influxes of tourists bring diverse values to the community and influence behaviours and family life. Individuals and the collective community might try to please tourists or adopt tourist behaviors.

Interactions between residents and tourists can impact creative expression by providing new opportunities or by stifling individuality.

Culture Tourism and its Impacts:

Culture, has been defined as "the whole complex of distinctive spiritual, intellectual, and emotional features that characterize a society or social group. It includes not only the arts and letters, but also modes of life, the fundamental rights of a human being, value systems, traditions and beliefs".

Culture tourism began to be recognized as a distinct tourism product category in the late 1970s, with the realization that a large number of people travel specifically to gain a better understanding of the culture or heritage of a destination. Nearly 40% of international travellers are now considered cultural tourists, who visit destinations based on cultural heritage of a place – rural, ethnic and spiritual factors.

The name 'India' comes from the word 'Indus', which has been derived from the Persian word for 'Hindu', and Sanskrit word 'Sindhu'.

- Now, India is popularly know as "Bharat", and also "Hindustan".
- Since ancient times, India has been known for its culture, heritage, and tradition.

One can find the traces of different cultures in music, dance, architecture, festivities, languages spoken, traditional beliefs and customs, food and many more like these. It is the development in these aspects of life that makes the heritage of India one of the most vibrant and most exhaustive.

Cultural tourism is the subset of tourism concerned with a country or regions culture, specifically the lifestyle of the people in those geographical areas, the history of those peoples, their art, architecture, religions, and other elements that helped shape their way of life.

India has a rich resource of both tangible cultural heritage in its monuments and sites and also an intangible cultural heritage in the form of its architecture, music, dance/drama, local rituals and traditions and other folk arts. An integrated circuit linking heritage monuments with culturally rich villages and towns around them should be formed to enable and strengthen the development of cultural tourism in India.

Cultural tourism includes tourism in urban areas, particularly historic or large cities and their cultural facilities such as museums and theatres. It can also include tourism in rural areas showcasing the traditions of indigenous cultural communities (i.e. festivals, rituals), and their values and lifestyle.

Our historical and archaeological monuments continue to be the biggest draw in attracting international tourists.

Music:

Classical music of India has its roots in beliefs of the people and an amalgamation with other systems has not erased this source. Careful intonation has always been at the core of Indian classical music. The chanting of sacred words and phrases like 'Om' required total precision because these chants were part of what it took to maintain the order of the universe.

The music of India includes multiple varieties of folk, popular, pop, classical music and R&B. Indian music covers a wide range of traditions and regional styles. Classical music largely encompasses the two genres – North Indian Hindustani, South Indian Carnatic traditions and their various forms of regional folk music.

Dances:

Dance in India cover a wide range of dance and dance theatre forms from the ancient classical or temple dance to folk and modern styles. There are hundreds of Indian folk dances such as Bhangra, Bihu, Ghumura, Sambalpuri, Chhau and Garba apart from special dances observed in regional festivals.

India offers a number of classical dance forms, each of which can be traced to different parts of the country and representing the culture of a certain region or a group of people. The beginning of the contemporary styles of classical dances can be traced to the period 1300-1400 A.D.

The dance forms range from temple dances like Bharatnatyam, oddissi and mohiniyattam, to kathakali, symbolizing the victory of truth over falsehood. Kathak and Kuchipudi are means to recite religious and mythological tales to the accompaniment of music, mime and dance. Manipuri, and Dandiya Raas represents the celebration of Radha-Krishna's togetherness.

Art and Crafts:

Indian art and craft can be classified into specific periods each reflecting particular religious, political and cultural developments. These are: 1. Ancient period (3500 BCE-1200 CE), 2. Islamic ascendancy (1192-1757), 3. Colonial period (1757–1947), 4. Independence, and the postcolonial period (Post-1947).

The talent of the Indian artisans' is till date visible in the age-old monuments/constructions. The sculptures boast of their creativity and hard work. The numerous sculptures on temple walls are all hewn out of hard rock and last to date. Rock-cut architecture was perfected by the Buddhists, and was followed by several Hindu rulers. In Southern India, Pallavas excelled in this art form.

The sculptures or idols in temples are made of granite and the Utsava murthis are made of bronze & panchaloha. Apart from these, there are the huge Iyyanar statues & horses exist in South Indian villages.

Indian Cuisine:

Indian Cuisine has caught the fancy of people across the globe. This can be capitalized on by developing culinary tour routes into different regions for enthusiasts to taste and learn to cook the authentic way. Also, it is proposed to create a highly skilled workforce of culinary professionals not only for India but also to promote Indian cuisine internationally. The Ministry of Tourism should work on a rating and recognition system for Indian Restaurants overseas, so that a customer is assured of its authenticity and standard.

The cuisine in India is classified into three major categories. Sattva, Rajas, and Tamas. Sattva stands for balance, Rajas stands for passion, and Tamas stands for indulgence. Food is consumed according to the lifestyle of the person. For example: When a person tries to lead his life in want of self-realisation, he would prefer a Satvic food, known as Sattvic diet, which would help to keep his mind in balance.

Pilgrimage:

India is a place of diverse pilgrimage centers associated with various religions such as Buddhism, Muslim, Hindu, Christianity, Sikhism, etc.

Wildlife:

India's great Wildlife Sanctuaries and National Parks need to be made an integral part of the Indian Tourism product. The tourist facilities at the parks need be enhanced and a proper site and visitor management plan be prepared so as not to disturb the ecological balance and disturb the local habitat but have a sustainable tourism product.

Flora and Fauna:

India's rich flora, fauna and natural wonders especially in the North Eastern States are yet to be exploited for tourism purposes and made an integral part of the Tourism Product mix. This was envisaged in the 11th Plan by involving the State Governments and local communities.

Festivals:

Many festivals are religious in origin, although several are celebrated irrespective of caste and creed. Some popular festivals are Diwali, Ganesh Chaturthi, Ugadi, Thai Pongal, Holi, Onam, Vijayadashami, Durga Puja, Eid ul-Fitr, Bakr-Id, Christmas, Buddha Jayanti, Moharram and Vaisakhi.

Mountain-Based Adventure Tourism

India offers the best Mountain Based adventure tourism in the world in the Himalayas. Already a lot of work has been initiated in this segment but they have to be made comparable or better than what is being offered in the Alpine Countries. Regulations and certifications for adventure tourism operators should be a must so that laid down standards of safety and conservation are adhered to.

Handicrafts

Indian textiles, handlooms and handicrafts, its furniture and jewellery are already popular abroad. Now with Indian designers also receiving global recognition, shopping has become an integral part of a tourist's itinerary. Hence the development of dedicated shopping centres and special interest shopping tours should be encouraged as it will help revive traditional crafts and craftsmen, textiles and weavers and give families livelihood.

Traditional clothing in India greatly varies across different parts of the country and is influenced immensely by local culture, geography and climate. Popular styles of dress include draped garments such as sari for women and dhoti or lungi for men; in addition, stitched clothes such as *churidar* for women and *kurta-pyjama* are also in vogue.

Indian Arts

Indian Art and Artists are gaining world recognition and the development of such a niche–based special interest product-mix will position India as a unique destination.

Architecture of India

Architecture of India especially situated in 6 cities/towns namely, Hampi, Agra, Konark and Khajuraho, Orccha and Datia along with Buddhist and Jain circuits.

Culture Tourism has a special place in India because of its past civilization as India has been considered the land of ancient history, heritage, and culture. Historical and archaeological monuments continue to be the biggest draw in attracting international tourists. This fact has been confirmed by a survey undertaken by the Pacific AreaTravel Association (PATA). In order to make all these well known so that foreign and domestic tourists make them part of their itinaries, we will have to take following steps:

- Conduct Tourism Impact Assessment studies under multi-disciplinary agencies to assess the socio-cultural, economic and political impact of tourism on the heritage site as well as the host community.
- Buildings that are abandoned or that continue to be left vacant are at the risk of physical decay through lack maintenance or they risk destruction through vandalism or fire.
- Identify ten new heritage circuits every year and follow up with action as suggested for existing sites.
- There is a need to identify museums in potential tourism circuits, and to make them visitor-friendly.
- Places of important religious pilgrimage may require substantial development of tourist facilities. To begin with, 11 places of pilgrimage namely four dhams of Uttaranchal – Kedarnath, Badrinath, Yamunotri and Gangotri; Sabrimala in Kerala; Kamakhya Temple in Guwahati (Assam); Dwarkadhish in Gujarat, Puri in

Orissa; Ujjain in Madhya Pradesh; Kanchi Kamkioti and Rameshwaram in Tamil Nadu should be taken up to identify and provide the required tourist facilities.

- Rural villages which have immense cultural heritage potential need to be developed to showcase India's vast heritage.
- A Special Task Force should be constituted to assess culture and heritage endowments in the North-Eastern States which need to be conserved and developed for tourism.
- The State Government alone cannot develop the heritage tourist circuits and there is a need to improve partnerships with the private sector by implementing the announced incentives and bringing synergy in inter-sectoral policies.
- On experimental basis, two heritage tourist sites should be given to private partners for on-site management to be administered within the permissible parameters.
- Other than the Ministry of Tourism, funds are available for cultural heritage with Ministries of Rural Development, Culture, Environment, Urban Development and Tribal Welfare.
- There is a tendency to focus on tangible heritage, but intangible heritage is no less important. If tangible heritage represents the "hard" culture of a community, then intangible heritage represents the "soft" culture – the people, traditions, folklore, oral traditions, music, dance, traditional games, mythology, rituals, customs, handicrafts, arts, festivals, events, storytellers, local markets, and also living human treasures.
- There is also a need to review the existing system of Guides Training, and specialized workshops need to be conducted for existing guides to become cultural heritage guides.
- Publicity material and other promotional measures for each circuit should be developed.
- Special incentives should be given to rural areas, hill areas and pilgrim centres and the States of North-East including Sikkim; Jammu and Kashmir; Uttarakhand and Himachal Pradesh. Incentives to be provided to Heritage Hokktels and reuse of heritage buildings to be promoted in new states.
- To conserve the object of tourism, i.e., the cultural entities or the heritage buildings, Conservation Management Plans must be prepared, approved and implemented at each protected heritage site, complete with manuals and guidelines.

Possible Cultural Impacts of Tourism Development

Positive	Negative
Facilitates intercultural understanding understanding and global communication. Improves understanding and image of different communities and cultures. Promotes cultural exchange. Facilitates meeting visitors (an educational experience). Preserves cultural identity of host population. Increases demand for historical and cultural exhibits. May lead to the preservation and revitalization of local ethnic and cultural identity.	Change or loss of local identity and values, brought about by several closely related influences, such as: **Commodification** Tourism can turn local cultures into commodities when religious rituals, traditional ethnic rites and festivals are reduced, sanitized and performed on demand to conform to tourist expectations, resulting in what has been called 'reconstructed ethnicity'. This can also lead a loss of traditional crafts and skills. The commercialization and bastardization of traditional cultural events, arts and crafts, can reduce or destroy their cultural value to both host and guest. **Standardization** Destinations risk standardization in the process of satisfying tourists' desires for familiar facilities. Tourists often look for recognizable facilities in an unfamiliar environment, like well-known fast-food restaurants and hotel chains. **Loss of authenticity and staged authenticity** Adapting cultural expressions, rituals, performances to the tastes of tourists or even performing shows as if they were 'real life' constitutes 'staged authenticity'. **Cultural deterioration** Damage to cultural resources may

contd....

arise from vandalism, littering, pilferage and illegal removal of cultural heritage items. Degradation of cultural sites may occur when historic sites and buildings are unprotected, the traditionally built environment is replaced or virtually disappears, or structures or places of religious/spiritual significance are displaced or desecrated to make way for tourist facilities.

Non-capitalist path of development have made the transition to socialism, bypassing capitalism.

Socio-economic structure: A sector of a country's economy that is a type of economy based on a certain form of ownership of the means of production and corresponding production relations. It coexists with other forms of economy. As a rule, one socio-economic structure is dominant, determining the character of the social system in the country. Typical of developing Asian and African countries is a multi-structural economy with a sizable share of feudal and semi-feudal relations and vestiges of primitive-communal and patriarchal economy.

Socio-economic view: The view that management's social responsibility goes beyond making profits to include protecting and improving society's welfare.

Sociological Approach: Tourism tends to be a social activity being an interaction between different communities – hosts and guests – and encounter between different cultures. The approach studies social classes, habits and customs of both hosts and guests in terms of tourism behaviour of individuals and/or groups of people and the impact of tourism.

Elements of culture include handicrafts, language, traditions, food, dress, art, architecture, leisure activities, music, dance, belief systems, types of work engaged in and technology used. etc. Certain types of society (small, unsophisticated, isolated) are much more vulnerable to the pressure for cultural change brought about by tourism than others.

The effects listed above are not related exclusively to tourism. There are various powerful external and internal forces leading to changes in the natural environment from industrialization and urban development. There are also cultural changes worldwide, from sources such as television, cinema, Internet, and written media that act independently of the tourism industry.

There are no universally accepted indicators of sustainability of a tourism product or tourism itself. However, these main types of impacts and associated indicators can form the basis of a Tourism Sustainability Index (March, 1993) that can serve as:

- a classification scheme for understanding tourism's impacts
- a basis for projecting the impacts from particular tourism development.
- a basis for impact assessment
- a basis for mitigating projected adverse effects of tourism development
- a basis for monitoring the impacts of tourism development

Much studies have been conducted to investigate tourisms role in communication between cultures, its effect on the physical products of culture such as crafts and arts and influence on customs and ceremonies in the host society.

Preservation of National Heritage and Environment:

Tourism helps preserve several places which are of historical importance by declaring them as heritage sites. For instance, the Taj Mahal, the Qutab Minar, Ajanta and Ellora temples, etc. would have decayed and destroyed had it not been for the efforts taken by Tourism Department to preserve them.

Communication Between Cultures:

Cross-cultural contact arising from tourism is thought to be function of at least three factors:

- Type of tourists the different categories of which in the third world are reflected on expected differences in their kind of interaction with local people.

- Clearly things such as length of stay, the environment under which the contact occurs, and language ability will help to determine the depth of communication, which takes place.
- The role of cultural brokers, who are intermeddling occupational groups such as interpreters and guide who are the conduit through which much of contacts occurs. Their activities are thought to have considerable effect on the manner and speed with which new ideas and influences are transmitted.

Effects of Tourism on Local Customs

Tourism has the ability to market its products as a commodity, part of which consists of promoting the cultural attractions of holidaying in an exotic environment. Although this process is criticised cheeping cultural events such as religious ceremonies, it is also responsible for the flow of funds into many local activities.

For all foreign tourists, any visit to India is a form of cultural tourism. There are however those with more explicit interests in the monumental heritage, the religious heritage, the natural heritage, traditional arts and crafts, music and dance and those who help in formulation its scope.

Tourism industry in India is growing and it has vast potential for generating employment and earning large amount of foreign exchange besides giving a fillip to the country's overall economic and social development.

The impact that tourism has on the cultural lives of communities is one of the most important issues debated by tourism researchers and academics today. There is an increasingly growing concern that tourism development is leading to destinations losing their cultural identity by catering for the perceived needs of tourists.

Although they take longer to appear, the cultural consequences of tourist activity have the potential to be much more damaging in the long term than environmental or social effects. In many countries, tourists are not sensitive to local customs, traditions and standards. Offence is given without intent, as tourists are short-stay visitors carrying with them their own cultural norms and behavioural patterns. They are usually unwilling to change these norms for a temporary stay – and may be unaware that these norms are offensive to the host community.

Commercialisation of traditional cultural events and customs is leading to 'fake folklore' for the tourists, but more importantly, with no cultural value for the local population or the visitors. The issue is the potential conflict between the economic and cultural interests, leading to culture being sacrificed for reasons of promoting tourism, i.e., creating an additional economic value at the price of losing a cultural value.

UNIT–V:

TOURISM RESOURCE POTENTIAL OF INDIA

11

Tourism Capacities and Handicrafts of India

Tourism is coming up as a major source of earning in the developing countries. India has been a spiritual and cultural destination for tourists from all over the globe from time immemorial. Man's instinctive wanderlust takes him from deserts to mountains and from rivers to monuments to satiate not only his physical but also his psychological needs.

Why India has become a popular country in respect of tourism products and what makes a tourist to come to India and how does one satisfy one's need? People would be coming for pleasure and recreation and may opt for festivals, wild life and sports. Tourists, who comes for leisure and relaxation, would go to hill stations, beaches, etc. Those who come for education, they would go to the places known for heritage and culture. One who comes to India for business, he/she opts for trade fair, conferences, etc. One who comes to India for health purposes, would seek yoga and andventure sports. Those tourists, who come for visiting friends and relatives, they would opt for shopping, soveneirs and fair and festivals.

We are proud to be citizens of India. It is the only country in the world, which can boast of all types of seasons thoroughout the year, and consists of hills, forests, snow clad mountains, rivers, deserts and the highest rainfall region in the world, amongst others.

Persons belonging to different religions of the world do not feel as strangers in India. India has Hindus, Muslims, Jains, Buddhists, Zorastrians and Jews, living together in harmony.

India is known to be a country of fairs and festivals. Apart from the traditional festivals like Deepawali, Eid, Christmas, Holi.

India has six thousand miles of coastline beaches which are sunny, have cocounut palms, birds and rich variety of underwater beauty.

India has almost all types of adventure sports facilities – water rafting, paragliding, trekking, scuba diving, sky diving, skiing, motor rallies, etc.

India has excellent arrangements for tade fairs, conferences, sports meets, etc., and above all, the slogan '*atithi devo bhav*'.

HANDICRAFTS OF INDIA

Introduction

Tourists do visit a country or a tourist spot may not be for the express purpose of shopping, but shopping is a part and parcel of tourist activity. Tourists thoroughly enjoy buying things that are peculiar to that particular region.

Handicrafts are an important part of shopping. These objects are made by the skill of the hand which is an admixture of tradition and creative craftsmanship. Moreover, handicrafts as souvenirs arouse nostalgia, because they are symbolic of the place, event or activity. They act as status symbol, are often utility item or of aesthetic value and sometimes decorative.

Handicrafts can be of several types. They may be designed for personal use like soap boxes. They could be religion oriented like *malas*, replicas of idols for worship, etc. Most places have specialized handicrafts like the puppets of Jaipur. Some handicrafts are steeped in tradition, like the carved miniatures available at Agra are said to be by the descendants of the makers of the Taj Mahal. All the types of handicrafts ensure employment to a large number of handicraftsmen and women.

Through these handicrafts, the tourists learn about the cultural heritage of the country. For example, when a tourist buys a statue of Natraj, the whole concept of Hindu religion becomes apparent to him. For the tourists these handicrafts revive treasurd memories of the tour which had been undertaken.

History of Handicrafts of India

Since time immemorial, Indian Handicrafts have been popular throughout the world. India Craft tours take you on an online tour to acquaint you with the forms of Handicraft artifacts available in India. The first references to Indian Handicrafts can be found from the Indus Valley Civilization. Works of art always portray the customs, traditions and beliefs of the people of that era. Being a work of art, crafts also exhibit religious beliefs and lifestyle of people.

Modern handicrafts evolved after much alteration in the traditional styles. Indus Valley Civilization showed a remarkable artistic skill and technical excellence in pottery, jewellery, sculpture making and weaving etc. The influence of the central Asian Culture on Indian craftsmanship is reflected in the sculpture of the Kushan king Kanishka. Mughals endowed India with a rich legacy of architectural and artistic heritage. The new occupations added during this era were glass engraving, carpet weaving, inlay work, brocades and enameling, etc.

Handicrafts of India broadly include –

1. Ceramics
2. Phulkari
3. India Painting Styles
4. Carpet Weaving
5. Handloom Textile Weaving
6. Tie and Dye
7. Papier Mache

The First International Conference on Tourism and Handicrafts was held from 13-15 May, 2006 in the Seminar Hall of Iranian National Broadcast in Tehran. This conference had been organized by the United Nations World Tourism Organization (UNWTO) and Iran's Cultural Heritage and Tourism Organization (ICHTO) in order to discuss the role of handicrafts in promoting tourism industry which will result in job creation and earning more currency through attracting more tourists.

The arts and crafts of a nation reveal its culture and heritage and India is one such nation which is quite affluent in awe-inspiring works of craft. Almost all the Indian states have their own ethnic craft traditions and most of them have been passed from generation to generation as legacies. The ingenuity of the craftsmen has lent an unending appeal to the various craftworks and craft in India is valued by tourists frequenting this country. Orissa is one such state that has kept its age-old tradition and culture alive by their inimitable craftworks and some of the tribes such as Kondhs, Koyas, Bondas, Santals, Gadabas, Juangas are known for the fine craft works. Every tribe is known for its unique art forms that range from weaving of handloom, saris, basket, stone carving, painting, metal work that are popular the world over. The stone carving on the walls of the Jagannath, Konark and the Lingaraja temples reveals the superiority of the artists. Each stone has been brought to life with the endeavor and art of the artists.

Crafts tourism in India, has gained immense popularity and is quite valued by not only the domestic but also the foreign travellers from all parts of the world. As far as handicraft tours of India are concerned, Orissa occupies a prominent place among all the other states of India and its craftsmen are specialized in the production of exquisite hand-made trousseau sarees. The craft in India is incomplete without a mention of earliest traditional weaving villages of Orissa and Nuapatna.

Apart from Orissa, the craft show in Rajasthan is also very popular and is valued by the tourists who are the true appreciators of craft works. The handicraft shops in Rajasthan are huge in number and house a large number of incredible craft items such as antiques, pottery items, dhurries and carpets, fabrics, furniture and wood carving items, gesso works, jewellery and gemstones, leather ware, metal crafts, paintings, puppets, and stone carvings.

Moreover, the paintings and the hand-made royal furnishings found in the royal mansions and also in the shops are quite famous.

The level of excellence and intricacy depicted through the various craft works is simply unparalleled and catches the attention of the most discerning aesthete. Craft in India is surely going to bring in something special for the tourists and they can surely take back some of the best craft works as souvenirs after their tour to India.

Of late, tour operators offering package tour to Kerala and Rajastahan include visit to handicraft fairs or villages in these states which produce handicrafts unique in nature. Other travel agents are following in their footsteps.

Every tourist place is having some unique items of art and handicraft associated with, however the potential of amalgamation of the tourism and Handicraft has not yet been understood, explored & developed in manner it should have been. The craft has the ability to create jobs, socio-economic opportunities, and enhanced quality of life in local communities; this gives an added recognition to the tourist spot as well.

The basis of these products is the large amount of easily accessible natural materials offered by the land. Handicrafts are the maximum representation of India's idiosyncrasy and one of its better cultural expressions.

For instance, those on tours to Kerala or Rajasthan states are likely to discover and be impressed by Indian handicrafts since these are popular destinations. In popular tourists, states an infrastructure has been laid down in bringing forth all elements of tourist attractions.

But as rest of India opens up to tourism, more and more states are gearing up to display and promote the local talent which produces unique works of arts. Be it jewellry, wooden statues, brass works and designer dresses. Those on travel to India must read and know about beforehand the craftsmanship popular in the parts of India they are visiting.

Tourists travel to learn – to experience personally – with their hands and eyes. The fundamental connection between handcrafts and tourism resonate particularly well in India, with ancient human settlement and abundantly rich culture. Handcraft instills a sense of hand-made and the unique richness of artisan craftsmanship.

Tourists purchase handcrafted souvenirs to represent our memories of connecting with and participating in other cultures. Through the purchase of locally made items, tourists create craft economy, upon which artisans often depend for their livehoods, encourages the production of natural products and binds communities together. At the very least, every traveller makes the purchase of a souvenir to share what they have learned with friends and family.

The travel industry has also recognized the importance of linking craft with tourism by investing in handcrafts for room furnishings and for lobby, lounge, spa and restaurant decor. That is why handcraft activities can increase the average length of stay by adding a day or more to a travel itinerary.

Learning and participating have become a paramount element of travel, as proven by the success of study and culture tours and special interest tours with crafts as a central focus. Shopping is no longer simply a form of entertainment, but a link to a foreign culture that greatly enriches the travel experience.

The Pushkar Fair in Rajasthan, Suraj Kund Craft Mela and others like it in India, have become a delightful carnival of culture and crafts, complementing traditional markets. Craftsmen perform skilled and essential repairs, and in a natural way preserve tradition and culture by making them familiar and popular.

The patronage of tourists helps such techniques survive through sales. Without a market, many traditional skills could eventually fade due to lack of demand. Tourism provides an opportunity to preserve the traditions that comprise the fabric of cultural heritage.

Tourists want to enjoy the shopping experience.They expect to buy a product that relates to their visit, perhaps to a specific site, or that embodies some aspect of the culture they have seen and experienced.

Tourists seek information through guide books with sections

on local shopping, maps, trend magazines, and informative, easily downloadable websites. Flight magazines can educate arriving tourists and direct them to featured locations.

A look at the figures on foreign and domestic visitors to handicraft production centers in countries such as India as well as their sales figures indicate that handicrafts are considered as art and cultural symbols of these countries. They can be important factors in attracting tourists, because every piece of handicraft demonstrates the historic, social, and cultural features of a country, region, or location in which it was produced and can play a significant role in introducing original, native art.

Handicrafts have much appeal as an economic stimulator. Low barriers to entry enable people to enter this sector with minimal capital and debt load. Government programs to provide seeding loans, training programs and assistance with the legal requirements to establish enterprises often yield positive results.

Crafts enable members of agricultural communities to supplement their income with off-season employment. Importantly, they provide much needed employment and income opportunities for people traditionally excluded from local economies, including women, members of ethnic minorities, young people, unskilled workers, people with disabilities and the elderly.

Crafts may also provide important income streams for museums and historic sites. Handicraft tourism can help diversify local economies, especially in rural areas of the less developed world.

Handicraft production is a socially responsible, sustainable activity that can eliminate much of the exploitation of unskilled workers found in so many parts of the world. As people directly involved in the production and distribution of the handicraft, workers also have a direct say in how they are treated.

The production of handicrafts allows a number of individuals to benefit from tourism without necessarily having direct involvement in the industry, enabling many people to achieve a balance between home duties and income generation.

Tourism may also provide an alternative market for goods traditionally produced within the community that are now in decline, providing a means of retaining employment.

Further, tourist interest in some handicrafts may foster renewed interest from the local market, leading to a revitalization of some businesses.

Crafts also provide an opportunity for communities to reconnect to their cultural heritage, disappearing traditions, activities and cultural practices.

Creating a positive link between the tourism sector and local communities is a further benefit of handicraft tourism. The industry is increasingly developing a social ethic with many operators in rural communities realizing that they must contribute something back to the community.

The contribution to the sustainable use of heritage assets is one benefit that is often overlooked.

Souveniring of artifacts and the illicit trade in antiquities continue to pose a threat to our collective tangible cultural heritage.

Fostering a craft industry to produce copy relics for sale to tourists enables them to acquire an authentic souvenir, generate income for local communities and conserve cultural heritage *in situ*, a triple benefit.

While handicrafts and tourism obviously create a variety of synergies that can benefit the resident, the community and the tourist, this practice is not without its risks. Successful and truly sustainable handicraft tourism involves being aware of these risks and developing program to mitigate them.

An over-riding question is who really benefits from handicraft tourism? In some cases, an unequal relationship exists, whereby the consumer and end retailer seem to gain a disproportionate benefit, while the artisan him or herself gains little. The more steps in the distribution process, the higher the end price. But, the artisan may see little of this price. The establishment of co-operatives is one solution that has worked for many aboriginal communities in many parts of North America, Australia and

Europe. The co-operatives assume responsibility for all or part of the distribution and, thus its members retain more benefits directly. But, personal observation suggests that many of them are poorly run and not as profitable as they could be.

Pricing strategies emerge as a second issue. Often, local artisans are unaware of the true value that the consumer places on the handicraft, the retail price charged overseas, base prices of local economic conditions in the tourists' home community and have little knowledge of the various approaches to pricing. As a result, they charge a cost-plus price rather than a price that reflects the true craftsmanship and scarcity value of the item. Many handicrafts purchased at source are grossly under-priced. This problem is not unique to handicrafts, but it is common along all micro businesses in the tourism and hospitality industry.

The popularity handicrafts amongst tourists may be a double edged sword that can lead to increased income, but may also result in the exploitation of the producers. How does the individual artisan cope with high demand for popular items, especially if cooperatives or wholesalers have accepted orders for these items?

Few have the ability to industrialize their production process and so, most end up simply working more hours. Demand pressures may convert an enjoyable part-time activity into a laborious full-time job where the returns do not match the effort.

The generic tourism literature also suggests that craft production can result in the commodification of culture for tourist use, the trivialization of local culture, the transformation of skilled craftsman into trinket makers and, ultimately to the creation or fostering of ethnic and/or gender stereotypes. Others may suggest that rather than fostering a re-birth of traditional culture, it may lead to the suppression of diversity and to the loss of traditional skills as craftsman and women have to shift their emphasis to the production of the most popular tourist goods.

The theft of cultural identity and traditions poses an even greater threat. Artists with no connection to a community in may copy a style of painting or other artwork and may produce 'authentic' goods for the tourist market. Tourists may think they are buying authentic goods from traditional craftsman when in fact they are purchasing copies of art work from people that have no cultural connection to the works being produced. This issue has arisen repeatedly with the production and sale of aboriginal art works of India.

Finally, the government also needs to examine its motivations for encouraging communities to become involved in community tourism. Tourism is often identified as an economic opportunity for rural communities not because there is any real tourism potential but because there is little potential for any other activity. Fostering community tourism represents a feel-good, low investment option whereby central governments can be seen to be doing something, and yet in reality are doing little.

12

Fairs and Festivals

India is the one of the main attractive place in all over the world and its history made this country so much popular. India is all about the land of God, Culture, and its historic places. There are lots of communities in this country and everybody has its religion and culture. This beautiful country is covered by The Great Himalayas in the north side and the south side is covered by the never ending ocean.

The west side is covered by the longest desert and the east side is covered by the long lasting green forests. Country is full of scenic hills, forests, beaches, and temples. India is full of arts, cultural songs, dances, and the long lasting crafts. Country is also known for its rivers and there beaches.

Indian is known for its classical dance, classical music and its folk and tribal dance forms. This makes the India incredible and attracts people towards this country. The culture and traditions of the Indians make this country so strong in any other country. Lots of festivals and local gathering make this country so much colourful and create the brotherhood between each and every person hearts.

The cultural history of the India is fully protected and there are lots of historic schools and colleges where the Indian people are studied about their culture and their traditions. Indian art and its historic infrastructure like Taj Mahal and the Red Fort make the India so proud and the helping people makes India so incredible.

The Vedic scriptures and literature give many references to festivals when celebrations were carried on to honor gods, rivers, trees, mountains, the coming of monsoons, the end of winter or the first flush of spring.

The ancient tradition of celebrating festivals goes back to the Vedic times of the Aryans. Ancient Indians used to express these occasions through the words SAMAJA (a gathering of people), UTSAVA (a festival) and YATRA (a pilgrimage or temple chariot procession). And today we use the word MELA (meaning a fair) rather than a SAMAJA.

The celebrations not only include fasting and prayers, but also equally events of social and cultural significance. Performances of music, dance and drama took place side by side with more rugged physical activities. Even today, festivals are symbolic of a link between the home, the villages and a larger outside world. Colour, contribution, enthusiasm, prayers and rituals are the characteristics of the festivals of India.

Travel to India is one of the great and perfect ideas. It is known for its culture, religious power, fairs and festivals and its tourist attraction. It is also one of the largest countries in the south Asia, with large population, and having prople from different religions. The Ganges and the Brahmaputra are the two longest rivers which originate from Himalayan origin. India is also known for its climate and variety of a habitat, flora and fauna. In India there are lots of ecological parks and protected areas where the diminishing breeds are fully sheltered.

Each part of the state has some local festival to commemorate an event, a deity, or an important personage. The fairs and festivals of this country are known for their beauty and liveliness, attracting both domestic as well as international tourists.

There are lots of tourist places where one must visit to witness cultural heritage, colorful fairs and festivals, peaks for adventure, technological parks and the science museums and the long-lasting yoga, ayurveda and natural health resorts. The cultural and fairs & festivals of the Indian history is so unique and old, and there are lots of tourist places where you must visit.

At some of the fairs, the ambience of romance is very real, for this is where the young gather to arrange the betrothals. For example at the tarnetai in Madhya Pradesh, the young men and women wear their best clothes, sing dance and make merry.

The Webster dictionary presents several meanings to the term "fair", but one of them which is relevant to the book is that, "fair" is competitive exhibition of farm products, livestock etc. often combined with entertainment and held annually. It is a periodic gathering of buyers and sellers in an appointed place. Fairs are exposition in which different exhibitors participate, often with a purpose of buying and selling or of familiarizing the public with the products.

Difference Between Fairs and Festivals:

An overview of literature on festivals and fairs reveals that there is a a vast difference between a fair and festivals.

Given below are few points that distinguishes these two concepts:

- A fair is celebrated on grand scale by more than one religious sect, tribe or a caste community.

  whereas festival is celebrated by one religious sub-group, group, tribe or a community with exceptions to few festivals.
- Fair consisits of a place which has people from various walks of life such as artisans, musicians, traders, vendors, toy sellers, cattle traders, devotees, medicine, men, drama, artists, snake charmers, acrobats, etc.

  whereas festival celebrations are usually accompanied by only one or two ethinic group.

Although arts and tourism linkages have been advocated by many, and certainly exist with regard to festivals, concerts and staged performances, there will always remain tension between these sectors.

"Festival tourism" is an important element in "event tourism", so much so that the term "festivalization" has been coined to suggest an over-commodification of festivals exploited by tourism and place marketers. Indeed, a marked trend toward treating festivals as commodities has emerged. In this approach, drawing heavily upon consumer behavior and other marketing concepts, motivations for attending festivals have been studied at length, and more recently the links between quality, satisfaction, and behavior or future intentions have been modeled. The roles of festivals in tourism include attracting tourists (to specific places, and to overcome seasonality), contributing to place marketing.

The fairs and festivals of India bring together people of all sects and religions. In these multifarious celebrations, processions are held, prayers are offered and people sing and dance. These are the very things which attract tourists from all across the world. One thing common to all of them is they celebrate humanity.

The travellers are attracted to the scale and elaboration of the merrymaking that populate the cultural scene of the country. The various festivals in the country can be categorized on the national, regional, local, religious, seasonal and social grounds. The popularity of Indian fairs and festivals are spread far and wide and attract a large number of foreign tourists.

Fairs and Festivals in India that attract the Tourists:

Many of the fairs and festivals of India are geared toward the tourist – the people who drive the economy of many of the states in India. India is a country that seems to have a festival on somewhere just about every day of the year. So, some research has been done and conclusions are as under:

- The harvest festivals of the south, the immersion of Ganesh in Bombay, the car festival of Puri, snake-boat races in Kerala, Republic Day in Delhi fascinate the tourists.
- In fact, they are fast becoming a major pull for tourists from all over the world as many people come to India to participate in them.
- These festivals originate from the religious beliefs, traditions and myths of a diverse class of people and bring out the true spirit of the Indian people and their society.
- Festivals across India generally celebrate the change of seasons, promote the culture or are of a religious nature. Like Mewar Festival and Holi signify the coming of the spring season. In the same way, Teej of Rajasthan, Onam in Kerala and Bihu in Assam celebrate in different seasons.

- At the same time festivals like Durga Puja, Janamastami, Eid-ul-Fitr, Christmas, Ganesh Chaturthi, Rath Yatra, Ram Navami and Vasant Panchami are few of the many popular religious festivals of India.
- India is also famous for the fairs which are organized from time to time.
- These attract people from different parts of India and abroad. In fact, many tourists plan their vacations to accommodate some popular fairs like Pushkar Fair, Urs Ajmer Fair and Surajkund Crafts Fair which are highly vibrant and vivid by nature. In the same ways the fascinating Kumbh Mela and the colorful Goa Carnival are extremely popular among the locals as well as the tourists.

Month-wise record of some important fairs and festivals, is as below:

January–Feburary:

National Kite Festival, Pongal, Id-ul-Fitr, Makar Sankranti/ Pongal: Mainly Tamil Nadu, Andhra Pradesh and Karnataka. 3 days and colourful: Tamil harvest festival. Republic Day: National: establishment of Republic 1950, on 26th January. Grand Military Parade and Procession of dancers, etc. Delhi. Vasant Panchami: National (Mainly in the Eastern region): Hindu – dedicated to Saraswati, the Goddess of Learning. Women wear yellow saris. Floating Festival: Madurai: Birthday of local 17th century ruler; elaborately illuminated barge carrying decorated temple deities at the Mariamman Teppakulam Pool amids chanting hymns.

Feburary–March

Shivaratri: National: Solemn worship of Hindu deity, Lord Shiva. Fasting and chanting. Special celebrations at Chidambarum, Kalahasti, Khajuraho, Varanasi and Bombay. Holi: Mainly northern, popularly called the festival of colors. Advent of Spring. Lively and much throwing of coloured water and powders. Public Holiday. Mardi Gras: Goa: Mainly three days during lent. Unique celebrations at this carnival. Ramnavami: National: Birth of Rama, incarnation of Vishnu. No processions. Plays and folk theaters. Mahavir Jayanti: National: Jain festival; birth of Mahavira, the 24th and last Tirthankara. Easter: Good Friday / Easter Sunday National.

March–April

Kumbh Mela: The oldest and most important of the Hindu festivals. It takes place every three years, at one of the four great holy cities; Nasik in Maharashtra, Ujjain (MP), Prayag (Allahabad) and Hardwar (both in UP). It is attended by millions of pilgrims who take a holy dip in the sacred Ganges River.

April–May

Baisakhi: Northern India, West Bengal and Tamil Nadu; Hindu Solar New Year. Bhangra dancing. Women wear yellow saris. Pooram: Trichur: New Moon. Spectactular sight of large number of elephants carrying ceremonial umbrellas going round the temple; midnight fireworks display.

Id-Ul-Zuha: (Bakrid): Muslim, National: The most celebrated Islamic festival in India, commemorating the sacrifice of Abraham. Id-Ul-Fitr (Ramzan Id): Muslim, National: Celebration to mark the end of the month of Ramajan. Meenakshi Kalyanam: Madurai. Marriage of Meenakshi with Lord Shiva. Colourful temple festival. Deities borne by colossal chariot. Ten day festival. Fair: Rajasthan: Urs Ajmer Sharif. Ajmer, 6 days. Religious cultural and commercial extravaganza dedicated to the Sufi. Music; no procession.

June–July

Rath Yatra: Mainly Orissa. Greatest temple festival in honour of Lord Jagannath (Lord of the Universe). Three colossal chariots drawn from Puri temple by thousands of pilgrims. Similar festivals, on a smaller scale, take place at Ramnagar (near Varanasi), Serampore (near Calcutta) and Jagannathpur (near Ranchi).

July–August

Teej: Rajasthan–Particularly Jaipur: Procession of the Goddess Parvati to welcome monsoon; elephants, camels, dancers, etc. Women wear green saris.

Raksha Bandhan: Northern and Western India. Legendary reenactment, girls tie rakhis or talismen to men's wrists. Colourful build up. Naag Panchami: Mainly Jodphur, Rajasthan and

Maharashtra. Dedicated to the green thousand-headed mythical serpent called Sesha. The day is also observed in many other parts of Western and Eastern India. Amarnath Yatra: Hindu: Lidder Valley, Kashmir at full moon. Pilgrims visit the place where Lord Shiva explained the secret of salvation to his consort Parvati.

August–September

Independence Day: 15th August. National: Independence Day. Prime Minister addresses to the nation from Delhi's Red Fort.

Janmashtami: National, particularly Agra, Bombay and Mathura; Lord Krishna's birthday.

Onam: Kerala's Harvest Festival; spectacular snake boat races in many parts of Kerala.

Ganesh Chaturthi: Mainly Pune, Orissa, Bombay, Madras, dedicated to elephant-headed God Ganesh. Giant models of the deity processed and immersed in water. Colourful, and a particularly worth visiting on the Day of immersion at Bombay.

September–October

Dussehra: National: The most popular festival in the country, celebrated in different ways in different parts of the country. In the north and particularly in Delhi (where it is known as Ram Lila), plays and music recall the life of Rama; in Kulu, the festival is also very colourful celebrated. In Bengal and many parts of Eastern India it is known as Durga Puja, and in the South as Navaratri.

Fair, Himachal Pradesh: Kulu Valley to coincide with Dussehra (10 days).

Gandhi Jayanti: National: Mahatma Gandhi's birthday. No processions.

Diwali: National: One of the most lively and colourful festivals in India. In some parts, it marks the start of the Hindu New Year. In Eastern India, the goddess Kali is particularly worshipped; elsewhere, it is Lakshmi, the goddess of prosperity, who is venerated.

Everywhere there are magnificent illuminations and fireworks. Gurpurab: Mainly in northern India. Anniversaries of ten gurus, spiritual teachers or preceptors of Sikhism. No procession.

November

Muharram: Muslim. Commemoration of Imam Hussain's martyrdom. Tiger dancers lead processions of colourful replicas of martyr's tomb. Colourful, particularly at Lucknow. Bihar: Largest cattle fair in the world; 1 month Sonepur, Patna; on banks of the Ganges. Pushkar Mela: Pushkar, near Ajmer, Rajasthan. Important and colourful. Camel and cattle fair, attended by Rajputs from miles around. Camel races and acrobatics, etc.

December

Christmas Day: National: Most exuberantly celebrated in Goa, Bombay and Tamil Nadu.

Besides the above festivals there are hundreds of festivals and fairs which are of regional significance, celebrated with equal pomp and colour.

Dominating this discourse has been the assessment of economic impacts of festivals and festival tourism, planning and marketing festival tourism at the destination level and studies of festival-tourism motivation and various segmentation approaches. The negative impacts of festivals and festival tourism is a more recent line of research.

"Event tourism" has been reviewed historically and ontologically by Getz (2008). Ritchie and Beliveau published the first article specifically about event tourism in the Journal of Travel Research in 1974, the topic being how "hallmark events" could combat seasonality of tourism demand. They examined the Quebec Winter Carnival and included citation of an unpublished study of the economic impacts of the Quebec Winter Carnival dated 1962, which is perhaps the earliest such study recorded in the research literature. Another early impact study was conducted by Vaughan in Edinburgh (1979).

Festival tourism is essentially instrumentalist, treating festivals as tools in tourism and economic development, or in place of marketing and the selling of attractions and venues. Looking ahead to the structured literature review, it can be seen that tourism is a theme running through all the elements of the framework. But it is most prevalent in the literature concerning outcomes (i.e. economic impacts) and motivations, marketing and evaluation, with many of these articles being published in mainstream tourism journals.

This is the most recent discourse or sub-field to develop in the research literature, even though professional practice of event management has a much longer history. The first major textbook on this subject was Goldblatt's "Special Events: The Art and Science of Celebration (published in 1990), followed closely by "Festivals, Special Events and Tourism" (Getz, 1991) and a year later by Hall's "Hallmark Tourist Events" in 1992. Numerous books have been published from the event practitioners point of view, and there are many texts on specific elements of events management including human resources, risks, logistics, and marketing.

13

Architectural Heritage of India

The first serious attempt to document India's architectural heritage was made in the late 18th and early 19th century by British soldiers, administrators, and civil servants. Spurred by a resurgence of renaissance ideals in contemporary Europe, men like Colin McKenzie and Alexander Cunningham travelled widely through the subcontinent documenting architectural and sculptural remains. Their specific interests varied but there was a general tendency to consider earlier Indian architecture superior, while the exuberant sculptural detail of later Hindu temples was considered degenerate. In the 200 years since those first attempts at serious research, there have been considerable advances in understanding the origins, patronage, and evolution of the many regional Indian architectural styles. However, our understanding of Indian architecture is still very basic and many hundreds of monuments and many dozens of regional styles wait to be studied and analysed in detail.

Art and Architecture of India

The art and architecture was produced on the Indian subcontinent from about the 3rd millennium BC to modern times. To viewers schooled in the Western tradition, Indian art may seem overly ornate and sensuous; appreciation of its refinement comes only gradually, as a rule. Voluptuous feeling is given unusually free expression in Indian culture. A strong sense of design is also characteristic of Indian art and can be observed in its modern as well as in its traditional forms.

The art of India must be understood and judged in the context of the ideological, aesthetic, and ritual assumptions and needs of the Indian civilization. These assumptions were formed as early as the 1st century BC and have shown a remarkable tenacity through the ages. The Hindu-Buddhist-Jain view of the world is largely concerned with the resolution of the central paradox of all existence, which is that change and perfection, time and eternity, immanence and transcendence, operate dichotomously and integrally as parts of a single process. In such a situation, the creation cannot be separated from the creator, and time can be comprehended only as a matrix of eternity. This conceptual view, when expressed in art, divides the universe of aesthetic experience into three distinct, although interrelated, elements – the senses, the emotions, and the spirit.

These elements dictate the norms for architecture as an instrument of enclosing and transforming space and for sculpture in its volume, plasticity, modelling, composition, and aesthetic values. Instead of depicting the dichotomy between the flesh and the spirit, Indian art, through a deliberate sensuousness and voluptuousness, fuses one with the other through a complex symbolism that, for example, attempts to transform the fleshiness of a feminine form into a perennial mystery of sex and creativity, wherein the momentary spouse stands revealed as the eternal mother.

The Indian artist deftly uses certain primeval motifs, such as the feminine figure, the tree, water, the lion, and the elephant. In a given composition, although the result is sometimes conceptually unsettling, the qualities of sensuous vitality, earthiness, muscular energy, and rhythmic movement remain unmistakable. The form of the Hindu temple; the contours of the bodies of the Hindu gods and goddesses; and the light, shade, composition, and volume in Indian painting are all used to glorify the mystery that resolves the conflict between life and death, time and eternity.

The arts of India expressed in architecture, sculpture, painting, jewellery, pottery, metalwork, and textiles, were spread throughout the Far East with the diffusion of Buddhism and

Hinduism and exercised a strong influence on the arts of China, Japan, Burma, Thailand, Cambodia, and Java. These two religions with their various offshoots were dominant in India until Islam became powerful from the 13th to the 18th century. With Islam, which forbids representation of the human figure in religious contexts, geometrical patterns became the most common decoration in the arts patronized by the Muslim rulers.

India is surely among the foremost as far as its architecture heritage is concerned. Different types of Indian architectural styles include a mass of expressions over space and time, transformed by the forces of history considered unique to India. As a result of vast diversities, a vast range of architectural specimens have evolved, retaining a certain amount of continuity across history.

With a past stretching back to 2500 B.C., there are innumerable examples to choose from. It is difficult to select truly representative monuments – those which clearly typify the spirit of their age and/or usher in a new style. The Indus and its tributaries were one of the earliest cradles of civilization. The Indus Valley Civilization is the first surviving evidence of architecture/ town planning in the sub-continent. It formed the earliest urban civilization on the Indian sub-continent, and one of the earliest in the world.

Its unique urban characteristics ensure it a place in the annals of world architecture. Indian architecture, belonging to different periods of history, bears the stamp of respective periods. Though the cities of Indus Valley provide substantial evidence of extensive town planning, the beginnings of Indian architecture can be traced back to the advent of Buddhism in India. It was in this period that a large number of magnificent buildings came up. Some of the highlights of Buddhist art and architecture are the Great Stupa at Sanchi and the rock-cut caves at Ajanta.

With the establishment of Hindu kingdoms in South India, the south Indian school of architecture began to flourish. The most notable achievements of the Pallava rulers were the rock-cut temples of Mahabalipuram and the temples of Kanchipuram. The Chola, Hoyasala and Vijayanagar rulers also did remarkable job in the field of architecture. The temples at Thanjavur, Belur and Halebid bear testimony to the architectural excellence of the South Indian rulers.

In north India, there developed a new a different style of architecture. This was called as the Nagara style architecture. In central India, the Chandela rulers built a magnificent temple complex at Khajuraho. With the coming of the Muslim rulers, there developed a new architectural style in India – the Indo-Islamic architecture. The Indo-Islamic style was neither strictly Islamic nor strictly Hindu. The architecture of the medieval period can be divided into two main categories. They are the Delhi or the Imperial Style and the Mughal Architecture. The colonial architecture exhibited itself through institutional, civic and utilitarian buildings such as post offices, railway stations, rest houses and government buildings.

ANCIENT ARCHITECTURE

Indian architecture is as old as the history of the civilization. The earliest remains of recognizable building activity in the India dates back to the Indus Valley cities. Among India's ancient architectural remains, the most characteristic are the temples, Chaityas, Viharas, Stupas and other religious structures. In ancient India, temple architecture of high standard developed in almost all regions. The distinct architectural style of temple construction in different parts was a result of geographical, climatic, ethnic, racial, historical and linguistic diversities.

During the Indus Valley civilization, the house was planned as a series of rooms opening on to a central courtyard. This courtyard served the multiple functions of lighting the rooms, acting as a heat absorber in summer and radiator in winter, as well as providing an open space inside for community activities. There were no openings toward the main street, thus ensuring privacy for the residents. An advanced drainage system is also in evidence. Drains started from the bathrooms of the houses and joined the main sewer in the street, which was covered by brick slabs or corbelled brick arches, depending on its width.

It is unfortunate that none of the structures of the Indus

Valley civilization survive intact today. Unlike Egypt and Mesopotamia, the Harappan people left nothing monumental, like the pyramids or ziggurats, for posterity to marvel at. This may be the reason that among the majority of books on architecture, the Harappan Culture hardly merits a note. However, the planning principles and response of the architecture to climate are a lesson to us all.

However, the most numerous of the surviving artifacts are a series of steatite (soapstone) seals, of which the best known are those of the Humped Brahmani Bull and Pashupati. Apart from this, there are some carved figurines – the bronze Dancing Girl and the statues of a priest and a male torso, again in steatite.

The Vedic texts (c.1500-900 BC) that talked about "nomadic invaders conquering mighty citadels... under the banner of their God, Indra". However, no trace of the 'mighty citadels' had ever been found. Then, in 1856, the bricks, certain steatite (soapstone) seals were found. Archaeologists, notably Sir John Cunningham, quickly confirmed their antiquity. The nomads that streamed in from the Northwest towards the middle of the second millennium B.C. overwhelmed the indigenous people of the subcontinent with their superior military technology.

No architectural examples of this period are surviving. The Aryans built no colossal monuments. So what is the importance of this period? It was early Aryan architectural forms that were translated into the architecture of India for thousands of years. Considerable information is given in the Vedas. These ancient texts were composed by the Aryan seers and handed down through generations orally. The great epics, the Mahabharata and the Ramayana, vividly picture village and town life during Aryavrata, or the Aryan age.

The Aryan hut, in its most basic shape, was circular in plan, with a thatched roof over a bamboo network of ribs. This was later elongated to become rectangular in plan, with roofing of bamboo as well, only this time curved in, in most of the sites, the central-western blocks were reserved for public architecture. Perhaps the most famous examples are the Great Bath and Granary at Mohenjo-daro. The Great Bath has been the subject of much debate over its exact function.

Rock Cut Architecture

The Rock-cut structures present the most spectacular piece of ancient Indian art specimen. Most of the rock-cut structures were related to various religious communities. In the beginning, remarkable Buddhist and Jain monuments were produced in areas such as Bihar in the east and Maharashtra in the west. Numerous caves were excavated by the Buddhist monks for prayer and residence purposes. The best examples of this are Chaityas and monasteries. Inside these rock-cut structures, monks carved windows and balconies and gates in the shape of huge arch-shaped openings.

Rock-cut architecture occupies a very important place in the history of Indian Architecture. The rock-cut architecture differs from traditional buildings in many ways. The rock-cut art is more similar to sculpture than architecture as structures were produced by cutting out solid rocks. Let's have a look at various specimen of rock-cut architecture in ancient India. Some prominent rock-cut structures of ancient India are Chaityas, Viharas, temples, etc.

Chaityas and Viharas

Chaityas and Viharas are those rock-cut structures that were hewn out for Buddhist and Jain monks. Chaityas were places of worship whereas Viharas were residence of monks. The Buddhist and Jain monks usually stayed away from the towns, therefore, they developed Chaityas and Viharas in the hillside. Most of the Chaityas and Viharas were constructed in western India. Some of the prominent places having Chaityas and Viharas are Karle, Nashik, Bhaja and Kanheri. The rugged hills of the Western Ghats were naturally suited to the creation of living space in the hillside.

Rock-cut architecture occupies a very important place in the history of Indian Architecture. This differs from 'building up' in many important ways. Firstly, the art is more akin to sculpture than architecture, in that a solid body of material (rock) is taken, the final product visualized and cutting/carving starts. Secondly, the mason is not overly concerned with spans, forces, beams, columns, and all the other architectural features – these can be carved, but are seldom playing any structural role.

The most remarkable aspect of the rock cut architecture at Karle and other such sites is its close similarity to wood construction. Here, you will find great imitation of every detail of wood in rocks. This throws light on the great skill of Indian craftsmen.

The rathas are today half-buried in the sand, silent monuments to the age of kings gone by, their silhouettes and graceful surface sculpture exhibit in every detail to the great temples of the south that would follow the most enduring achievements of Indian civilization, undoubtedly in its architecture. Indian architecture, which has evolved through centuries, is the result of socio-economic and geographical conditions. Different types of Indian architectural styles include a mass of expressions over space and time, transformed by the forces of history considered unique to India. As a result of vast diversities, a vast range of architectural specimens have evolved, retaining a certain amount of continuity across history.

Indian architecture, belonging to different periods of history, bears the stamp of respective periods. Though the cities of Indus Valley provide substantial evidence of extensive town planning, the beginnings of Indian architecture can be traced back to the advent of Buddhism in India. It was in this period that a large number of magnificent buildings came up. Some of the highlights of Buddhist art and architecture are the Great Stupas at Sanchi and the rock-cut caves at Ajanta.

India is surely among the foremost as far as its architecture heritage is concerned. Different types of Indian architectural styles include a mass of expressions over space and time, transformed by the forces of history considered unique to India. As a result of vast diversities, a vast range of architectural specimens have evolved, retaining a certain amount of continuity across history.

Its unique urban characteristics ensure it a place in the annals of world architecture. Indian architecture, belonging to different periods of history, bears the stamp of respective periods. Though the cities of Indus Valley provide substantial evidence of extensive town planning, the beginnings of Indian architecture can be traced back to the advent of Buddhism in India. It was in this period that a large number of magnificent buildings came up. Some of the highlights of Buddhist art and architecture are the Great Stupa at Sanchi and the rock-cut caves at Ajanta.

BUDDHIST ARCHITECTURE

Indian architecture found its earliest expression in brick buildings that were contemporary with buildings that were constructed of wood. The wooden structures disappeared over the centuries, but they were succeeded and imitated in stone buildings, which have survived.

The oldest architectural remains in India are buildings of burnt brick found at Mohenjo-daro and Harappa (now in Pakistan), dating from about 2500-1750 BC. The subsequent Vedic period, which precedes the beginning of historical styles, is represented by burial mounds at Lauriya Nandangarh, in Bihar State, and rock-cut tombs in Malabar, Kerala state.

The establishment of historical styles began about 250 BC in the time of the Indian king Asoka, who gave imperial patronage to Buddhism. Accordingly, the monuments of this time were built for Buddhist purposes. A characteristic Buddhist construction was the tope, or stupa, a memorial mound encased in masonry, with an altar and parasol at the top, corridors around the base, and four entrances marked by gateways. The best example of these structures, commemorative of the death and entering into Nirvana of Buddha, is the Great Stupa in Sanchi in the state of Madhya Pradesh. Other Buddhist structures are the dagoba, a relic shrine, said to be the ancestral form of the pagoda; the lat, a stone edict pillar, generally monumental; the chaitya, a hall of worship in basilican form; and the vihara, a monastery or temple. Chaityas and viharas were often hewn out of living rock. Architectural details such as capitals and moldings show influence from Middle Eastern and Greek sources. Notable examples of early rock-cut monuments in Maharashtra State are the Great Chaitya Hall at

Karle (c. early 2nd century AD) with its elaborate sculptured facade and tunnel-vaulted nave, and various temples and monasteries at Ajanta and Ellora.

The earliest structural sramana monuments were Buddhist stupas, built in about the 3rd century BC but then enlarged and elaborated over centuries to magnificent complexes, such as at Sanchi, Amaravati, Sarnath, and Bharhut. This concept of extending and adding to a core religious site over time is a common theme across regions and religions in India. Both rock-cut and structural Buddhist and Jaina monuments continued to be built till about the 9th c.AD in India and till much later outside India. Buddhist architecture are the vast maha-viharas at Nalanda and Paharpur built in eastern India during the Pala era, the extensive rock-cut complexes at Ellora and Ajanta.

Considerable information is given in the Vedas. These ancient texts were composed by the Aryan seers and handed down through generations orally. The great epics, the Mahabharata and the Ramayana, vividly picture village and town life during Aryavrata, or the Aryan age. A third quarter was reserved for the merchants, and the last for tradesmen who could display their wares. From these modest beginnings, early Hindu architecture gradually metamorphosed into the magnificent Buddhist stupas and the rock-cut caves at Ajanta.

Ashoka proclaimed Buddhism as the State religion and spread its message to the four corners of the land through state-funded monasteries, grants, and his famous rock-edicts, which dot the face of modern Orissa and central India.

The caves of Ajanta and Ellora, much of Buddhist architecture, were directly influenced by the simple village structures of the Aryan villages. In addition, carvings on the Stupas at Barhut and Sanchi, depict Aryan village life vividly.

The Rathas of Mahabalipuram:

The Rathas at Mahabalipuram are yet another great specimen of rock-cut architecture in ancient India. These Ratha temples at Mahabalipuram were constructed during the reign of Pallava rulers.

The Pallavas were founders of the Dravidian Style of temple architecture. They were the founders of what later became known as the Dravidian Style, which became the style prevalent all over South India during mediaeval times. The town of Mahabalipuram is home to a curious experiment: to determine which form of temple is best. This led to the sculpting, out of monolithic rock, scaled-down replicas of actual temples, which are now known as the Rathas of Mahabalipuram or the 'Seven Pagodas'. The rathas are not very large, the biggest measuring 42 feet by 35 feet, and the tallest is 40 feet high. With one exception, all the rathas are modeled on two types of structure: the Buddhist vihara and chaitya.

The cave architecture in India is believed to have begun in the third century BC. These caves were used by Buddhist and Jain monks as places of worship and residence. Initially the caves were excavated in the western India. Some examples of this type of cave structure are Chaityas and Viharas of Buddhists. The great cave at Karle is one such example, where great Chaityas and Viharas were excavated by hewing out rocks. The Karle caves are big in size and the interior is lighted up by great windows.

Besides the caves at Karle, many caves were excavated at other places. These were excavated not only by Buddhists or Jains but also by Hindus. Some of the famous and prominent caves are at Nashik, Kanheri, Gaya (Barabar Hills), Bhaja, Nagarjunikonda, Badami, Elephanta and Ellora. These caves house some of the amazing murals, sculptures and architectural structures. The Elephanta caves contain Maheshmurti, Shiva in three aspects of Creator, Preserver and Destroyer. This is undoubtedly one of the finest single piece Indian sculptures. There are numerous such great examples of Buddhist, Hindu and Jain rock temples at Ellora but the most spectacular of all splendid is the Kailasha temple. The Kailasha temple is hewn of rocks.

Maharashtra is home to the spectacular and amazing Ajanta and Ellora group of caves. The caves at Ajanta and Ellora were cut out of rock, by hand, and rank amongst some of the most outstanding specimens of ancient Indian architectural heritage. In all, there are 34 caves at Ellora and 29 caves at Ajanta.

Ajanta:

Ajanta caves were rediscovered in the 19th century by British officers. The Ajanta caves depict the story of Buddhism, spanning the period from 200 BC to 650 AD. The caves at Ajanta served as secluded retreats to the Buddhist monks. Beautiful wall frescos and sculptures speak volumes of the advancement of Indian art in ancient period. Some of the caves at Ajanta house panels depict stories from the Jatakas, stories about several incarnations of the Buddha. Cave number one contains wall frescos that include two great Bodhisattvas, Padmapani and Avalokiteshvara. Other wonderful paintings in Ajanta are the flying apsara, dying princess and Buddha in preaching mode.

Ellora:

At Ellora, the caves are 34 in number. The Ellora caves are carved into the sides of a basaltic hill. The caves at Ellora contain some of the finest specimens of cave-temple architecture and exquisitely adorned interiors. Structures in the Ellora caves represent the three faiths of Hinduism, Buddhism and Jainism and were carved during 350 AD to 700 AD. The nobility, serenity and grace of Buddha are visible in the Buddhist caves of Ellora. Ellora caves also contain images of Vishwakarma, the patron saint of Indian craftsmen. The Kailasha temple in Cave 16 is indeed an architectural wonder, the entire structure having been carved out of a monolith.

The scheme of the Kailash temple is basically divided into four main parts: the body of the temple itself, the entrance gateway, an intermediate nandi shrine and the cloisters surrounding the courtyard. Much of the imposing character of the main shrine is due to its substantial plinth, which on first examination seems to be a floor by itself. Above and below this, the sub-structure is heavily molded, while the central space is occupied by a frieze of elephants and lions.

The Kailash temple is not only the single largest work of art executed in India, but as an example of rock-cut architecture, it stands unrivalled. One gradually becomes aware of the stupendous labor that it involved (over a hundred years), and finally, the sculpture that adorns it. Standing within its walls, one cannot help but be aware of the spiritual energy that went into its creation a jewel hewn out of the rock itself.

Stupa:

A trip through rural India reveals the countryside to be dotted with shrines of all sizes, shapes and denominations. However, if we look at the modest examples, we will find that they need not be masonry structures – a stone, a tree, a mountain or even an animal will suffice. A variety of natural objects have been conferred divinity because of their association – real or imagined – with a mythological event, or with the 'relics' of some historical/ mythological figure.

Thus, it was that during Ashoka's time, the first Buddhist 'shrines' were mere piles of stone or rubble containing relics of the Buddha. Over time, it became necessary to 'upgrade' these structures, in conformity with Buddhism's rising status. As is common with ancient structures the world over, for structural reasons, it was necessary to have a wide base, tapering towards the top. The form chosen for the Buddhist Stupa was that of a sphere – as much for the shape's metaphysical associations as for the fact that it was an antipode to the square/rectangular form of Hindu temples.

Even after Ashoka, assistance from the mercantile class, who had little interest in Brahmanism, was still available, and thus the Buddhist monks could, over the years, transform their humble centers into truly magnificent works of art. The foremost among these centers was Sanchi, near modern Bhopal. The Sanchi Stupa basically is a dome, surmounted by a finial or 'harmika', with a circumambulatory path around it, delineated by a railing or 'vedika'. As mentioned earlier, the spherical shape of the Stupa was a structural culmination of rubble masonry piled up, and also had metaphysical connotations with the apparent shape of the universe. The harmika on top represented the Bodhi Tree under which the Buddha first gained enlightenment. And the path around, provided a passage for monks who could circle the Stupa, chanting endlessly.

A structure as large as Sanchi Stupa attracted large numbers of monks for penance and meditation. In addition, there were a large number of visitors who made a pilgrimage to this, the most holy site of the Buddhists. A natural consequence was the gradual development of a large complex of buildings around the Stupa. These were typified by the vihara and the chaitya. The magnificent ruin still attracts a large number of tourists today.

TEMPLE ARCHITECTURE OF INDIA

As temples form the backbone of Indian medieval architectural heritage, it would be appropriate to discuss their basic architectural features before we move on to different styles of Indian architecture. Despite the vastness of the land, Indian temple architecture is remarkably uniform. It is, however, often distinguished into two chief styles, each having numerous sub-styles. The Northern or Indo-Aryan style is marked by a tower with rounded top and curvilinear outline while the Southern or Dravidian style has the tower usually in the shape of a rectangular truncated pyramid.

Perhaps the most important part of the ancient Indian temples is decoration. It is reflected in the multitude details of figured sculpture as well as in the architectural elements. Another important component of Indian temples was the garba-griha or the womb chamber, housing the deity of the temple. The garbha-griha was provided with a circumambulation passage around. However, there are also many subsidiary shrines within temple complexes, more common in the South Indian temple.

In the initial stages of its evolution, the temples of North and South India were distinguished on the basis of some specific features like sikhara and gateways. In the north Indian temples, the sikhara remained the most prominent component while the gateway was generally unassuming. The most prominent features of South Indian temples were enclosures around the temples and the Gopurams (huge gateways). The Gopurams led the devotees into the sacred courtyard. On the other hand there were many common features in the Northern and the Southern styles. These included the ground plan, positioning of stone-carved deities on the outside walls and the interior, and the range of decorative elements.

Some of the best examples of the north Indian style (Nagara style) of temple architecture are the Khajuraho Group of temples, Sun temple, Konark, Sun temple at Modhera, Gujarat and Ossian temple, Gujarat. The finest examples of Dravidian style (south Indian style) are temples of Tanjore, Madurai, Mahabalipuram, Badami, Pattadakal and Kanchipuram.

However, the first example is that of a modest structure at Tigawa, near modern Jabalpur. This has all the main characteristics of early Hindu temples – an inner garba-griha surrounded by an ambulatory path or cella, an outer portico with columns in the front, and above all, a flat roof of stone.

This temple is notable for the vitality of the carving on its outer columns. There is indeed a certain crudeness in its construction, an over-use of stone, far more than structurally necessary. This may be attributed to the mason's unfamiliarity with the new material. However, there is no concealing the vitality and sheer exuberance of the sculpture, nor the signs that this was done in an age of plenty, with optimism and security writ large. Of the numerous similar examples, this is undoubtedly the finest.

The early Gupta Age reached its zenith with the construction of a superb little Shiva Temple at Deogarh, in Jhansi district. This temple is remarkable for a number of reasons. First and foremost, an effort is seen to augment the grandeur of the shrine by a raised structure above the garba-griha, discarding the hitherto-used flat roof. Thus, the upper part of the sanctum assumes a pyramidal shape, which when built would have been at least 40 feet (unfortunately, not much of the temple survives). Placing the whole structure on a pedestal, thus adding five feet more, further increases the appearance of height. The second noteworthy point is the portico – which does not face only in one direction. Instead there are four, one in each direction. There is also the usual carved exuberance on the pillars.

The initial Hindu sanctuaries are from the Gupta period such as the Vishnu temple at Deogarh, Parvati temple at Nachna Kuthara, the brick-built Lakshmana temple on the banks of the Mahanadi at Sirpur, and the Varaha sculpture in the rock-cut cave at Udayagiri, all from about the 5th cAD. The Gupta style was adopted and transformed by several regional empires. Perhaps the finest examples are of the Western Chalukyas at Badami, Aihole, Pattadakal, and Alampur, where there are rock-cut and structural Hindu temples from the 7th cAD.

Further south, the Pallava dynasty also built several rock-cut and structural shrines in and around their capital at Kanchipuram, the finest examples being temples and rock-cut sanctuaries at Mamallapuram and the 8th c Kailasnatha temple at Kanchipuram.

North Indian Style Evolves

The only remnants now of its former glory are a handful of small stone temples.

The shikhara was now the logical culmination of a plan that included all the basic features of the later temples at Khajuraho and Bhubhaneswar. Two are raised on high plinth, like the temples at Khajuraho, but their shikharas are like the early Orissan examples. The builders at Osian added a mandapa or open assembly hall for devotees to congregate. Another feature was a rectangular wall around the temple, at each corner of which was a subsidiary shrine.

Teli-ka-Mandir at Gwalior

This temple in the fort at Gwalior is unique. The name, of course, literally means Oil-man's temple. In its conception, it resembles more a shrine than a temple, as it consists of a sanctuary only – there is neither mandapa nor pillared pavilions that make up the composition of a full temple.

This consists of two temples, one much smaller than the other, but with the same architectural style. The larger temple is but a portion of the original conception, as only the main hall remains, the shikhara that was about 150 feet in height, having disappeared.

Temples at Bhubhaneswar:

Over a period of seven hundred years, the city of Bhubhaneswar itself had more than seven thousand temples. The

Orissan craftsmen reverted to the familiar shikhara, albeit with a change in profile. Ignoring the elliptic curve of the Gupta temples, the Orissan shikhara was endowed with a more 'shoulder like' profile, or spire.

The need was soon felt for attaching a mandapa or covered hall to single room shrines where worshippers could congregate. In the 8th century temple of Parasurameshwar, the earliest known example of such a modification was found. A lifetime was required to study the rules and more, if possible.

All the temples of Khajuraho are set on broad terraces. In profile, they display a unity of composition and graceful silhouettes that exceeds any preceding examples. But the most distinctive feature of the silhouette of a Khajuraho temple is without doubt its distinctive shikhara. For some historians this is evidence of the decadence of the Chandela kings, a hypothesis backed up by the fact that the Chandela dynasty did not survive for long thereafter.

The Sun Temple, Konark, if it had been successfully completed, would have been the biggest temple in India by far. Yet it seems that the conception of the structure exceeded the available structural skill. For even before completion, the foundation of the temple started sinking under the great weight above, and the 200 feet high shikhara could never be finished. What remains of the temple now is the mandapa, which alone is colossal.

These rules sometimes assumed ridiculous dimensions. The most basic acts of building were no longer to be based on technical considerations but rather on mythological ones. Thus the Vastu-shastra was sometimes more of a hindrance than a help to the craftsmen.

It is in this situation that the genius of the Indian craftsman came to the fore. In a situation that could easily have been stifling, the mason and stonecutters came forth and created beauty simply by the plasticity of their sculpture and the sheer brute force of their forms.

Thus Brahma, the creator, occupied pride of place in the center and lesser gods were relegated to the edges. A humanistic façade was given to the square by showing it to be able accommodate a figure in a convoluted yogic posture.

It is interesting to note that this idea, that of the human figure was started being the basis of a system of proportion.Very simply, the central square could be used for the garba-griha, while the surrounding grid formed the pradakshina-path and outer wall, and so on.

Hindu Temple architecture has remain unsurpassed to this day. Some other associated features are:

1. The Bundelkhand region ruled by the Chandelas, especially the town of Khajuraho.
2. Bhubhaneswar, which produced its biggest temple ever.
3. Konark, on the eastern coast of Orissa.
4. Modhera, in Gujarat.

Development of Temples in South India:

Almost contemporaneously, another similar movement was taking place in the south under the vigorous direction of the Chalukyas (AD 450 to 650). The main effort of this dynasty was at Aihole, in Bijapur district. Here the Durga temple, also at Aihole, is an example of the form of a Buddhist Chaitya hall, adapted to suit the Brahminical ritual. Gradually, as the masons gained greater confidence, temple forms all over the country started crystallizing. Just as in a church, a temple too has its distinctive element.

The origin of the Shikhara is the subject of intense debate, due to its prominence and characteristic form. Some theories on its derivation: from the sphere of the Buddhist stupa, from the domed huts of central India, and also from the pyramidal covering on a ceremonial chariot of the Aryans.

In the 10th and 11th centuries, the South too witnessed the construction of massive temples. The Great Temple at Thanjavur was 180 feet high from the ground, with a spire of 130 feet, fully 70 feet higher than the tallest spire so far attempted. This soaring height was capped by an enormous domical monolith, weighing at least 80 tons.

In this temple, two mandapas in front of the Vimana are also proportionately built. It was also true, of course, that the form chosen was far more prudent, a comparatively stable pyramid rather than the complex curvilinear profile of the shikhara. Growing chola power was accompanied by a patronage for the arts, the building of new cities and improvement in material life of the city-states as a whole.

The Temples in the South became famous for:

- "The rigid and geometrically perfect Vimana";
- Innovation of the Mandap i.e. huge flat-roofed hall has processional aisles that remain at ground level.
- South India temples could be discerned from afar by the distinctive shape of their Gopurams dominating the skyline.

Thus an ancient, venerated shrine could often find itself in the position of being reduced in appearance to a fortress, that too a most utilitarian one. These temple cities and their sociological implications will be the subject of architecture.

Despite constrained by the huge battlements thrown up around, temples in south India contained massive Gopurams. The new wall had its own huge Gopurams. The Gopuram, was erected primarily to emphasize the importance of the temple within the city precincts without in any way altering the form of the temple itself. The temple-city had evolved from a place of pilgrimage to the hub of political, cultural, social and secular activity of the region. The temple-city had evolved from a place of pilgrimage to the hub of political, cultural, social and secular activity of the region.

The Meenakshi Temple at Madurai:

Thus, it came to pass that the Meenakshi temple was designed as a series of concentric courtyards, orparikramas. The spaces around the shrine became hierarchical, diminishing in religious value; the further one went from the main shrine. The outermost ring had buildings of a more practical nature – accounts, dormitories, kitchens, shops selling items for rituals, maintenance areas and 'parking' for the increasing number of chariots.

The Hall of a Thousand Pillars:

With temple building losing its architectural challenge and becoming more and more a town planning exercise, the craftsman was restricted to working on pavilions, halls and Gopurams, the last of which grew ever larger and imposing. The huge hall in the Meenakshi temple needed 985 pillars to support its roof. This is the famous 'Hall of a Thousand Pillars'.

The Corridors of Rameswaram:

Rameswaram, on a tip of land jutting out into the sea, is a maze of huge pillared verandahs. Not only is the temple surrounded by corridors, but it is also linked to the entrances by covered passages. Rameswaram, thus has the distinction of possessing the longest corridors in the world.

To add to its distinctiveness, the Hoysala temple in plan composed of numerous cellas or garbha-grihas served by a common mandapa. The plan of each of these cellas was a star. The departure from the accepted square form of the temple is understandable when we analyze the plan and see that it is made up of a grid of rotating squares. The resulting outline thus emerges as a star. The mandapa remained a square, though it was now distinguished by circular columns, the shafts of which had been lathed and thus acquired a number of parallel knife-edges.

The site of Vijaynagar is spectacular, a city carved out of low lying hills and massive boulders, the treacherous terrain provided ample defense with only a few well-defended accesses. The Tungabhadra river meanders gently through, and at night, the boulder-strewn landscape has an almost magical quality.

Fortifications, outlying fields and a fifteen mile long aqueduct were the defense against a siege. This city has been the subject of many an impassioned travelogue by foreigners – Portuguese and Persians.

"The city of Bidjanagar (Vijayanagar) is such that the pupil of the eye has never seen a place like it." To add to its distinctiveness, the Hoysala temple in plan composed of numerous cellas or garbha-grihas served by a common mandapa. The plan of each of these cellas was a star. The departure from the accepted square form of the temple is understandable when we analyze the plan and see that it is made up of a grid of rotating squares. The resulting outline thus emerges as a star. The mandapa remained a square, though it was now distinguished by circular columns, the shafts of which had been lathed and thus acquired a number of parallel knife-edges.

The site provided ample raw material for building, and the huge massifs of rock were often themselves sculpted to produce a unique architecture that is part organic, part man-made and often is difficult to distinguish from natural features.

Hampi shows us a change from the normal centralized temple with outlying ancillaries, in the sense that the religious buildings are scattered around in small units, each with its own importance and function, the planning of the whole obeying the diktat of the terrain.

The merging of the Dravidian and North Indian styles created a temple that is unique, so much so that it is often classified as the Hoysala style. The early experiments were found on the extreme edges of the kingdom, around ancient Dwarasamudra. The profile of the temples at Ittagi, Gadag and Lakhundi reveals that the craftsman's most visible contribution was a subtle merging of the two spire forms – the horizontal tiers of the pyramidal south Indian vimana and the round-shouldered elegance of the northern shikhara.

By the 14th century A.D., considerable political changes had taking place. The most threatening was evidence of a new, irresistible force from the north – the all-conquering hordes of Islam.

Materials and Construction:

Indian temple architecture has often been called sculpture on a mass scale rather than true architecture. The Indian mason relied on gravity and mass for his structure to stand, and the piling of massive blocks one on top of the other ensured stability without using mortar. This has made Indian temples poetry in stone, mute sentinels to the skill of their unnamed builders.

Temple Layout and Chief Structural Components

- The Hindu temple is laid out on an **east-west alignment**; the temple **entrance** is on the **eastern side** and the **sanctuary** is on the **western side.**
- The **entire temple** complex is placed on a high plinth or **platform** to symbolize its significance.
- The chief temple structures (moving from east to west) include:
- **Ardha-mandap** (This is a largely open entrance vestibule, entered by passing under a gopuram, symbolic of the passage from the world of the profane to the sacred. Temple-goers ascend stairs, pass under the gopuram to the level of the ardha-mandapa, and then proceed into the mandapa).
- **Mandapa.** (The mandapa is positioned directly between the entrance vestibule and the garbha griha; it is a hall, in which devotees assemble (to view the deity) and ritual dances are performed).
- **Garbha griha.** (The square-shaped garbha griha holds the core sanctuary, where deity resides. The vimana, the main tower of the temple, sits directly above the garbha griha).
- In the Northern Indian Temple style, garbha griha is the core of the temple complex, positioned directly under the mountain tower (vimana); it houses the resident deity. The overall plan of the temple is dictated by this central square, as its form is mirrored by surrounding structures.
- The square form is associated with divinity, whereas the circle is associated with humanity.
- It is interesting to note that the apsidal form used as the floorplan for Buddhist sanctuaries (chaitya) fuses the circular with the square; this was likely the inspiration for the use of these basic, symbolic architectural forms.
- Temples venerating Shiva (and his consort, Parvati) display stone images of his mount, Nandi (a seated bull), facing the main shrine.
- Temples dedicated to Vishnu (and his consort, Lakshmi) display stone images of his mount, Garuda (a mythical bird), facing the main shrin.
- The Southern temple style – There are often three entrances to the South India temple, on the east, north, and south sides of the external ardha-mandapa. This compares with the Northern temple's single eastern entrance.

- The progression of rooms follows the same pattern as in the North: In the interior mandapa is shown in yellow highlights and the garbha griha sanctuary is shown in red highlights.
- Later, in the Southern style's development, the internal mandapa was replaced by vast hypostyle halls, with as many as one thousand pillars.
- Later, even the external ardha-mandapa was expanded, becoming a small hypostyle hall that fed an even larger one.
- South India Temples are usually encircled by protective, concentric enclosure walls with entrances through large **Gopurams.**
- **Gopurams** dwarf the enclosed temples.
- The temple-cities now even more accurately symbolized the divine city (the temple proper) surrounded by its mountain ranges (city walls).
- Southern Style Temples are known as – Pyramidal shaped towers for temples.
- North Indian temples are known as Meru shaped temples.
- The clearly visible horizontal lines indicative of the storeys contrast with the Northern style's strong vertical lines.

Importance of Guilds:

Two institutions that greatly influenced temple construction brought about this close coordination. The first was the seni, or guilds. Initially a system of apprenticeship, the guilds slowly became hereditary and knowledge of temple construction and sculpture was passed down through the generations from father to son. A large project necessitated a guild being obliged to settle on the site for a long period, sometimes a generation or more. Thus, "a large architectural undertaking became an art center from which a local school and style were derived".

The second influence was that of the silpas, treatises codifying rules for Art, Sculpture and Architecture and the Vastushastra in particular, a book setting down the rules of architecture. The silpas were committed to memory and passed down the generations simply by learning them by heart. Thus the workmen had infallible rules, by following which they could be assured of success.

As early as the 7th century B.C., Indian craftsmen had organized themselves into guilds, to protect their special knowledge, and to gain for themselves better working conditions, and finally to ensure a minimum standard of quality of workmanship.

In the senis, heredity was the route by which traditional knowledge was passed on through the generations. As soon as a boy was old enough to hold tools, he was set to work on a rough block of stone and so commenced his long apprenticeship. This was the father's sole gift and heirloom to his sons who in turn ensured that his name and style would live on.

A temple project would often be of such magnitude that more than one generation of master cutters and masons would be required to finish it. So a clan of stonecutters would settle around the building site for years. The temple site attracted young men hoping to learn as well as find work. Thus it became the focus of activity for miles around. Over the years, regional variations introduced for the building of a particular temple led to the evolution of a new style or 'school' of temple building, much like the gharanas that exist in Indian classical music even today. Hence we find distinct schools of art and architecture even within North Indian temple construction – the Orissan, Chalukyan, Gujarati, Kashmiri, and of course, the same situation in the temples of the south, which were further divided into many regional variations and schools of construction. In all these, the Vastushastra was the giver of cohesiveness, which ensured overall similarity of form and function, but also, as we have seen, was responsible for fettering the imagination of the craftsmen.

Entire families of skilled craftsmen were now presented with two choices – the first of which was to work for their new masters and abandon the idea of building a temple as an offering to God. This resulted in the fusion of Persian and Indian building styles.

MEDIEVAL PERIOD ARCHITECTURE

While the impressive Hindu temples were being built, Islamic architecture made a sudden but pronounced appearance in north India in the late 12th century. Rapid Islamic military expansion across the country was complemented by prolific building of mosques, forts, tombs, and victory towers by successive pre-Mughal dynasties from the 13th to the 16th centuries. Though Muslim raids had started since the 8th century A.D., it was not until 1192 A.D. that Delhi got its first Muslim ruler - Qutb-u-Din Aibak – the founder of the so-called Slave dynasty. The new Muslim rulers feverishly started building activity as another sign of their missionary zeal. The coming of the Turks inaugurated a new era in the history of Indian architecture. They brought with them architectural ideas developed in Persia, Arabia and Central Asia.

"Nothing could illustrate more graphically the religious and racial diversity, or emphasize more decisively the principles underlying the consciousness of each community, than the contrast between their respective places of worship, as represented by the mosque on the one hand, and the temple on the other... Compared with the clarity of the mosque, the temple is an abode of mystery; the courts of the former are open to light and air, with many doorways, inviting publicity, the latter encloses 'a phantasma of massive darkness', having somber passages leading to dim cells, jealously guarded and remote... architecturally the mosque is wholly visible and intelligible, while the temple is not infrequently introspective, complex and indeterminate."

"On the one hand was the rhythmic mind of the Hindus, while on the other the formal mind of the Muslims.

Main Features of the Islamic Architecture:

The distinctive features of the Islamic architecture are seen in the standardized architecture of the mosque and the mausoleum. The mosque consisted of a large, rectangular open courtyard surrounded by arcades on all four sides. The mehrab which faces Mecca indicates the direction to the prayer. The call to worship was made from a tall tower or minaret. There were many minarets in some mosques.

The arch in the gateway and other places was another characteristic feature. The dome was another prominent feature of the mosque and the mausoleum. The ancient Indian buildings were decorated with beautiful carving and sculpture while the Muslim buildings were marked by simplicity and lack of a adornment. The two styles were gradually synthesized into a new and unique style.

Architecture under the Sultanate:

The Turkish rulers utilized the services of the local designers and craftsmen who were among the most skilful in the world. The new fusion that started to take place avoided the extreme simplicity of the Islamic architecture and the lavish decoration of the earlier Indian architecture. The Quwwat-ul-Islam mosque and the Qutb Minar are the most renowned monuments of India. Ala-ud-din Khalji enlarged the Quwwat-ul-Islam mosque and built the Alai Darwaza. Decorative element was introduced to beautify the building.

The buildings of the Tughlaq period were significant from the point of view of the development of architecture. They were not beautiful but massive and very impressive. The regional kingdoms in Bengal, Jaunpur, Gujarat, Malwa and Kashmir developed their own distinctive styles of architecture. With the arrival of Turks during the thirteenth century came a new technique of architecture – the architectural styles of Persia, Arabia and Central Asia. The engineering features of these buildings were the domes, arches and minarets. The palaces, mosques and tombs built by the rulers had these features which were blended with the features of the indigenous architecture and a new synthesis in architecture was achieved. This happened because the Turkish rulers of Delhi utilized the services of the local Indian craftsmen who were very skilful and had already constructed beautiful buildings.

In the buildings that came up, we find the simplicity of the Islamic structure as well as the detailed sculptures and designs they made on their own indigenious structures. A middle path was followed in all their designs in the architecture of this period.

The earliest building of this period is Quwwatul Islam Mosque at Delhi and the Qutub Minar. The latter is a tower, whose height is 70 metres. It is a tapering tower that has five stories. There are beautiful engravings of calligraphy both in the mosque and on the tower.

Many other buildings were later constructed by the Sultans. Ala-ud-din Khalji enlarged the Quwat-ul-Islam mosque and built a gateway to the enclosure of the mosque. This gateway is called the Alahi Darwaja and is one of the most beautiful architectural design even today.

Decorative elements were used to make the building outstanding in its beauty. He also built the Hauz Khas in Delhi which was a hydraulic structure. The tomb of Mohammad Tughlaq, Firoz Tughlaq and the forts of Tughlaqabad are some examples.

Though their buildings were not beautiful but had very strong walls, massive as well as impressive. During the Afghan rule the tombs of Ibrahim Lodi at Delhi and Shershah tomb at Sasaram were built. The architecture of this period also shows how indigenous styles were adopted and utilised by the builders. During these years, the Turks were still in the process of settling down. The rulers were threatened by the Mongols, who made sudden invasions from the north. This is why the buildings of this period are strong, stand practical.

Regional Kingdoms:

With the establishment of regional kingdoms in Bengal, Gujarat and the Deccan, beautiful buildings having their own style were constructed. The Jama Masjid, the Sadi Saiyyad Mosque and the shaking towers at Ahmadabad are a few examples of this architecture. In Mandu (Central India), Jama Masjid, Hindola Mahal and Jahaz Mahal were built. In the Deccan, the Sultans erected a number of buildings.

The Jama Masjid at Gulbarga, Madarsa of Mahmud Gawan at Bidar, Ibrahim Rauza, Gol Gumbaz at Bijapur and the fort at Golkunda are just a few famous buildings. Gol Gumbaz has the largest dome in the world.

All these buildings vary in design and style from the buildings of north India.

In Bengal, the oblong shape of many structures and the peculiar style of roof construction were some of the distinctive features of the regional architecture of Bengal like the Adina mosque and the tomb of Jallal-ud-din at Pandua, Khil Darwaza and Tantipara mosque Gaur.

In Jaunpur, the Atala mosque build by the Sharqui rulers had a gigantic screen covering the dome while the tomb of Hoshang Shah at Malwa is made entirely of marble and is made of yellow and black marble inlay work beautifully done by craftsmen.

The rulers of Vijayanagar, an empire which was established during this period also erected many beautiful buildings and temples and had a number of achievements to their credit.

Though only ruins remain, but the temples of Vithalswami and Hazar Rama at Hampi are good examples.

Bahamani:

The Bahamani sultans borrowed from the styles of Persia, Syria, Turkey and the temples of Southern India. The Jama Masjid at Gulbarga is quite well known. The courtyard of this mosque is covered with a large number of domes and is the only mosque in India which has a covered countryard.

Mughals:

The process of synthesis was completed under the Mughals. Babur and Humayun erected a number of buildings with the help of Persian architects but those were not very impressive.

The advent of the Mughals brought a new era in architecture. The synthesis of style which began earlier reached its zenith during this time. The architecture of Mughal style started during Akbar's rule.

The Mughal architecture began in the reign of Akbar. The first important building of Akbar's reign is Humayun's tomb at Delhi. It has a main gateway and the tomb is placed in the midst of a garden. Many consider it a precursor of the Taj Mahal. The Bulund Darwaza reflect the grandeur of the mighty Mughal empire. This building was made following Akbar's victory over Gujarat. The two significant features of the Mughal architecture are the large gateways, and the placements of the building in the midst of a large park are evident here.

Akbar also built forts at Agra and Lahore. The crowning achievement of the reign of Akbar was the building of his new capital at Fatehpur Sikri. The buildings at Fatehpur Sikri have been built in a variety of styles. The arch of the Buland Darwaza is about 41 metres high and is perhaps the most imposing gateway in the world. The tomb of Salim Chishti is built in white marble. The palace of Jodha Bai was built in the style of ancient Indian architecture.

During the reign of Jahangir, the mausoleum of Akbar was constructed at Sikandara which was inspired by the Buddhist viharas. After a long time, the minar became architecturally significant here. He built the beautiful tomb of Itimad-ud-daula which was built entirely of marble. Shahjahan was the greatest builder amongst the Mughals. He used marble extensively.

Shah Jahan was the greatest of the Mughal builders. His reign marks the highest development of Mugal architecture. Some of the finest monuments of our country were built during his time. The list of Shah Jahan's buildings is very large. The most magnificent of Shah Jahan's buildings is the Taj Mahal built in memory of his wife, Mumtaz Mahal. The only notable buildings of the reign of Aurangzeb are the Badshahi mosque at Lahore and the Moti Masjid at Delhi. The new style of architecture had a significant influence on the construction of Hindu temples and the secular buildings of the Rajputs during this period.

Decorative design in inlay work, beautiful arches and minarets were the features of his buildings. The Red Fort and Jama Masjid of Delhi and above all the Taj Mahal are some of the buildings built by Shahjahan. The Taj Mahal, the tomb of Shahjahan's wife, is built in marble and reflects all the architectural features that were developed during the Mughal period. It has a central dome, four elegant minarats, gateway, inlay work and gardens surrounding the main building.

The Mughal style of architecture had a profound influence on the buildings of the later period. The buildings showed a strong influence of the ancient Indian style and had courtyards and pillars. For the first time in the architecture of this style living beings – elephants, lions peacocks and other birds were sculptured in the brackets.

Monuments Built by Akbar at Fatehpur Sikri:

The Mughal architecture began in the reign of Akbar. He erected many important buildings. The crowning achievements of his reign was the building of his new capital city of Fatehpur Sikri., 40 km from Agra. Fatehpur Sikri is a romance of stones. The Arch of the Buland Darwaja is the most imposing gateway in the world. The tomb of Saint Salim Chisti is exquisite in its beauty. Jodha Bai Palace is a fine example of ancient Indian architecture.

The Jama Masjid was built with the influence of the Persian style. The Dewan-i-Amm and the Dewan-i-Khas are famous for their planning and decoration. The Ibadat Khana and Panch Mahal are another notable buildings. The Panch Mahal is a pyramidal structure in five storeys. It was build on the pattern of a Buddhist Vihara.

From 1526, the Mughal architecture gave a totaly different dimension to tomb building. These are built on platforms and are surrounded by gardens laid out with ornamental fountains. A famous example is the mosque at Fatehpur Sikri – three domes of 290 ft by 470 ft and with two royal tombs.

Another famous tomb is Akbar's tomb in Sikandra (A.D. 1593-1613). The Taj Mahal, Agra (A.D. 1630) built by Shah Jahan is considered one of the 'Wonders of the World'. It is a royal tomb in marble built on a platform 18ft high and 313 ft. square. Each corner is marked by a minaret 133ft high. The central dome is 80 ft. high and 58ft. in diameter. Marble is inlaid with semi-precious stones like jasper and a gate. It stands by the bank of the river Jamuna in the middle of marble terraces, fountains and lakes flanked by cypress trees. Mughal architecture declined with the failing political power of the Mughal empire.

A unique architectural development in the Mughal time was the beautiful gardens developed around the tombs and other buildings. The Shalimar Gardens in Kashmir and lahore were developed by Jahangir and Shah Jahan respectively. The Mughals encouraged cultural and architectural growth of India.

COLONIAL INDIAN ARCHITECTURE

Beside the aura of sophistication of the west, the British brought with them the traditional European architectural styles. The British were much more comfortable with the comfort part than the intricate designs. That is why most of the monuments built by them usually carry a very simple and sober look, when compared to the rest.

Yet, if its artistry you are looking for, then check out the Churches of Old Goa, which has got the largest collection of Goa's churches. Secondary option can be Delhi, which got a total new look at the 'Raj' times. Or, visit the city of Calcutta, the first capital of the East India Company and it was this city from where the British started off their monumental expeditions.

The colonial influence can be seen in office buildings. Europeans who started coming from sixteenth century AD constructed many churches and other buildings. Portuguese built many churches at Goa, the most famous of these are Basilica Bom Jesus and the church of Saint Francis. The British also built administrative and residential buildings which reflect their imperial glory. Some Greek and Roman influence can be observed in the colonnades or pillared buildings. Parliament House and Connaught Place in Delhi are good examples.

From the mid-nineteenth century, it became a norm for the Anglo-Indian church builders to follow the model set by the revivers of the many combinations of Gothic in England. In many cases, imperialism was the sole guiding force rather than practicality. On many occasions, heavier styles than Gothic were employed. This can be seen in the Mutiny Memorial Church at Kanpur and the last garrison church in New Delhi.

The architect Lutyens, designed Rashtrapati Bhavan, formerly the Viceroy's residence. It is built of sandstone and has design features like canopies and jaali from Rajasthan. The Victoria Memorial in Calcutta, the former capital of British India, is a huge edifice in marble. It now houses a museum full of colonial artefacts. Writers' Building in Calcutta, where generations of government officers worked in British times, is still the administrative centre of Bengal after independence.

Some Gothic elements can be seen in the church buildings like St. Paul's Cathedral in Calcutta. The British also left behind impressive railway terminals like the Victoria Terminus in Mumbai.

In Delhi, the Austrian architect, Stein, designed The India International Centre where conferences are held by leading intellectuals from all over the world and more recently, the India Habitat Centre which has become a centre of intellectual activities in the capital.

The Victoria Terminus, once the headquarters of the Great Indian Peninsular Railway, was the culminating masterpiece of the phase. It was increasingly hybrid in style. The Classical and Baroque style furthered the innovation in architecture. Its best exponent was Walter Carnville's Calcutta General Post Office. The innovation in colonial architecture did not stop here; in Victoria Memorial, William Emerson tried to emulate the Taj Mahal in material if not in form. This was an indication of 'Indo-Saracenic' hybridization and was being increasingly employed at different places like St. John's College, Agra and the Madras High Court, Madras.

Line all other aspects, colonization of Indian also had an impact on architecture style. With colonization, a new chapter in Indian architecture began. The Dutch, Portuguese and the French made their presence felt through their buildings but it was the English who had a lasting impact on architecture. In the beginning of the colonial rule, there were attempts at creating authority through classical prototypes. In its later phase, the colonial architecture culminated into what is called the Indo-Saracenic architecture.

The Indo-Saracenic architecture combined the features of Hindu, Islamic and western elements. The colonial architecture exhibited itself through institutional, civic and utilitarian buildings such as post offices, railway stations, rest houses and government buildings. Such buildings began to be built in large numbers over the whole empire. Colonial architecture in India followed developments not only from metropolis but also took inspiration from existing architecture in India.

The Italian Gothic was seen to be well adapted to conditions in India. The architecture style recommended by Sir Gilbert Scott for Bombay University proved crucial in making the colonial architecture look more 'Indian'. Perhaps this was the beginning of a truly imperial style that reached its apex at New Delhi. The great public building campaign launched in Bombay in the second half of the nineteenth also resulted into great development of colonial architecture. In this phase Sir Gilbert Scott's buildings were significant products. Other remarkable landmarks produced during this phase were William Emerson's Crawford Market, the Bombay high court and the Victoria terminus (now Shivaji terminus).

THE SCHOOLS OF ART

The Gandhara School of Art (50 BC to 500 AD)

The Gandhara region extending from Punjab to the borders of Afghanistan was an important centre of Mahayana Buddhism up to the 5th century A.D. The region became famous throughout the world since a new school of Indian sculpture known as the Gandhara School developed during that period. Owing to its strategic location the Gandhara School imbibed all kinds of foreign influences like Persian, Greek, Roman, Saka and Kushan. The origin of Gandhara art can be traced to the Greek rulers of Bactria and Northwest India. But it was during the reign of Kanishka that the art received great patronage.

The Gandhara School of Art is also known as the Graeco-Buddhist School of Art since Greek techniques of Art were applied to Buddhist subjects. The most important contribution of the Gandhara School of Art was the evolution of beautiful images of the Buddha and Bodhisattavas, which were executed in black stone and modelled on identical characters of Graeco-Roman pantheon.

Hence it is said, "the Gandhara artist had the hand of a Greek but the heart of an Indian." The most characteristic trait of Gandhara sculpture is the depiction of Lord Buddha in the standing or seated positions. The seated Buddha is always shown cross-legged in the traditional Indian way. Another typical feature of the Gandhara Art is the rich carving, elaborate ornamentation and complex symbolism. The best specimens of Gandhara art are from Jaulian and Dharmarajika stupa at Taxila and from Hadda near Jalalabad in modern Afghanistan. The tallest rock-cut statue of Lord Buddha is also located at Bamiyan in modern Afghanistan and dates back to 3-4 century AD.

The Mathura School of Art:

The Mathura School of art flourished at the holy city of Mathura, especially between 1-3 A.D. It established the tradition of transforming Buddhist symbols into human form. Buddha's first image can be traced to Kanishka's reign (about 78 A.D.). The earliest sculptures of Buddha were made keeping theMathura Style yaksha prototype in mind. They were depicted as strongly built with the right hand raised in protection and the left hand on the waist. The figures produced by this school of art do not have moustaches and beards as in the Gandhara Art. These figures can be seen in the museum of Mathura. The standing Buddha figures resembles the yaksha figures and indicates the Kushan influence. The seated figures are in the padmasana posture. The Mathura School not only produced beautiful images of the Buddha but also of the Jain Tirthankaras and gods and goddesses of the Hindu pantheon. Many scholars believe that the Mathura School of Art, although of indigenous origin, was greatly influenced by the Gandhara School of Art. The Guptas adopted the Mathura School of Art and further improvised and perfected it.

The Amravati School of Art:

This school of art developed at Amravati, on the banks of Krishna River in modern Andhra Pradesh. It is the site for the largest Buddhist stupa of South India. Its construction began in

200 B.C. and was completed in 200 A.D. The diameter of the stupa at the base was 51 metres. The height of the dome was 31 metres and its outer railing was 5 metres wide. The stupendous stupa could not withstand the ravages of time and its ruins are preserved in the London Museum.

Conclusion

Although Buddhism finally waned in the land of its birth, yet it was destined to spread throughout Asia on the basis of the simplicity of its message and the humaneness of its teachings. However, the fertile land of the Gangetic plain was its progenitor. The formal and metaphysical principles evolved at Sanchi in India inspired countless generations of Buddhist architecture throughout South-East Asia. Sanchi, Nalanda, and Bodh Gaya are today world-famous, with countless Buddhists the world over making pilgrimage to India to see the land where the Buddha gave his first sermon and set rolling the Dharma Chakra, or the Wheel of Truth.

After the reign of Ashoka the Great, there was an interregnum of relative anarchy, with the collapse of two powerful dynasties, the Kushanas (236 AD) in the north, and the Andhras (225 AD) in the south. As pointed out in our previous article, Buddhism too suffered from a lack of political patronage during this period, leading to its slow decline, despite the valiant efforts of its monks. Also notable was a corresponding slowdown in the arts and literature. Thus, in its effects, this period in Indian history may be said to be analogous to the end of the Greek empire in Europe (which coincidentally was almost contemporaneous).

However, the cyclic nature of history demands a renaissance after every Dark Age. It was no different in India – the age that followed has been described as the greatest intellectual awakening in the sub-continent. A large part of the country came under the political control of the Gupta dynasty, which reached its zenith around 400 AD. The culture of the Guptas and their innate Brahmanism gave a fillip to the arts, and in the field of architecture, fundamental progress was made.

Architecturally, we may discern a new sensibility, a break from the mere copying of forms carrying over from wood construction, to a new sensitivity in the handling and use of stone. This is the first time that the use of dressed stone masonry is made, a major step in the evolution of building construction. With this, a radically different type of architecture began to evolve.

Hitherto, it seems that all Brahminical shrines were impermanent. Stone reliefs on the Stupas in Bharhut and Sanchi depict non-Buddhist rituals being held in the open, with merely a shed for shelter, '... formed of posts and beams covered with reeds and mats'. However, with time, Indian deities gradually became anthropomorphic and needed to be housed in some more permanent abode.

Thus, we see the Indian temple passing through various stages, corresponding to the need – clearings in forests, a reed hut, and finally a sanctuary of first wood and then of brick. Eventually, by the Gupta period, a garba-griha of stone evolved. Although the final form of the temple itself is small and unimpressive compared to the juggernauts that followed in the mediaeval age, yet they contained the nucleus of the architecture to follow. We can best illustrate the point by discussing a few seminal examples.

14

Performing Arts in India

The performing arts are the art forms which use the artist's own bodily gestures, facial expressions, and presence as a medium to create some physical art object. Performing arts include the dance, music, opera, drama, and circus art forms. The Natya Shastra, written during the 2nd century, has laid the structure of music, dance and drama.

The performing arts are a division of art that includes any creative endeavor where the artist uses an aspect of their physical being, such as their body or voice, as the presentation medium in front of an audience. In India, various facets of performing arts are all pervading bringing colour and joy to numerous festivals and ceremonies, and reaffirming the faith of the people in their heritage. These facets have been responsible for sustaining the long continuities of ancient traditions. It thus exemplifies the complex, organic interaction of all aspects of life implicit in all tribal and folk art forms; art is not seen as something apart from life, a mere ornamentation or entertainment, but as an intrinsic part of it.

The different types of performing arts are theater, musical theater, dance, music, acting, magic and circus acts. Performing arts involve using facial expressions, voice, and body language to communicate a creative fabrication India is a land of rich culture and heritage. Since the beginning of our civilization, music dance and drama have been an integral aspect of our culture. From the Vedic era to the medieval period, performing arts remained an important source of educating the masses. The Vedas laid down precise rules for the chanting of Vedic hymns. Even the pitch and the accent of singing different hymns have been prescribed. There was more of exemplary presentation through them than education or social reforms. Under the patronage of kings and rulers, skilled artisans and entertainers were encouraged to specialize and to refine their skills to greater levels of perfection and sophistication.

Gradually, the classical forms of Art evolved for the glory of temple and palace, reaching their zenith around India around 2nd C.E. onwards and under the powerful Gupta empire, when canons of perfection were laid down in detailed treatise – the *Natyashastra* and the *Kamasutra* – which are still followed to this day. Through the ages, rival kings and nawabs vied with each other to attract the most renowned artists and performers to their courts. Changing trends in performing arts rarely manifest themselves with dramatic abruptness. More often than not, they creep up silently, diverting the flow of continuing traditions and practices stealthily but resolutely.

As the relentless tidal wave of globalisation swept across the world in the last two decades, Indian performing arts too were swept, tossed high and hurled down, without many even noticing that some of the great rivers of performing traditions and systems had changed course or, at times, been reined in forcefully. Looking back on some of these changes, particularly in the sphere of Indian music, it may be worthwhile to begin by examining a few words, terms and phrases that provide clues to some of the many ways in which globalisation has impacted the performing arts in India.

While the classical arts thus became distinct from their folk roots, they were never totally alienated from them, even today there continues a mutually enriching dialogue between tribal and folk forms on the one hand, and classical art on the other; the latter continues to be invigorated by fresh folk forms, while providing them with new thematic content in return. Other than in academic discussions, performing arts in India and its practitioners are today referred to most commonly as being part of the "entertainment industry." This may seem innocuous enough to some, but the usage of the term and its passive acceptance in most circles definitely indicate a paradigm shift in the manner in which the arts are viewed by society at large.

That today the arts must entertain and amuse in the manner defined by showbiz, and that they must form part of organised industry is the clear and unambiguous message conveyed by this shift. For creators and artistes who, in an ideal world, create art driven by an artistic urge or by that inexplicable creative charge that propels artistes towards their respective forms of expression, this shift from being an individual artiste or part of an artistic community, to being absorbed into or discarded by the politics and commerce of the entertainment industry, has had a far-reaching impact.

India is a land of rich culture and heritage. Since the beginning of our civilization, music, dance and drama have been an integral aspect of our culture. Initially, these art forms were used as medium of propagation for religion and social reforms in which music and dance were incorporated to gain popularity. From the Vedic era to the medieval period, the performing arts remained an important source of educating the masses. The Vedas laid down precise rules for the chanting of Vedic hymns.

Martial art forms throughout the country have been stylized to quasi dance forms, notable among which are the martial dances of the North-eastern hill tribes, the Lazim dances of Maharashtra, the Kalaripayattu of Kerala, and the highly stylized masked Chhau dances of Orissa, West Bengal and Bihar.

Performing arts in India and its practitioners are today referred to most commonly as being part of the "entertainment industry." This may seem innocuous enough to some, but the usage of the term and its passive acceptance in most circles definitely indicate a paradigm shift in the manner in which the arts are viewed by society at large. That today the arts must entertain and amuse in the manner defined by showbiz, and that they must form part of organised industry is the clear and unambiguous message conveyed by this shift.

For creators and artistes who, in an ideal world, create art driven by an artistic urge or by that inexplicable creative charge that propels artistes towards their respective forms of expression, the shift from being an individual artiste or part of an artistic community, to being absorbed into or discarded by the politics and commerce of the entertainment industry, has had a far-reaching impact.

In a globalised world, Indians are fast losing touch with the charm and beauty of regional languages and dialects. Once a form that enjoyed massive popularity, the *ghazal* today faces a bleak future. Some exponents of this genre made attempts to modify the form to suit popular taste and preference. In the process, some abandoned the complex and evolved poetry of the great masters of Urdu, and opted to present simple texts that could be enjoyed by even those who did not fully comprehend the grandeur of classic Urdu poetry. While this strategy brought them some amount of fame and popularity for a short period of time, it did not, by any means, save the *ghazal* from becoming nearly extinct.

Other exponents attempted to use catchy and even slightly westernised tunes with musical interludes and backing orchestras that would be more appropriate for hip hop or Indi pop. Music videos too did not help the floundering form and ultimately the *ghazal* specialists ended up branching out in other directions. Some took to *bhajans,* others to playback and still others accepted anything that came their way.

What is art? "Art is an expression of all characteristics of the human mind aesthetically". Love, humor, pathos, anger, heroism, terror, disgust, wonder and serenity are the nava rasas or nine basic emotions which are fundamental to all Indian aesthetics.

These characteristics, i.e. the varied human emotions, are known as 'RAS'. In Hindi, 'ras' literally means a sugary juice. It signifies the ultimate satisfaction of 'aanand'. Human emotions can be categorized into nine sub-headings or 'navras'. They are:

1. Hasya — laughter
2. Bhayanak — evil Shringar — aesthetics
3. Rudra — chivalrous

4. Karun — pathos
5. Vir — courage
6. Adbhut — astonishing
7. Vibhatsa — terrifying glory
8. Shaanti — peace
9. Shringaar — decorating one's self

Art reflects human emotions and human beings spontaneously express their frame of mind through various art forms. Thus, the intellectual mind merges with the artistic streak, giving birth to art. The expression is reflected in various styles like singing, dancing, drawing.

Music:

Music evokes a particular emotion or mood. The classical music tradition in India has always been a form of meditation, concentration and worship. The melodious sounds of music can evoke the innermost emotions and moods of the audience, connoisseurs and non-connoisseurs alike.

Folk theatre and dance-drama were the common roots of both classical dance and theatre, the traditions of both of which were elaborated upon the Natyashastra. Kalidasa is India's most famous poet and dramatist, and his plays are still performed today. Nawab Wajid Ali Shah, the last ruler of Awadh, was a noted playwright and staged elaborate dramas at his court. Another major text is Matanga's Brihaddesi compiled between eight and ninth century AD. In this work, ragas were first named and discussed at great length. Sangeet Ratnakara written by Sarangdeva in the thirteenth century mentions 264 ragas. A variety of string and wind instruments were invented over the period of time.

In ancient texts, references have been made to flutes, drums, veena, and cymbals. Many rulers such as Samudragupta, King Bhoja of Dhara and King Someshavra of Kalyana patronised music. The Gupta monarch Samudra Gupta was himself an accompolished musician. In some of his coins, he is shown playing on the Veena. Music was also associated with the worship of Gods and Goddess in the temples.

In the 12th. century, Jayadeva of Orissa produced the most brilliant raga kavya, the Gita Govinda, each song of which was set in a raga and was composed on the theme of love of Radha and Krishna. Abhinavagupta's (AD 993-1055) Abhinavabharati provides useful information about music.

Tamil music has a number of terms and concepts parallel to what is found in Sanskrit texts. The Saivite Nayanars and Vaishnavite Alvars too set their psalms (poems) to music.

Similarly, in the medieval period, the Sufi and Bhakti saints encouraged music. Qawwalis were sung in Sufi khanqahs and devotional music like kirtan and bhajan became popular with the Bhakti saints. Names of Kabir, Mirabai, Surdasa, Chandidasa, Tulsidasa, Vidyapati are closely associated with religious music. Great scholars like Amir Khusrau contributed equally to the promotion of music. The legendary ruler of Malwa, Baz Bahadur and his wife Rupmati introduced new ragas.

Kitabe Navras written by Ibrahim Adil Shah II during the seventeenth century is a collection of songs in praise of Hindu deities as well as Muslim saints. The most famous musician of Akbar's court was Tansen and there was nobody to match him, even though there were all kinds of singers. Baiju Bawra was also a well known musician during Akbar's time. The patronage given to these artists by the ancient and medieval rulers have been instrumental in keeping the traditions alive. In fact the Mughal rulers were great patrons of music. Pundarika Vittal was a great scholar of music who wrote the famous Ragamala. Hindustani Music was also enriched by devotional songs sung by Mira Bai, Tulsidas and Surdas.

Music is composed of two essential ingredients – the Raga, or musical mode and the Taal. Two classical types of music, Carnatic (southern Indian) and Hindustani (northern Indian) have been introduced after the 5th. century and had been influenced by Bhakti traditions. The Muslims invaders influenced the Hindustani instruments, styles and schools of performance. The legends associated with Hindustani Music are Amir Khusro (13th century), Miyan Tansen (16th century) and Venkatamakhi (17th century). Thyagaraja and Shyama Shastri are associated with Carnatic Music.

HINDUSTANI CLASSICAL MUSIC

Hindustani classical music may be traced back to the period of the Delhi Sultanate and to Amir Khusrau (AD 1253-1325) who encouraged the practice of musical performance with particular instruments. He is believed to have invented the sitar and the tabla and is said to have introduced new ragas. Most of the Hindustani musicians trace their descent to Tansen. Different styles of Hindustani music are Dhrupad, Dhamar, Thumri, Khayal and Tappa.

It is said that Tansen's music had the effect of magic. He could stop the rising waves of the Yamuna and, by the force of his '*Megh Rag*' he could cause the rain to fall. In fact, his melodious songs are sung in every part of India even now with great interest. Some of Akbar's courtiers patronised musicians like Baiju Bawra, Surdas etc.

The most popular ragas are: Bahar, Bhairavi, Sindhu Bhairavi, Bhim Palasi, Darbari, Desh, Hamsadhwani, Jai Jayanti, Megha Malhar, Todi, Yaman, Pilu, Shyam Kalyan, Khambaj. India also has a rich variety of musical instruments of different types. Amongst the stringed instruments, the most famous are sitar, sarod, santoor and sarangi. Pakhawaj, tabla and Mridangam are precussion or tal giving instruments. Likewise, flute, shehnai and nadaswaram are some of the chief wind instruments.

The musicians of Hindustani classical music are usually associated to a gharana or a particular style of music. Gharanas refer to hereditary linkages of musicians which represent the core of the style and distinguish them from the other.

The gharanas function in gurushishya parampara, that is, disciples learning under a particular guru, and transmitting his musical knowledge and style, will belong to the same gharana. Some famous gharanas are Gwalior gharana, Kirana gharana, and Jaipur gharana.

Devotional music like kirtan, bhajan, ragas contained in the Adi Grantha and singing in the Majlis during Muharram also deserve a special place in Indian music. Along with this, folk music also shows a very rich cultural heritage.

Carnatic Music:

The compositions in Carnatic music may be attributed collectively to three composers who lived between AD 1700 and 1850. They were Shyam Shastri, Thyagaraja and Mutthuswami Dikshitar. Purandardasa was another great composer of Carnatic music.

Thyagaraja is revered both as a saint and an artist and epitomises the essence of Carnatic music. The main compositions are known as kriti and are devotional in nature. The three great musicians experimented with new forms.

Some notable musicians of this period are Maha Vaidyanath Ayyar (1844-93), Patnam Subrahmanya Ayyar (l854-1902) and Ramnad Srinivasa lyengar (l860-1919). Flute, veena, nadaswaram, mridangam, ghatam are some of the instruments to accompany Carnatic music.

Despite contrasting features between Hindustani and Carnatic music, one can find some Tilana in Carnatic, which resembles Tarana of Hindustani. Both lay stress on tala or talam.

Modern Indian Music:

With the British rule came Western music. Indians adopted some of their instruments such as violin and clarinet to suit the demands of Indian music. Orchestration of music on stage is a new development. Use of cassettes replaced oral transmission of tunes and ragas.

Performance, which were earlier limited to a privileged few have now been thrown open to the public and can be viewed by thousands of music lovers throughout the country. Music education no longer depends on the master-disciple system but can be imparted through institutions teaching music.

Famous Musicians:

Amir Khusrau, Sadarang Adaranga, Miyan Tansen, Gopal

Nayak, Swami Haridas, Pt. V.D. Paluskar, Pt. V.N. Bhatkhande, Thyagaraja Mutthuswami Dikshitar, Pt. Omkar, Nath Thakur, Pt. Vinaik Rao Patwardhan, Ustad Chand Khan, Ustad Bade Ghulam Ali Khan, Ustad Faiyaz Khan, Ustad Nissar Hussain Khan, Ustad Amir Khan, Pt. Bhimsen Joshi, Pt. Kumar Gandharva, Kesarbai Kerkar and Smt. Gangubai Hangal are all vocalists.

Among the instrumentalists Baba Allauddin Khan, Pt. Ravi Shankar, Ustad Bismillah Khan, Ustad Alla Rakkha Khan, Ustad Zakir Hussain are some of the well known musicians.

Folk Music:

The folk music and dances of agricultural communities celebrate the rhythms of daily life, the turn of the seasons, the highlights of the agricultural calendar, religious festivals and important events that punctuate the flow of life, such as births and marriages.

While folk music and dance share common themes and concerns, there is a wide variety of forms. Along the entire Himalayan region, from Kashmir to Darjeeling, folk dancers link arms and sway gracefully in undulating movements, celebrate the sowing of the wheat crop; few can resist the infectious beat of the Dholak, the two-sided drum, and pairs of dancers take turns to execute complex acrobatic movements in the centre of a circle of abandoned dancers.

Women perform the Giddha, also characterised by its spontaneous energy. Rajasthani women, their faces covered with flowing veils, are swirls of colour as they pirouette in the Ghoomar dance, while their counterparts in Gujarat perform the famous Garba, dancing in a circle with batons. Their men perform the Dandiyaras, a more vigorous version of the same dance, leaping and crouching in twirling patterns.

The women Lavani dance from this area is notable for its unabashed sensuality. There are also several forms of dance-drama or folk theatre, such as the Nautanki of Rajasthan, Uttar Pradesh and Bihar, the Bhavai of Gujarat, the irreverent Tamasha of Maharashtra, the Bengali Jatra, the spectacular Yakshagana of

Karnataka and Theyyam of Kerala, all of which narrate legends of local heroes, kings and deities.

Besides classical music, India has a rich legacy of folk or popular music. This music represents the emotion of the masses. The simple songs are composed to mark every event in life.They may be festivals, advent of a new season, marriage or birth of a child. Rajasthani folk songs such as Mand and Bhatiali of Bengal are popular all over India.

Ragini is a popular form of folk songs of Haryana.

Folk songs have their special meanings or messages. They often describe historical events and important rituals. Kashmir's Gulraj is usually a folklore and Pandyani of Madhya Pradesh is a narrative put to music. Muslims sing Sojkhwani or mournful songs during Muharram and Christmas carols and choral music are sung in groups on the festive occasions.

DANCES OF INDIA

Together these dances have formed a vast reservoir from which the classical dances have drawn sustenance. There are seven major classical dance styles — Bharatnatyam from Tamil Nadu and Karnataka, Kathakali, a classical dance-drama from Kerala, Manipuri from Manipur, Kathak from Uttar Pradesh, Odissi from Orissa, and Kuchipudi from Andhra Pradesh and Sattriya from Assam which has recently been included in the fold of Classical Dances.

Dances of India:

The Rig Veda mentions dance (nrti) and danseuse (nrtu) and compares the brilliant dawn (usas) to a brightly attrived danseuse. In the Brahmanas, Jaiminiya and Kausitaki dance and music are mentioned together. The Epics are full of references to dances on earth and heaven.

In India, religion, philosophy and myth can not be divorced from their art forms. Dance and music are tied inextricably to ceremony of any kind. Weddings, births, coronations, entering a new house or town, welcoming a guest, religious processions, harvest time, any or all of these are occasions for song and dance.

Music and dance are probably the most elemental art forms, spontaneously expressing the entire gamut of human emotions and experiences. There are tribal belts throughout India, and although each tribe has its own distinctive music and dances, they all share a similar form, with men and women forming separate rows with linked arms and executing intricate leg movements in a gradually increasing tempo that builds up to a crescendo of vigour.

Like music, Indian dance has also developed a rich classical tradition. It has a great power of expression and emotions while telling a story. In India, the art of dancing may be traced back to the Harappan culture. The discovery of the bronze statue of a dancing girl testifies to the fact that some women in Harappa performed dances.

In traditional Indian culture, the function of dance was to give symbolic expression to religious ideas. The figure of Lord Shiva as Nataraja represents the creation and destruction of the cosmic cycle. The popular image of Shiva in the form of Nataraja clearly shows the popularity of dance form on the Indian people. There is not a single temple at least in the southern part of the country which does not show the sculptures of the dancers in their different form. In Southern India, Bharatanatyam and Mohiniattam developed as an important aspect of the rituals in temples. Yakshagana, a form of Kathakali in Kerala, tells us stories of Ramayana and Mahabharata whereas Kathak and Manipuri are mostly related to the stories of Krishna and his leela (exploits). Performance of Odissi is related to the worship of Lord Jagannath. Though the Krishna leela and the stories related to Lord Shiva was the theme of Kathak, this dance came to be performed in royal courts in medieval times. Romantic gestures contained in Thumri and Ghazal, that were also performed with accompanists for the kings, reflect this aspect. Manipuri dance was also preformed for religious purposes.

Basic Components of the Classical Dances:

To understand the intricacies of classical dances and to excel in these dance forms, there needs to be a basic understanding of the components of these fascinating dance styles. In the Natya Sastra, a book on classical dances, it is made clear that drama and acting are considered inseparable from the dance and music. They are totally interdependent.

The Dance itself may be divided into three main parts:

Nritta: This refers to pure technical aspects of dance. These are the movements without any special meaning or mood, and used to show the basic adavus or fundamentals and the intricacies of complicated timings, rhythms, posture and footwork.

Nritya: That form of dance, comprising movements of the body, hands, limbs, together with facial expressions, and filled with Rasa or Flavor, which may express small episodes, just a sentence, or a whole drama.

Natya: The combination of both dancing and acting. This, then is the basic foundation of the entire dance.

The science of dramaturgy further showed that the dance was composed of a series of enchanting combinations of three main elements of bodily gesture, namely:

The Limbs;

The Face;

The Whole Body.

These three main components had to express between them one uniform whole in which speed, grace, symmetry, body control, versatility, eye expressions, facial expressions, thought, word and song followed in a natural stream of harmony.

The meaning of the dance was further detailed in the three forms:

Bhava or Mood : This part of the dance was to be gracefully described by the glances and play of the eyes and eyebrows; the Hastas of hand gestures, accompanied by the relevant facial expression.

Raga or Melody : The song and melody used during the dances have direct impact on the expression of the dance and its mood.

Situated on the northeastern region of India, **Manipur** presents a beautiful picture of nature and charm. The word Manipur is derived from the words "Mani" a jewel and "pur" a place. Center of Manipuri dance is based in Imphal, the capital of Manipur.

This is a very graceful and spiritual dance form and is not seen very often. For centuries, people of Manipur have expressed their emotions and faith through dance and music. Initially, many dances were devoted to Lord Shiva and his wife Goddess Parvathi. However, through times the dances of Lord Krishna, and his lover Radha have gained more popularity.

This dance style is characterised by the graceful movements and the richness of Bhava (mood), raga (melody) and Tala (Rhythm). Every hand gesture and every inflection of the body is very calculated to convey a story and an in-depth message.

The costumes are elaborate and colorful. The Manipuri dance contains both Lasya or the graceful dancing and the Thandava, the forceful dancing.The music is composed to Hindustani tunes or the North Indian tunes. Unlike Bharatha Natyam or Kuchipudi, these dances do not have any exaggerated movements, postures, or extrovert expressions, but a fine balance of hips and body. Tilting the head slightly, forming a rhythmic unison with hands, feet and the body, this dance style is a symbol of grace. However, the hand gestures or hasthas used in this dance style do overlap with Bharatha Natyam and Kuchipudi dance forms from south India.

Through years, the classical dance form, Manipuri has retained its heavenly beauty and rich content. This dance lives through its people as a vital part of their social, religious and spiritual existence. Their deep religious faith and strict discipline in dancing has contributed to the continuation and retention of such purity in this style. If guided by the set timing of the drum, helps manages the energy of the dancer.

Rules and regulations for the performance of the Indian dance made it an exact science and art, where nothing was left to the arbitrary whim of the dancer. Yet, it could be mastered so perfectly that each dancer's individuality and ability in expression, grace, technical knowledge and personality, emotional feeling and confidence, gave distinction to her/his performance.

Mohiniyattam, the dance form is said to have originated in Kerala. It is closely related to Bharatha Natyam of Tamil Nadu, which was originally called "Dasiyattam". Originated as the temple dance performed by Devadasis, it portrays feminine love in its myriad forms – carnal, devotional and maternal – with accent more on Lasya and Bhava (expressions). In the main items Cholkettu, Padavarnam and Padam, mudras (hand gestures) and facial expressions are more important than the rhythmic steps. Costumes and ornaments of Mohiniyattam have much in common with female characters of Koodiyattam and Kathakali.

Originally, Mohiniyattam was performed only in a temple's premises and royal courts. The first reference to Mohiniyattam is found in 'Vyavaharamala' composed by Mazhamangalam Narayanan Namboodiri, of 16th century AD. Major contributions to this art form were given by Maharaja Swathi Thirunal, Irayimman Thampi and Kuttikunju Thankachi.

Most of the dances of Mohiniyattam are similar to Bharatha Natyam and Kuchipudi, though subtle differences of style are obvious. The language used in the lyrics is a pleasant mixture of Malayalam and Sanskrit, known as Manipravalam. Formerly, the Padams were especially composed to include only Sringararasa (expressions of love). Now days, artists are using any classical or semi-classical compositions, even from other languages within India. The real beauty of Mohiniyattam comes through when mature ladies enact the romantic Padams specially written to present the Ashta Nayikas (eight heroines): *Swadheena Bharthruka, Khanditha, Abhisarika, Vipralabdha, Kalahandtharitha, Vasakasajja, Proshithabharthruka, and Viraholkhanditha.*

The accompaniments for Mohiniyattam are vocal, veena, venu, maddalam and Idakka. Other instruments are also not unusual. Primary emphasis is placed on gestures and facial expressions. The mudras (hand gestures) are almost always same as those employed in Kathakali. The artists try to enact the lyrics almost in its entirety, like in Kathakali. It is hoped, someday this beautiful style would be propagated as other dance styles.

Kathakali –This South Indian classical dance style is often confused with the name Kathak, a North Indian dance style. Kathakali is a classical dance-drama of Kerala in South India that dates from the 17th century and is rooted in Hindu mythology.

Kathakali actually means, "Story-Play", and it has been a highly specialized dance style for ages. This dance style has been considerably influenced by the old Sanskrit dramas of Kerala called Kudiyattam, and also Krishna Atam or the dramatic stories of Lord Krishna. The themes of these compositions were based on the stories of the Puranas with their beauty of parables and moral lessons.

The facial makeup and the elaborate costumes and dance movements of the kathakali dancers are awesome and fascinating. The movements are very powerful and hypnotic.

Kathakali is a harmonious combination of five forms of art:

1. Literature (Sahithyam)
2. Music (Sangeetham)
3. Painting (Chithram)
4. Acting (Natyam)
5. Dance (Nrithyam)

All the five forms of art have a very important place in this dance style. Its literature is poetic and dramatic. Like Bharatha Natyam and Kuchipudi, Kathakali dance style also composes its music using the Carnatic or Southern school of classical music.

To act, the use of the eyes and eyebrows is far more evolved and involved than in Bharatha Natyam or Kathak or any other school of the classical dance. Eyes and eyebrows are constantly used to aid the process of communication in the most effective manner with great intensity.

During the drama, the dancers do not speak, but they use varied hand movements known as 'Mudras' and mime to constitute a complete sign language. The movements are explosive, accompanied by a nonstop drumming that begins before the performance and lasts throughout the whole dance-drama.

This is Kerala's rich contribution to the Indian classical dances, drama and art. This unique dance form can be seen in mythological or classical Malayalam movies.

Kuchipudi – Simhanandini is the dance of Parashakthi or the supreme power represented in the form of a woman. This item is generally performed before starting the procession of the large vehicle called Rath, during the car festival (Rathosthavam) at the temples. Initially, the dancers describe the greatness of Parashakthi and pray for her compassion upon all as Mother Goddess and then they depict the destruction of the cruel demon Mahishasura. Finally, the dancer paints the picture of a lion on the rangoly powder (colorful powders) by her dancing feet followed by Simhanandini tal (beat). This beat is ancient and very difficult. The jathi (technique) contains 128 matras, including six types of rhythmic modes.

After the abolition of the Devdasi system at temples in 1939, dancers worked diligently to keep the dance dramas alive. Many groups ended splitting and became solo dancers. Many people who are settled outside India are playing an important role in bringing these dance dramas back to life. Due to the attractiveness of these dance dramas vs. solo dances, more and more dance dramas are being choreographed. It still leaves a lot of room for these ritual dances. It is hoped these dances will be learned by the younger artists, before the tradition dies.

As far as performance of Bharatha Natyam Arangetram is concerned, it is felt that the key to a successful arangetram is planning, and only planning. This planning includes many things such as dance practices, setting the date, finding a venue, invitation cards, budgets, ordering costumes, preparing for lunches and dinners, etc.

In the medieval period, Kathak dance form was promoted by the Muslim rulers. We hear of these performances in the courts of most of the Mughal rulers. In the south, temples, 'court' and other parts of the building provided an important stage for all dancers. Some rulers of the north like Wajid ali Shah was a great patron of music and dance and here the seeds of the Lucknow gharana or 'school of dance' was sown. In the modern period, we find maximum dance forms in the south Indian classical dance stream. They are Kucchipudi, Bharatnatyam, Mohiniatyam, Kathakali. On the eastern and architecture side, Odissi dance flourished greatly.

Well-known Dancers of Modern India are:

- Pt. Birju Maharaj,
- Pt. Shambhu Maharaj,
- Sitara Devi,
- Pt. Gopi Krishna,
- Pt. Lacchu Maharaj.
- Saroja Vaidyanathan,
- Padma Subhramaniam,
- Geeta Chandran,
- Kelucharan Mahapatra,
- Sanjukta Panigrahi,
- Kiran Sehgal,
- Madhavi Mudgal,
- Swapna Sundari,
- Satya Narayan Sarma,
- Raja Reddy,
- Radha Reddy,
- Sonal Mansingh,
- Bharata Matangamuni,
- Naradamuni,
- Pt. Sharangadeva,
- Pt. Somnath,
- Pt. Ahobala,
- Pt. Vyankatmakhi,
- Pt. Ramamatya,
- S.M. Tagore,
- Acharya K.C.D. Brihaspati.

In the last few decades, the status of dance as well as its performers has changed. Young people have started learning dance to enrich their personal qualities. In some of the schools, colleges and universities separate departments have been established for imparting training in dance. Several renowned classical dancers have been awarded national awards like the Padmashree and the Padmabhusan.

Throughout the different periods of history starting from the dancing figure found in the Indus valley civilization to the present, Indian people have expressed their joys and sorrows by singing and dancing through various art forms. This art form has been used to express their love, hatred, their aspirations and their struggle for survival which ultimately led to the enrichment of our culture.

Folk Dance:

Such is the impact of this aspect of globalisation that most forms of Indian music desperately try and conform to the successfully globalised Hindi film song. From the *Bihu* of Assam, to the *Biraha* of Uttar Pradesh and Bihar, most folk forms are undergoing a Bollywood makeover. On television channels catering to regional viewership, music videos provide ample proof of this homogenising which has undoubtedly had a tragic impact on the diverse forms of musical expression in the country. Music from Rajasthan and Punjab have for long found favour with popular taste, but even the music from these two states finds itself being sifted for tunes and song types that will conform to the norms of entertainment and industry as set out in a globalised world. Therefore, songs with slow tempo or complex rhythms are usually rejected and what is retained are the songs that can be converted into dance tracks with a primal beat.

Along with classical dance forms, folk dance also flourished. In most of the regions, the local dance form became very popular. Manipuri dance, Santhal dance, Rabindranath dance, drama, chhau, ras, gidda, bhangra, garba are some of the folk dances that have flourished in India. They are equally popular and have extreme acumen and innovation.

Practically every region of our country has developed their own rich tradition of folk dances. For example, the Bihu dance of Assam, Mask dance of Ladakh, Wangla of Meghalaya, Bhutia or Lepcha dance of Sikkim. Similarly we also have some dances which are called martial dances like Chholia of Uttranchal, Kalari paittu of Kerala, Thang-taa of Manipur among the more famous ones.

Changing trends in performing arts rarely manifest themselves with dramatic abruptness. More often than not, they creep up silently, diverting the flow of continuing traditions and practices stealthily but resolutely. As the relentless tidal wave of globalisation swept across the world in the last two decades, Indian performing arts too were swept, tossed high and hurled down, without many even noticing that some of the great rivers of performing traditions and systems had changed course or, at times, been reined in forcefully. Looking back on some of these changes, particularly in the sphere of Indian music, it may be worthwhile to begin by examining a few words, terms and phrases that provide clues to some of the many ways in which globalisation has impacted the performing arts in India.

Features of Folk Dances:

Generally people nourish a wrong notion as to the word 'folk', and perceive it as anything that relates, to village. But folk comprises of the common people irrespective of place urban or rural. folk dances are common man's dances.

The folk dances are simple, natural and spontaneous expression of every day theme and feelings. Language is colloquial dialect, dress simple and theatrical atmosphere spontaneous. Themes of folk dances relate to nature, every day activities and basic human joys and fears. Folk dances are a mixture of dialogue, dance, music, song, clowning moralizing and prayers. Audience participation is natural and common in folk dances.

Folk dances are primarily for the purpose of entertainment but they are also used for social, political, moral or religious purposes. Literate or illiterate, young or old, men or women all can easily identify themselves with this form. The emergence of powerful and glamorous electronic media and urban elite both have started affecting the purity of folk dances. There is need to protect these folk dances from vulgarization from them. Integrated approach should be practiced to create synergic effect by combining technology and traditional form of folk dance so as to keep the essence of folk-form intact.

Difference between Folk & Classical Dances

Following are some of the basic differences between Folk Dances and Classical Dances:

- Number of participants — Folk Dances are usually group dances where classical dances are primarily SOLO.
- Language — Unlike Classical scripts, language in folk dances is colloquial dialect.
- Classical dances use refined, developed and literary language.
- Dress — Elaborate dresses with high artifacts and ornamentation are used in classical dances. Simple, but colorful, evety day dresses are used in folk dances.
- Format — Natural original theatrical atmosphere is the key to the credibility and spontaneity of folk dances. Sophisticated, refined elaborate and artificial theatrical atmosphere exists in classical Dances.
- Theme — Classical dances usually have the stories from mythology or society, where as theme in folk dances moves around nature, agrarian activities and every days joys and sorrows.
- Audience participation — Because of the natural and spontaneous nature of folk dances, they allow, instigate and welcome the participation of audience. In case of classical dances, spectators can enjoy but cannot participate in the dance.

It is not surprising then, to find that traditional forms including classical, folk and tribal forms, which have enjoyed niche and regional following, have been slowly edged out towards extinction. In a nutshell, such is the impact of globalisation that the West, which not so long ago revered traditional Indian arts and music, albeit for their perceived spirituality and exoticism, is now increasingly becoming a consumer of Bollywood music!

Why is the classical Indian dance proper a solo dance? Factory-produced latex flowers can be compared with the dance styles that are suitable for group performances where the dancers perform identical movements at the same time. To achieve the perfect "synchronization," the movements have to be as plain ("perfect-shaped") as the latex orchids (or one of the 3 words "Dance" on the right). Live flowers are never perfect-shaped and never have "geometric" appearance. If you are half-blind, the easiest method of detecting latex flowers is to smell them. No fragrance, no rasa. "Recakas impearl the Nritta, make it shine and cause complete aesthetic satisfaction," says Padma Subrahmanyam. Recakas are like spices in food. Well, the food has to be bland enough to please the western palate.

Classical dances are based fully or partly on the principles and techniques embodied in the ancient Hindu scriptures and technical texts on dance and allied arts. The earliest of these known scripts is Bharatha's Natya Shastra believed to have been written around the 2nd. century B.C. Most of the prevailing systems of classical dancing governed by elaborate techniques with a high degree of refinement have had their origin in the dances of the common people.

A classical art evolves over a long period of time. It is not created overnight. Its technique is structured and stylized, predetermined and codified, and its projection conforms to a particular pattern. Emotion is not impulsive but is ruled by the intellect. The technique can only be imbibed through instruction.

It has also stood the test of time. It is dance that stems from the inspiration and the work of the individual rather than the collective; it is dance that not only affords appeal to the senses but also stimulates the intelligence of the performer and spectator alike.

On the other hand, folk dances express the mood of the moment, the celebration of birth, a harvest, or a festival. It is usually group effort and often the performers can imbibe the technique in less time as it is comparatively simpler. Folk dances all over the world have become more sophisticated, more structured and more complicated with elaborate group choreography, but its projection is spontaneous and rarely associated or driven by literary instruction like classical dance. Folk dance forms such as

Bhangra, Garba, are specific to a region, the language is also specific to that region and songs are traditional tunes sung by the common people of the region.

Classical dance in India is particularly characterized by an oral tradition of instruction from the guru or teacher to the sishya or disciple, known as the guru-sishya parampara which has kept various intricate arts alive for thousands of years.

The difference between classical dancing and folk dancing is mainly that there is a deliberate attempt at artistry in the former. Sophistication along the norms of the scriptures of advance theories on dance and dramaturgy are strictly adhered to. The concept of portraying emotion, the grace of the individual dances and the virtuosity of the isolated poses are all important in classical dances. Emphasis has been given to different aspects of the dance, namely pure bodily movement, aids to dance like theme, song, instrumental music, the expression of emotions, moods and sentiments, the dress, ornaments, makeup and the stage.

India has a rich variety of folk dances. They are highly developed and reflect the temperaments and moods of the localities in music and costume. Nature silently and unobstrusively has moulded these dances just as the lives of people who dance them. Religious colouring is seen in almost all of these folk dances, even in those performed in connection with harvests, sowing of seeds, festivals etc., so much so that their secular nature is always at doubt. There is difficulty in classifying these dances as social, religious and martial.

Many of these dances are performed by man alone, some exclusively by women. There are also dances in which men and women perform together. Most of folk dances are performed to the accompaniment of songs which are sung by the dancers themselves or occasionally by a group of musicians. Some dances are performed to the accompaniment of musical instruments only.

In several dances, the performers form a circle and clap as they dance. Sometimes, instead of clapping they strike small sticks which they hold in their hands. The costumes and ornaments are peculiar to the places to which they belong. The eloquent, effortless ease which the dances are executed and the overwhelming buoyancy of spirit are wonderful. In these folk dances, there is no difference between the performers and the audience. Almost all of these folk dances are simple but beneath this simplicity is a profundity of conception and directness of expression which are of high artistic order.

Indian folk dances are full of variation and multiplicity in terms of themes, forms, and styles. Folk dances continue to be a distinct category that can be characterized by the overwhelming spontaneity of participation without an artificial barrier between the actors, performers and the audience.

Folk dances play an important role and provide the best medium to express the feelings and emotions to common man. Indian folk dances are roughly classified as per the states boundaries, e.g., Bhangra is a famous folk dance of Punjab, performed only by males. Dashavatra is a folk art of Goa & Konkan region that describes the ten incarnations of Lord Vishnu.

These folk dance forms have contributed significantly in the development of the classical dance forms of the country too. Therefore, India has a large number of folk dances, with different regions of the country having their own set of dances. Folk dances are particularly prevalent in tribal, rural or comparatively less developed areas, where dance is regarded as an integral part of their lives.

Folk dances are dances of ordinary people and mostly are traditional in nature. Depending upon customs, every village has its own folk dances performed on specific occasions such as the birth of a child, to celebrate the arrival of new seasons, weddings and festivals. Therefore, folk dances can be classified, as harvest dances, celebration of arriving season, ceremony-based dance such as wedding dances, dances that are performed exclusively to show joy and happiness, ritualistic dance, etc.

In many cultures, the term ethnic dance or traditional dance is used to indicate folk dances. Although every single term has its own context for interpretation, the latter terms may encompass significance of ceremonial dances.

The terms ethnic and traditional are used when it is required to emphasize the cultural roots reflected from that particular dance. In this sense, nearly all folk dances are ethnic ones. But some dances form cross ethnic boundaries such as Kuravanji, a folk dance of Tamil Nadu which originated in the neighboring state of Andhra Pradesh and still termed as Folk one. However, not all-ethnic dances are folk ones. The simplest example of these are ritual dances or dances of ritual origin.

There is no such separate genre as folk dancing. Rather, there is a large body of unrelated non-classical dance forms. The only thing common among these dance forms is their origin in rural areas.

It may be academically desirable to separate tribal from simple folk dances, however this is generally not done. Artists do not concern themselves with these academic matters. Indian folk and tribal dances are product of different socio-economic set up and traditions of that particular region. The skill and style, steps of the dances influence the final performance of the dance in each case.

It would be more appropriate to categorize these folk dances into two categories: folk and tribal. The difference between the two is cultural. Folk dances are the rural extensions of the larger Indian population. Examples are the Bhangra of Punjab and the Garba of Gujrath. However, the tribal dances are dances by India‘s aboriginal populations. These people, known as adivasi, have a culture, which is very different from the larger Indian population. So, attempting to relate Indian tribal dances with Indian folk dances is not right.

It is very usual, that on special occasion, the villagers will gather, sing and dance, accompanying themselves on a variety of folk instruments for gaining music. Such special occasions include harvesting, planting, marriages and religious holidays, etc.

It would be more correct to divide these folk dances into two categories: folk and tribal. The difference between the two is cultural. Folk dances are the rural extensions of the larger Indian population. Examples are the Bhangra and the Garba. However, the tribal dances are performed by India's aboriginal populations.

These people, known as adivasi, have a culture which is very distinct from the larger Indian population.

The following is a very short and incomplete list of folk and tribal dances:

- Bihu is a folk dance from Assam. It is a very brisk and aggressive dance performed by both boys and girls.
- Bagurumba is a folk dance from Assam. It is performed by the Bodos and is known for its colourful attire.
- Bhangra is a folk dance from the Northwest Indian state of Punjab. It is a lively, powerful dance.
- Chah Baganar Jumur Nach is a dance from Assam. It is a dance of the tea gardens.
- Changu dance is a folk dance found in Odissa and Andhra Pradesh. It derives its name from the changu, which is a simple tambourine (daf) that is used to accompany this dance.
- Daankara is a stick dance, similar in some ways to the dandiaya raas of Gujarat. However, the daankar is also performed in Punjab.
- Dandaria is a folk dance of Andhra Pradesh.
- Dasakathia is a folk theatre of Odissa. It is performed by a pair of performers who entertain the audience with dance, songs, and stories.
- Dhamal is a folk dance of Punjab as well as of Andhra Pradesh.
- Gair is a dance of Rajasthan. It is performed by groups of dancers moving in and out with an almost military precision.
- Garba is a folk dance from Gujarat. It is traditionally danced at marriages and during the time of Navaratri festivals.
- Gatka is a folk dance utilising swords, daggers, or sticks performed in the Punjab.
- Geendad is a folk dance of Rajasthan. It is very similar to the Gair.
- Ghoomar is a folk dance of Rajasthan. It derives its name from its characteristic pirouettes.
- Ghanta Patua is a folk dance of Odissa. Its name is derived from the large brass gongs known as ghanta. It is performed in the Hindu month of Chaitra. This dance is most notable because it is performed on stilts.
- Giddha is a folk dance of Punjab, generally performed by women.
- Gobbi a folk dance of Andhra Pradesh.

- Jhoomar is a dance of the Mundas and Mahantas of Odissa.
- Jhuma a slow version of bhangra performed at weddings and other festive events.
- Julli is a folk dance performed in Punjab that is done sitting down.
- Kacchhi Ghodhi is a folk dance of Rajasthan that is performed with a dummy horse.
- Kandhei
- Kavadi is a folk dance of Tamil Nadu. It is played with a wooden pole upon which are tied two pots. The stick is then balanced upon the shoulder.
- Karagam is a folk dance of Tamil Nadu. It is played with a pot balanced on the head.
- Kela Keluni is a dance performed by the Kelas of Odissa.
- Kikli is a women's folk dance of the Punjab.
- Kushan is a folk theatre of Bangladesh and West Bengal.
- Laathi Nauch is a folk dance of North-East India and Bangladesh. This was originally based upon a system of martial arts that uses large sticks (laathi). However, in some cases, it has evolved into a game (Lathi Khelna) or a dance (Laathi Nauch).
- Luddi is a very characteristic form of Bhangra.
- Mathuri is a folk dance of Andhra Pradesh.
- Raas is a folk dance from Gujarat. It is traditionally danced at marriages and during the time of Navaratra festivals.
- Saami is a women's folk dance of the Punjab.
- Sakhi Nata is the puppet dance of Odissa.
- Terahtali is a folk dance of Rajasthan. It is performed by women while they are seated.
- Therukoothu is a folk theatre from the south Indian state of Tamil Nadu.
- Yaksha Gana is a folk theatre from the south Indian state of Karnatika.

Musical Instruments used to accompany Folk Dances:

Andelu;	Banam;	Bansuri;
Bombashi;	Charchari;	Chenda;
Chikara;	Chimpta;	Daf (Duf, Daphu, Daffali);
Damaru;	Dramyen;	Dhad;

Dhak (Daklu); Dhol; Dholak;
Dholki (Nal); Diggi; Dotar ;
Dota (Dotora); Ektar; GetchuVadyam
(Gettuvadyam); Ghatam; Ghungharu;
Goga Dhol; Gol Kathi (Dancing Stick);
Gopichand(ektar); Gummeta (Dakki, Budike);
Harmonium; Idakka and Udaku (Udakai);
Jaspuria; Jhorka & Korka; Kamancha;
Kanjira; Kartal; Kasht Tarang;
Katho (Khomok); Kend; Khol (Mridang);
Madar; Madda; Manjira;
Mukhavina; Murchang; Nagada;
Nissan, Mawaloti, or Lohati; Nout;
Ottu; Pena (a.k.a. Bana); Phara;
Pung; Pungi; Rabab (Kabuli Rabab);
Ravanhasta; Sambal; Santur;
Sarangi; Saringda; Shankh;
Shehnai; Shuddha Madalam;
Tamak; Tasha; Thanthi Panai;
Timki; Tumbak; Tuntuna (Chohokhode);
Urumili.

Drama:

The first form of Indian theatre was the Sanskrit theatre. Indigeneous tradition as well as modern research trace the origin of Indian drama to the Vedas. Drama is a performing art, which has also been practised since times immemorial. Drama could spring from a child's play. The child enacts, mimics, and caricates which was definitely the beginning of drama. In the Ramayana we hear of drama troupes of women while Kautilyas Arthshastra mentions musicians, dancers and dramatic shows.

Since early times, mythological stories of war between the gods, goddesses and the devils is known. Bharata wrote Natyashastra and created the plays known as Asura Parajaya and Amrit Manthan. *Natyashastra* is one of the greatest texts written in the field of drama and other performing arts. *Natyashastra* makes distinctions between ten kinds of plays. An "act" (*anka*) is generally understood as a cohesive dramatization of events that occur within the course of a day. However, the *Natyashastra* does not demand that these events run contiguously.

The two principal genres of Sanskrit drama include five to ten acts each.

The *Nataka* corresponds most closely with Tragedy, although there are some distinct differences. As in Tragedy, the characters of *Natakas* are divine-gods and demons – and royalty, and stories are not invented but taken from "history" as found in the Mahabharata and the Ramayana. *Natakas* concern stories of cosmic import, reiterating the divine roles of kings and sages of myth.

Natakas do not end badly. Where the Tragic hero falls, the hero of a *Nataka* triumphs. Sanskrit plays, in general, including *Natakas*, affirm a celestial order that sustains a temporal order that serves the cosmic good. Kalidasa's *Shakuntala* is the best known example of *Nataka*.

Prakarana, the other principal category that includes five to ten acts, roughly corresponds with Aristotelian comedy. *Prakarana* plays concern middle-class characters who are invented by the playwright. The stories take place outside of palaces and royal circles, in the lanes and houses of town, and are concerned with middle-class interests in money, love, legal justice, and bourgeois honor. With plots hanging on the complications of mistaken identities, petty revenge, theft, and political intrigue, *Prakarana* plays also end happily. At least, like *Natakas*, *Prakaranas* affirm the identities of their middle-class heroes, and their place in a permanent cosmic order. Shudraka's *Mrcchakatika* (*Little Clay Cart*) is the best known example of *Prakarana*.

The Samavakara and *Ihamrga*, for instance, use fewer than five acts, and exclusively concern divine characters. Furthermore, *Ihamrga* plays only concern war over a woman.

The *Vyayoga* and *Anka* plays are one-acts, concerned only with the events of a single day. The *Anka* is to revolve around sorrow, and is expected to involve, especially, the lamentation of female characters. Bhasa's *Urubhangam* may be an example of *Anka*.

It is not very correct to say that ancient Indian literature includes only the religious classics of Hinduism, Buddhism and Jainism. Jain narrative literature in the Prakrit language is full of erotic stories and realism. The next epoch is that of the great Bhasa who wrote plays based on the stories of Udayana, the Ramayana and Mahabharata, Swapana Vasabdatta being his masterpiece. In the second century B.C. Patanjali's Mahabhasya refers to several aspects of drama i.e. the actors, the music, the stage, rasa in the performances called Kamsavadha and Balibandha.

Vedas give importance to yajna (sacrifice). Purusa sukta of the Rigveda (10.90) describes the whole creation as a yajna extended by the divine forces of nature. Etymologically yajna means the worship of the divine, coordination and giving (sacrifice). These three elements together, vision, coordination and giving provide a basic paradigm for any creative act.

While referring to drama, Bharata has mentioned nat (male artists), and nati (female artist), music, dance, musical instruments, dialogues, themes and stage. Thus, we find that drama achieved a great level of perfection during the age of Bharata. For Bharata, drama is a perfect means of communication. He also started the concept of an enclosed area for drama. There is mention of a community called shailoosh which had professional drama companies.

The practice of singing heroic tales became popular. As a result, professional singers called kushilavas came into existence. Sanskrit dramas were performed mostly in this language. However, characters belonging to *Kamasutra*, Kalidasa's *Abhijnan Shakuntalam* were all written in Sanskrit and were significant plays of those times.

In the context of drama, two types developed the classic drama, which had intricacies of theme and subtle nuances of dramatic traits and folk theatre. It was of spontaneous and extempore nature. Local dialect was used in folk theatre, and hence in different provinces, many types of folk theatres developed. Even in Sanskrit dramas, local dialect was used in case of common folks and women formed part of any drama. Acting with accompaniment of music and dance was the popular practice. Many names were given to the forms of folk theatre in different provinces.

Two types of drama developed i.e. the classic drama, which had intricacies of theme and subtle nuances of dramatic traits and folk theatre. It was of spontaneous and extempore nature. Local dialect was used in folk theatre and hence in different provinces many types of folk theatres developed. Acting with accompaniment of music and dance was the popular practice. Instruments like dhol, kartal, manjira, khanjira were some props used in folk theatre.

The medieval period was rich in music and dance but theatre did not get much prominence.

However, Wajid Ali Shah, a great patron of art was also an important patron of drama. He enthused artists to participate in theatre and supported them. In the southern region, folk theatre with the use of local dialects was more popular.

With the advent of the British, the country changed the character of the society. In the eighteenth century a theatre was established in Calcutta by an Englishman. Vidyasundar, a popular drama of the medieval period, was influenced by jatra. Geet Govinda, an exemplary work by the great poet Jayadev, weaved stories of Krishna in kirtania natak and jatra style. Side by side, folk theatre like jatra, nautanki, khyal (Rajasthani folk), and naach also flourished. Dramas began to depict tragedies, comedies and the complexities of urban life. Dramas were now written in different regional languages. The stages evolved by educated Indians were different from traditional open air theatre. The stages now had rolling curtains and change of scenes. A Parsi company founded in Bombay showed that theatre could be used for commercial purposes. A similar situation appeared in the case of writing of drama. A Russian named Horasim Lebedev founded a Bengali theatre which marked the beginning of modern Indian theatre in India. English drama, especially by Shakespeare, influenced Indian drama.

At present, a lot of experiments are taking place in the field of drama. Western influences are very clear in the works of Shambhu Mitra, Feisal Alkazi, Badal Sarkar, Vijay Tendulkar and others.

For the content and thematic aspect of dance and drama, we must examine the works of creative literature. The most important literary event, which influenced not only dance and drama but painting also, was the composition of Jayadeva's Gita-Govinda in the 13th century. Its great impact can be seen on dance and drama forms all over India – from Manipur and Assam in the east to Gujarat in the west; from Mathura and Vrindavan in the North, to Tamil Nadu and Kerala in the South.

Presently drama are flourishing in the country. National School of Drama and many Natak Academies are also working hard to protect, develop and popularize drama at the national and even international level.

CINEMA

Dhundiraj Govind Phalke (1870-1944), affectionately called Dadasaheb Phalke, is considered as the 'father of Indian Cinema'. Central in Phalke's career as a filmmaker was his fervent belief in the nationalistic philosophy of swadeshi, which advocated that Indians should take charge of their own economy in the perspective of future independence.

His first production 'Raja Harishchandra' was screened at Coronation Cinema in Mumbai on 3 May, 1913 marking the beginning of Indian cinema. Regarded as the father of the Indian cinema, Phalke went on to make several silent films but became the first casualty when the silent era passed.

Inspired from an imported film – Life of Christ – Phalke started mentally visualising the images of Indian gods and goddesses. What really obsessed him was the desire to see Indian images on the screen in a purely Swadeshi venture. He fixed up a studio in Dadar Main Road, wrote the scenario, erected the set and started shooting for his first venture Raja Harishchandra in 1912. The first full-length story film of Phalke was completed in

1912 and released at the Coronation cinema on April 21, 1913, for special invitees and members of the Press. The film was widely acclaimed by one and all and proved to be a great success.

While Amirt Manthan (1934) opposed the senseless violence of Hindu rituals, Dharmatama (1935) dealt with Brahmanical orthodoxy and caste system. Originally titled Mahatma, the film was entirely banned by the colonial censor on the ground that it treated a sacred subject irreverently and dealt with controversial politics. Amarjyoti (1936) was an allegory on the oppression of women in which the protagonist seeks revenge. It could perhaps be called the first women's lib film in India.

In the middle of the Second World War in 1945 came 'Kismet' starring Ashok Kumar which became one of the biggest hits in the history of Indian cinema. It came with some bold themes – the first anti-hero and an unmarried pregnancy. It clearly showed that the filmmakers of the era were bolder than the times in which they were living in. By the 1940s, the winning formula at the Box Office had been thought – songs, dance, drama and fantasy.

A close relationship between epic consciousness and the art of cinema was established. It was against this backdrop that filmmakers like V. Shantaram, Bimal Roy, Raj Kapoor and Mehboob Khan made their films.

Among the leading film-makers of Mumbai during the forties, V. Shantaram was arguably the most innovative and ambitious. From his first talkie Ayodhya ka Raja (1932) to Admi (1939), it was clear that he was a filmmaker with a distinct style and social concern whose films generated wide discussion and debate. He dealt with issues like caste system, religious bigotry and women's rights. Even when Shantaram took up stories from the past, he used these as parables to highlight contemporary situations.

Tamil cinema emerged as a veritable entertainment industry in 1929 with the creation of General Picture Corporation in Madras (Chennai). Most of the Tamil films produced were multilingual productions, with versions in Telugu, Malayalam and

Kannada until film production units were established in Hyderabad, Trivandrum and Bangalore. The first talkie of South India, Srinivas Kalyanam was made by A. Narayanan in 1934.

Madan Theatres of Calcutta produced Shirin Farhad and Laila Majnu (1931) – well composed and recorded musicals. Both films replete with songs had a tremendous impact on the audience and can be said to have established the unshakeable hold of songs on our films.

Fifties saw the rise of great directors like Mehboob, Bimal Roy, Guru Dutt and Raj Kapoor who changed the fate of Indian cinema. These directors entered the film industry during the 1930s and '40s, which were traumatic years for the Indian people. The fight for independence, famines, changing social mores, global fight against fascism all contributed to the ethos in which the directors grew up.

Raj Kapoor's 'Awara', the story about a man caught in the centre of a nature Vs nurture debate brought him immense glory. The film went on to become not just a national but international success, especially in the then USSR. The film also got nominated in the Cannes film fest in 1943. The actor filmmaker effectively used Chaplin's character (the one he used in Awara) in later films like 'Shri 420'.

The golden period also produced some of India's most critically acclaimed films and memorable actors of all time. Among those in Bollywood's hall of fame are Guru Dutt, Mehboob Khan, Balraj Sahani, Nargis, Bimal Roy, Meena Kumari, Madhubala and Dilip Kumar.

Changing social norms and changing economies influenced movies and the companies that made them. In the 70's, a genre was born – masala movie. Masala films were the demand of the time. The genre promised instant attraction and had great entertainment value.

While Indian commercial cinema enjoyed popularity among movie-goers, Indian art cinema did not go unnoticed. Adoor Gopalakrishnan, Ritwik Ghatak, Aravindan, Satyajit Ray, Shaji

Karun and several other art film directors were making movies that gave India international fame and glory. This was Bollywood's prime period, a time when director Ramesh Sippy gave us his iconoclastic 'Sholay' (1975).

80's saw the emergence of several woman directors such as Aparna Sen, Prema Karnath and Meera Nair. And then in 90's, it was a mixed genre of romantic, thrillers, action and comedy films. A stark upgrade can be seen on the canvas as technology gifted the industry Dolby digital sound effects, advanced special effects, choreography and international appeal. Indian cinema finally found global mass appeal at the turn of the 21st century. As the world became a global village, the industry reached out further to international audiences.

Such is the impact of globalisation that the West, which not so long ago revered traditional Indian arts and music, is now increasingly becoming a consumer of Bollywood music.

Other than in academic discussions, performing arts in India and its practitioners are today referred to most commonly as being part of the "entertainment industry." This may seem innocuous enough to some, but the usage of the term and its passive acceptance in most circles definitely indicate a paradigm shift in the manner in which the arts are viewed by society at large.

That today the arts must entertain and amuse in the manner defined by showbiz, and that they must form part of organised industry is the clear and unambiguous message conveyed by this shift. For creators and artistes who, in an ideal world, create art driven by an artistic urge or by that inexplicable creative charge that propels artistes towards their respective forms of expression, this shift from being an individual artiste or part of an artistic community, to being absorbed into or discarded by the politics and commerce of the entertainment industry, has had a far-reaching impact.

In India, various facets of performing arts are all pervading bringing colour and joy to numerous festivals and ceremonies, and reaffirming the faith of the people in their heritage.The performing arts is the art form which uses the artist's own bodily gestures, facial expressions, and presence as a medium to create some physical art object.

Performing arts has a well-placed status in the culture and tradition of Indian society. Indian performing arts are well acclaimed by people from across the globe. Love, humor, pathos, anger, heroism, terror, disgust, wonder and serenity are the nava rasas or nine basic emotions, which are fundamental to all Indian aesthetics. Based on the nava rasas or the nine basic emotions, the Indian performing arts exist.

Based in Pembroke Pines, Florida, the Association of the Performing Arts of India (APAI) was formed to preserve and promote Indian Classical music and dance through concerts, classes and lecture-demonstrations of Indian Classical music and dances. Since 1998, APAI has been the sole organization in the South Florida region to consistently host artistes of major international stature within the realm of Indian Classical music and dance, while also serving the needs of the local community through educational outreach.

In the last fifteen years, in furtherance of the goal to educate Indian community about the Indian Classical music and dance, APAI has presented fifty plus concerts and many lecture-demonstrations to schools, libraries, universities and community colleges. January through April 2009, a course was offered on Indian Classical Dance - "*Bharat Natyam*" - at Florida Atlantic University, Boca Raton, Florida.

15

Geography and Tourism

Tourism is described by Heeley 'as being an amorphous, archaic and monstrously large focus of enquiry.' Jafari defines tourism as 'the study of man away from his usual habitat, of the industry which responds to his needs, and the impacts that both he and the industry have on the hosts' socio-cultural, economical and physical environments. Finally, tourism may be defined in terms of particular activities selected by choice and undertaken outside the home environment. Tourism may or may not involve overnight stays away from home. It has also been argued that tourism is highly multi-disciplinary and touches almost every aspect of man and society.

Geography can be described as a measurement or analysis of the location of customers. Proximity to major customer groups is often important to a retail travel agency. Most outlets draw the primary portion of their clients from their surrounding communities. In analyzing the geographic distribution of its customer base, the agency seeks the answers to the following questions: exactly where do the agency's clients come from? What region? What city clients come from? What section of the city or town? In recent years, the population of affluent city dwellers in many areas has shifted lives but also where it works. If business clients who live in a suburb work in a different city, it is of little value to the market commercial travel during working hours in the suburb where they live. The Northeast and Middle Atlantic

States are growing less rapidly than the Pacific and Mountain states. The most rapid population growth is in the Sun Belt.

It is a well known fact that the general tourism objectives are holiday, relaxation, entertainment and fun, curiosity, adventure, etc. However for some tourists the specific objectives are, to name a few, sea, hill resorts winter sports, wild-like areas, hiking, sports of scenic beauty, and the like.

Undoubtedly, the desire to know and see the unseen regions of the world is as old as human civilization itself. Travellers, voyagers, expeditionists, pilgrims, preachers, etc. all have been in a way precursors of the modern tourist. Nevertheless, a close relationship between geography and tourism is something of recent origin.

Untill the 17th century, mountains were feared and despised by Europeans as uncivilized, inhospitable, and dangerous regions that had been forsaken by God. Now it is not uncommon to witness the advertisements like "Visit our resort lodge/hotel with the windswept Mountain Wilderness Area at your doorstep". The tourist is attracted by the thought of being close to a real science beauty without incurring extra costs. It seems to be one of the products of the tremendous developments which took place in the field of geography during the two World War periods.

Tourism now is more and more related to spatial conditions. Geography, therefore plays a very important role in the spatial interplay of tourist demand and satisfaction. It is closely related to the structure, form, use and conservation of landscape. The spatial distribution of innumerable natural objects, the various physical and cultural phenomena and man's urge to see and experience them at leisure in order to derive pleasure bring tourism in closer contact with geography.

There are regions with lofty and snow-clad mountains, vast stretches of green gassy plains, dense forests, leafless sandy deserts, expansive swamps, the lands of midnight and rising sun, morning calm, active volcanoes, thick fog. scorching heat and perennial snow. Each of them arouses human curiosity, gigantic waterfalls, huge lakes, expansive glaciers, meandering rivers, cascading streams, gorgeous valleys, sunny beaches etc. are such creatings of nature which throw challenge to human genius and provide opportunities to pleasure seekers.

Way, where and route are the things which oblige a tourist to think about geography. However, one need not be a professional geographer. Geography is not a subject which is to be crammed. Every one is expected to be aware of some broad concepts of geography. A tourist should definitely know, for example, places where earthquakes are frequent, areas of landscape, areas of strong wind, etc.

It would not be wrong to say that birth of tourism in Europe was mainly due to love for nature. People wanted to escape from the humdrum of urban life. Even scientists were enamoured by nature. Saints in India found peace in the caves of Himalyas. Poets like Wordsworth were attracted by nature. One finds solace there. Geography can be equated with nature or physical geography with which man is always attached Going out to enjoy nature not for any monetary gains or business but simply to relax and enjoy is fast becoming the order of the day.

The surface of the earth is not the same everywhere. There are high mountains, flat plains, sandy deserts, swampy regions and rocky plateaus. Also, there are different types of climates in different parts of the world. There are regions of very high and very low temperatures and lands where rainfall is a daily affair as also regions where not a single raindrop falls for years and years together. There are regions of healthy as well as unhealthy climates. Nature has endowed the earth with vast forest, mineral and marine resources though unevenly distributed.

All these facts arouse man's inquisitiveness and a strong desire to see and enjoy them. One may like mountain or sea shore or desert, but nature is always at the back of every person. Persons surrounded by immense greenery like to visit deserts to see sand dunes or nights of the sands while those from hot tropical areas love to visit and enjoy the colder ice-capped land scape, and so on. At the same time, degree of enjoyment may differ from tourist to tourist.

Some may keep the memories for a long time, while for others it may be a short lived feature. But in such type of tourism one has to move in a very organised and planned way especially in regard to the programme, itinerary, routes, availability of funds, etc. In the shortest time, one would like to cover the longest route.

Every tourist has ones own category, own likes and dislikes. There can be two possible major categories of tourists, namely, tourists of a developed country, and those of an underdeveloped country. Tourists from developed countries by and large, like to go for natural beauty whereas an underdeveloped country tourist would like to see industrial and other advancements of a particular country. One may like or dislike, however, every tourist sees the area of natural beauty in way or the other.

Different geographical tourist sites and the purpose or a particular desire to fulfil which a tourist visits them can be categorized as:

> Mountains providing scenic beauty, grandeur of nature; hiking expeditions; lakes and peaks; health resorts; winter sports; summer hill resorts; hill forts and castles and above all snow; streamlined coasts with breathtaking beaches providing facilities for sea–sports; sunbathing and marine parks; grand rivers offering radiant canyons, gorges; waterfalls; and the pleasure of boating and enjoying the turbulent waters; while the vast, deserts with their lost ruins and dune landscapes. Furthermore, splendid glaciers offering a variety of snow sports; rich foresets with abundant, wild life; and the exotic savannas with lovely game sanctuaries and adventurous safaris are just to name a few.

The matrimony of geography with tourism is wide and varied and its applications numerous. A new place can adversely affect the biorhythm of a tourist. Therefore, his tour programme should he so designed so as to allow temporary dislocations and yet maintains the rhythm of his biological being.

Apart from the enjoyment excitement that a tourist looks forward to, he should also keep in mind some relevant information of practical wisdom which can be of immense help in making his trip successful. For instance, while travelling abroad he should be aware of the change in time and concepts of standard and zone times. For this he should refer to a world time chart and also plan his excursion in such a way so as to utilize the maximum available day time. Besides, the abrupt changes of the clock, a tourist should also be ready to face severe changes in the physical and cultural environment of the new places and hence requires caution in selecting his dietry items.

The geographical knowledge of a place is of immense relevance to the very concept of tourism, be it local or global, and for a tourist to be geographically aware of the place being visited by him, the art of map reading and interpretting is a must. He should be well equipped with the knowledge of the fundamentals of map reading like, the scale of the map, its orientation and grid reference besides the conventional map symbols. The immense growth in tourism during the past few decades has resulted into the availability of tourist map classified as maps of specific places and the regional maps. The maps related to the specific places give varied information pertaining to the locations of airport, railway station, bus and taxi stand, star hotels, banks, medical centres, PT and places of interest, besides the brief outlines of history. The regional maps, on the other hand, are meant to acquaint the tourists with air, rail, road linkages and distances between places, roadside amenities like petrol stations, wayside motels; quality of roads, railway; classified symbols for places of interest; main urban centres with overnight stay facilities.

The geographical site tourism offering numerous exciting extravaganzas has become so popular as to cause unacceptable degradation of the natural environment. The tourists in numbers acceptable to a profit-minded entrepreneur would likely destory any vestige of a "natural", "wild", or "primeval" environment. More often than not people cannot distinguish between a truly natural and a natural-appearing environment and even if they do, the difference is not very important to them.

Hence, efforts are on to artificially created geographical sites which not only provide an excellent substitute and accommodate larger numbers of tourists but also help a great deal in preventing disastrous effects. Such sites, if carefully planned, designed, constructed and maintained coupled with prohibition on activities like camping and open fires, can host a surprisingly large number of day hikers with a negligible negative impact on the physical environment.

The geographical site tourism besides providing the tourist some enchanting enjoyment, adventure and luxury also inflicts on him some obvious additional costs which can be mental, physical as well as monetary. Possibly the greatest cost that he may have to bear would be the hard, unremitting labour of walking, riding, or paddling, a lower level of comfort, lack of sanitary facilities and nearly continuousl exposure to some severe climatic extremities like cold, heat, rains, insects and other harsh environmental elements.

Thus, it can arguably be concluded that the utility of the alloyage of geography and tourism is multifaceted. Tourism can not only be seen as an industry for profit-making but also as an important and unmatched source of bringing into light the geographical heritage of low profile places coupled with adventure, recreation, attractiveness, compatibility and a modern sense of peregrination.

16

Buddhist Circuits

Introduction

Buddhist Circuits means a pilgrimage to all the important places attached with Lord Buddha and Buddhism. Buddhism has the strength and power to transform the lives of people of all walks of life forever. In this regard, the efforts made towards legendary commitment to Buddhism by King Ashoka cannot be forgotten. Buddhism travelled to Sri Lanka, Nepal, Bhutan, Tibet and the countries of South East Asia, even to far-flung Central Asia, China and Japan, under the umbrella of royal patronage and the dedication of its vast community of monks, teachers and artists.

Buddhism is embodied in the concept of the four noble truths and the three jewels (Buddha, Dharma, Sangha) via the eight-fold path to salvation and peace. Anticipating his death in his 80th year, Buddha urged his followers, especially his chosen disciples, to continue his work after his imminent Mahaparnirvana – the attaining of nirvana (enlightenment). As a reminder of his difficult journey and its ultimate goal, he prevailed upon them to visit the four important places that were the cornerstones of his great journey – Lumbini, Bodhgaya, Sarnath, and Kushinagar.

The spread of Buddhism down the centuries was to leave in its wake a wealth of symbolic structures, including sculpted caves, stupas (relic shrines), chaityas (prayer halls) viharas (monasteries), mahaviharas (universities) and numerous art forms and religious literature. Pilgrim tourists want to have myriad experiences of significant places important for Lord Buddha's birth, his teachings, spiritual struggle, attainment of enlightenment, great meditations, and message of peace and non-violence, both in Nepal and India.

The Buddhist Circuits are the places of all high significance holy sites of Buddhism; where Lord Buddha was born, attained Enlightenment, preached first sermon and reached nirvana.

In this regard Lumbini, Bodhgaya, Sarnath and Kushinagar are the primary pilgrimage places of Buddhist Circuits associated with the life and teachings of the Lord Buddha. There are numerous other sites where the Buddha and the saints that followed travelled during his life after his transformation, which are held in deep veneration. Visitors can travel through this Buddhist Circuit today, to savor the splendid beauty and great appeal of Buddhism.

The greatest impetus to Buddha's teachings came from the Indian King Ashoka who went on a great pilgrimage visiting the important sites that are directly associated with his life, in the footsteps of Lord Buddha. Primary amongst these holy places are Lumbini in Nepal, and Bodhgaya, Sarnath and Kushinagar in India. There are other places of lesser significance on the footsteps of Lord Buddha visitor circuit associated closely with Buddha's life. Amongst these are Buddha's monsoon retreats of Vaishali, Rajgir and Sravastii in India, and his early home at Tilaurakot in Kapilavastu Nepal. A discussion on some of them follows.

Vaishali:

Vaishali is also known as Vesali. Five years after the Enlightenment in Bodh Gaya, Lord Buddha came to Vaishali, the capital of one of the first republican states in the Ganga. Vaishali is bound by the hills of Nepal on the north and the river Gandak on the west. The Buddha preached his last sermon before his death at Vaishali in Bihar, 60 km away from its capital Patna. It was here that he told his disciple Ananda about his imminent demise. The Second Buddhist Council was held in Vaishala about 110 years later.

Nalanda:

In the 5th century CE, a monastic university was established at Nalanda that was eventually to develop into the greatest ancient centre of Buddhist learning. Students from China and Korea, Sri Lanka and Indonesia and from all regions of India came to Nalanda to study. Buddha gave his first sermon at Sarnath after achieving enlightenment, about 10 km from the ancient holy city of Varanasi. The sermon, setting in motion the wheel of the teaching (*dharamchakrapravartna*) revealed to his followers the four noble truths, the concept of the three jewels of Buddha, Dharma and Sangha via the eight fold path, for inner peace and enlightenment. It was here that the Buddha established his first disciples (*sangha*) to promote his new doctrine. The splendid Dhamekha Stupa at Sarnath was originally erected by King Ashoka, as was the famous lion capital pillar, now the proud symbol of India.

Bodh Gaya:

Bodh Gaya (The Mahabodhi Temple Complex) houses all the major pilgrimage spots. A flight of steps leads to the inner courtyard through a beautifully carved granite torana (gateway). A large circular stone with the Buddha's footprints is kept in a small shrine on the left. Seven spots within the complex precincts are especially sacred because it was at these spots that the Buddha spent a week each, meditating, after his Enlightenment.

It was in Bodhgaya in Bihar, India that Prince Siddhartha found Enlightenment (nirvana) under the bodhi tree after meditating for 49 days. No longer a bodhisattva (mentor), he became Lord Buddha, the Enlightened One.

Primary points of homage are the Mahabodhi Temple, the Vajrasan throne donated by King Ashoka, the holy Bodhi Tree, the Animeshlochana chaitya, the Ratnachankramana, the Ratnagaraha, the Ajapala Nigrodha Tree, the Muchhalinda Lake and the Rajyatna Tree. The spiritual home of all Buddhists, devotees from many Buddhist countries have built temples around the complex in their characteristic architectural styles. Bodhgaya today is a vibrant and inspiring tourist attraction.

Varanasi:

Varanasi (also Benaras) is located in the north Indian state of Uttar Pradesh and extends latitude 25°20' N and longitude 83°00' E. Sandwiched between the rivers Varuna and Ashi as they join the Ganges, Varanasi takes its name from its location. It is also called Kashi, the city of light, but the British, in an endeavor to simplify matters, had coined their own name for the place – Benaras.

Dharmekh Stupa is the most conspicuous structure at Sarnath. Colonel Cunningham bore a shaft from the top centre of the stupa and discovered a stone tablet on which an inscription is written with the word Dhamekha, and mentions that this is the spot where the Buddha delivered his first sermon.

Kushinagar:

Kushinagar is also known as Kasia or Kusinara. The founder of Buddhism, Lord Buddha passed away at this place near the Hiranyavati River and was cremated at the Ramabhar stupa. It was once a celebrated center of the Malla kingdom. Many of its stupas and viharas date back to 230 BC-AD 413, when its prosperity was at the peak. The Mauryan emperor Ashoka added grandeur to this place by getting the magnificent statue of Buddha carved on a single piece of red sandstone.

At Kushinagar close to Gorakhpur in eastern Uttar Pradesh, India en route to Kapilavastu, Lord Buddha fell ill and left this world in 543 BC. His mortal remains were preserved in eight commemorative chortens, and then further distributed by King Ashoka into 84,000 stupas across his kingdom and beyond. Important places to see here are the Mukatanabandhana stupa and the Gupta period reclining Buddha statue in red sandstone.

Besides the above, four major high significant Buddhist pilgrimage sites, there are other places that hold special meaning in the life of Lord Buddha.

Sravasti:

Sravasti or Savatthi was the capital of the mighty Kosala kingdom during Buddha's time. It is situated in the Uttar Pradesh and ten miles distance from Balrampur. It was at Sravasti that the Buddha displayed his great miracle sitting on a thousand Pettaled lotus in front of an audience consisting of the king of Kosala. There the Buddha displayed the multiplied forms of himself a million times going up to the highest heavens, in order to confound the Tirthikas and to establish his supremacy. This was a unique feat performed by the Buddha and as the locality of this unprecedented event Sravasti acquired foremost celebrity.

Lumbini:

Lumbini is in southern Nepal, where Queen Mayadevi gave birth to Prince Siddhartha. It is just a short distance from the Shakya capital of Kapilavastu. Pilgrimages focus on the sacred garden which contains the site of the birth, the Mayadevi temple, the Pashkarni pond and the Ashoka pillar. Designed by Japanese architect Kenzo Tange, the sacred garden of Lumbini is a World Heritage site with monasteries from many Buddhist nations. It is recognised as a supreme pilgrimage site and symbol of world peace. Lumbini, the Lord Buddha's birthplace, evokes the same kind of holy sentiment to the millions of Buddhists all over the world as does Jerusalem to Christians and Mecca to Muslims. For centuries, Buddhists all over the world knew Lumbini was where the Buddha was born, however, the exact location remained uncertain and obscured until as recently as 1886 when a wandering archaeologist came across a stone pillar and ascertained the exact location.

The historic importance of the pillar is evidenced by the inscription engraved on it, in Brahmin script. It reads that Emperor Ashoa (sometimes spelled Ashoka) visited the site in the twentieth year of his ascendancy to the throne (around 300 BCE), and as homage to the birthplace, erected the pillar.

South of the Ashoka Pillar is the famous sacred pool "Puskarni" believed to be the same sacred pool in which Maya Devi took a holy dip just before giving birth to the Lord and also where the infant Buddha was given his first purification bath.

The single most important place in Lumbini is the stone slab located deep in the Sanctum Sanctorum. Revealed after hard and meticulous excavations under three layers of ruins over the site of a famous Maya Devi temple, the stone slab marks the exact spot of the birthplace of Lord Buddha.

In addition to the Ashoka Pillar, the other shrine of importance is the bas-relief image of Maya Devi, kept in a small pagoda-like structure. The image shows Maya Devi, mother of the Lord, supporting herself by holding on with her right hand to a branch of the Sal tree, with the newly born infant Buddha standing upright on a lotus pedestal on an oval halo. Two other celestial figures are depicted in an act of pouring water and lotuses from heaven.

Rajgir and Nalanda University:

About 70 km from Bodhgaya, Rajgir was Buddha's monsoon retreat for 12 years whilst he spread his doctrine. It was at the holy Griddhikuta Hill that he expounded the precepts of his Lotus Sutra and the Perfection of Wisdom Sutra. The Saptaparni Caves set on Vaibhar Hill were the venue of the First Buddhist Council, held to compile the teachings of the Buddha in its authentic form, after his death. The world-renowned university of Nalanda is another important landmark site.

Different Tour Operators/Travel Agents have proposed following itineries to cover all the important places related to Lord Budha.

Complete Buddhist Circuit from Bodhgaya:

Day 01:	Arrive Bodhgaya and evening worship at the Main Temple. O/N Hotel.
Day 02:	After breakfast drive to Patna via Rajgir and Nalanda. O/ N Hotel.
Day 03:	Drive to Kushinagar via Vaishali and Kesaria. O/N Hotel.
Day 04:	Drive Kushinagar to Bhairahawa/Lumbini. O/N Hotel.
Day 05:	After Breakfast drive to Lumbini for the sightseeing tour and after lunch drive to Sravasti. O/N Hotel.
Day 06:	Morning sightseeing tour of Sravasti and after lunch drive to Vanarasi. O/N Hotel.

Day 07:	Morning boat ride at River Gages. After breakfast drive to Sarnath and return to Vanarasi. O/N Hotel.
Day 08:	Drive Vanarasi to Bodhgaya. Evening worship at main Temple. O/N Hotel.
Day 09:	Morning sightseeing tour of main temple, Kala Charka Ground, Dhungeshori, Sujata Village and Sujata Temple. O/N Hotel.
Day 10:	Transfer to airport for departure.
Day 11:	Morning worship at Main Temple and afternoon fly back to Kathmandu. O/N Hotel.
Day 12:	Morning free for last moment shopping before transferring to airport for departure.

Four Gateways:

Lumbini

Day 01:	Arrive Kathmandu. Transfer to Hotel. O/N Hotel.
Day 02:	Morning tour of Bouddhanath, Swyambhunath & Patan Durbar Square. Late afternoon flight to Lumbini. O/N Hotel.
Day 03:	Sightseeing tour of Lumbini – visit Maya Devi Temple, Ashok Pillar, Lumbini Garden, sacred pond & other ruins. O/N Hotel.
Day 04:	Drive Lumbini to Varanasi. O/N Hotel.
Day 05:	Morning Boat ride on River Ganges. Visit Sarnath. Drive to Bodhgaya. O/N Hotel.
Day 06:	Full day tour of Bodhgaya visiting Mahabodhi Temple & Tree, Niranjana River, Sujata Kuti, Big Buddha Statue and some international temple. O/N Hotel.
Day 07:	Drive to Rajgir via Nalanda. Visit Nalanda University, Vulture peak, Jeevak Van and Bhimbsar Jai. O/N Hotel.
Day 08:	Drive to Kushinagar via Vaishali. Visit Ahoka Pillar, Monkey tank, Kutagar Shala, Relic Stupa and Coronation Tank. Also visit Mahaparinirvan Temple, Mathakunwar Shrine and cremation stupa at Kushinagar. O/N Hotel.
Day 09:	Drive to Sravasti via Kapilvastu. Visit ruins at Kapilvastu and vist Jetvan, Gandh Kuti, Sudath Kuti, Angulimal Kuti etc at Sravasti. O/N Hotel.

Day 10:	Drive to Lumbini and catch evening flight to Kathmandu. O/N Hotel.
Day 11:	Transfer to airport for departure.

Varanasi:

Day 01:	Arrive Varanasi. Transfer to Hotel. O/N Hotel.
Day 02:	Morning Boat ride on River Ganges. Visit Sarnath. Drive to Bodhgaya. O/N Hotel.
Day 03:	Full day tour of Bodhgaya visiting Mahabodhi Temple & Tree, Niranjana River, Sujata Kuti, Big Buddha Statue and some international temple. O/N Hotel.
Day 04:	Drive to Rajgir via Nalanda. Visit Nalanda University, Vulture peak, Jeevak Van and Bhimbsar Jai. O/N Hotel.
Day 05:	Drive to Kushinagar via Vaishali. Visit Ashoka Pillar, Monkey tank, Kutagar Shala, Relic Stupa and Coronation Tank. Also visit Mahaparinirvan Temple, Mathakunwar Shrine and cremation stupa at Kushinagar. O/N Hotel.
Day 06:	Drive to Sravasti via Kapilvastu. Visit ruins at Kapilvastu and vist Jetvan, Gandh Kuti, Sudath Kuti, Angulimal Kuti etc at Sravasti. O/N Hotel.
Day 07:	Drive to Lumbini. O/N Hotel.
Day 08:	Sightseeing tour of Lumbini –visit Maya Devi Temple, Ashok Pillar, Lumbini Garden, sacred pond & other ruins. O/N Hotel.
Day 09:	Drive Lumbini to Varanasi. O/N Hotel.
Day 10:	Transfer to airport for departure.

Bodhgaya :

Day 01:	Arrive Bodhgaya and evening worship at the Main Temple. O/N Hotel.
Day 02:	After breakfast drive to Patna via Rajgir and Nalanda. O/ N Hotel
Day 03:	Drive to Kushinagar via Vaishali and Kesaria. O/N Hotel
Day 04:	Drive Kushinagar to Bhairahawa/Lumbini. O/N Hotel
Day 05:	After breakfast drive to Lumbini for the sightseeing tour and after lunch drive to Sravasti. O/N Hotel
Day 06:	Morning sightseeing tour of Sravasti and after lunch drive to Vanarasi. O/N Hotel

Day 07:	Morning boat ride at River Gages. After breakfast, drive to Sarnath and return to Vanarasi. O/N Hotel
Day 08:	Drive Vanarasi to Bodhgaya. Evening worship at main Temple. O/N Hotel
Day 09:	Morning sight seeing tour of main temple, Kala Charka Ground, Dhungeshori, Sujata Village and Sujata Temple. O/N Hotel
Day 10:	Transfer to airport for departure.

Kolkata:

Day 01:	Arrive Kolkata. Take train to Bodhgaya or fly to Patna. O/N Hotel.
Day 02:	Full day tour of Bodhgaya visiting Mahabodhi Temple & Tree, Niranjana River, Sujata Kuti, Big Buddha Statue and some international temple. O/N Hotel.
Day 03:	Drive to Rajgir via Nalanda. Visit Nalanda University, Vulture peak, Jeevak Van and Bhimbsar Jai. O/N Hotel.
Day 04:	Drive to Kushinagar via Vaishali. Visit Ashoka Pillar, Monkey tank, Kutagar Shala, Relic Stupa and Coronation Tank. Also visit Mahaparinirvan Temple, Mathakunwar Shrine and cremation stupa at Kushinagar. O/N Hotel.
Day 05:	Drive to Sravasti via Kapilvastu. Visit ruins at Kapilvastu and visit Jetvan, Gandh Kuti, Sudath Kuti, Angulimal Kuti etc. at Sravasti. O/N Hotel.
Day 06:	Drive to Lumbini. O/N Hotel.
Day 07:	Sightseeing tour of Lumbini – visit Maya Devi Temple, Ashoka Pillar, Lumbini Garden, sacred pond & other ruins. O/N Hotel.
Day 08:	Drive Lumbini to Varanasi. O/N Hotel.
Day 09:	Morning Boat ride on River Ganges. Visit Sarnath. Drive to Bodhgaya. O/N Hotel.
Day 10:	Train to Kolkata & Depart.

17

Location-Based Tourism

BEACH TOURISM

Along its 7000 km of coastline, India boasts of a number of beautiful beaches. The tranquil environment with abundant greenery around is just perfect to relax and refresh the drained mind and body. Lie on the smooth sandy beaches and soak the warmth of the sun or simply take a quiet walk barefooted on these beaches. The calming effect will easily penetrate deep into your body. The vast stretches of sea water have a unique ability to carry away all your worries and heartaches along with its waves. You can also watch the sun rise and set far in the horizon and appreciate the beauty that is reflected as a reflection in the water.

And for all those who are more venturesome and yearn for a lot of challenging activities, the beaches have plethora of options to choose from. Swim along with the waves of the ocean water or dive deep into the water to discover a magnificent and colourful marine world. Also, catch the good waves and duckdive the bigger ones while surfing. Cruising in the ocean water is for those who wish to explore the vastness and deepness of the water body without getting wet.

In brief, a beach tour in India will now be on the itinary most of the tourists coming to india and will provide them a thing to enjoy. Moreover it provides action and fun. Take a beach trip to India to actually experience what makes the beaches in India attractive to so many tourists.

India holds a number of travel theme in its kitty and these days, Beach Tourism is the talk of the town. The country has about 6,000 kms long coastline and houses some of the world's finest beaches, which allures holiday-makers to lose themselves in the azure sea. The romantic sea-shores hugs the dramatic high and low tides and captures the closest attention of the several sybarite, water-sport lovers, love-birds and nature-lovers. Catch-hold of some popular beach destination in India.

Popular Beaches in India:

Know more about the exotic Indian beaches, beach resorts in India, beach activities in Lakshadweep, Andhra Pradesh beaches, Goa beaches, Kerala beaches, Karnataka beaches, Andaman and Nicobar Island, Maharashtra beaches.

India has a coastline of 6000 km, as a result it has many beaches on both sides of the peninsula. Considering the total beach area India has, Indian beaches are very under-utilized as tourist spots. Some beaches that have become popular attract international travellers.

Of all the nature's paradise the most irresistible temptations are the beaches. Who doesn't want to wear those golden sand grains and wrap the blue or green water as well as surf the sea? And that's why the beaches in India are called as the amalgamation of sun, sand and surf. India is home to some of the most beautiful and finest beaches of the world offering plenitudes of opportunities for sunbathing, water sports and fishing.

Karnataka Beaches:

The fascinating palm-growth, the slanting coconut groves bordering the 320 kms long coastline features the number of beaches in Karnataka. The most popular Karwar, Malpe, Maravanthe, Bhatkal and Murudeshwar offers some promising water-sports and fabulous attraction of the rolling hills, silver-sand beach and above all, the calm aura.

Andhra Pradesh Beaches:

Besides the magnificent attraction in Andra Pradesh, a look into its mesmerizing beaches goes beyond imagination. Of the eleven beaches in the state, tourist attraction lies in the recreational activities on the bank of Bheemunipatnam, Ramakrishna, Manginapudi, Mypad and Rishikonda.

Andaman and Nicobar Island:

The isolated Andaman and Nicobar Island beaches are best known for its ultimate geographic location and exquisite marine lives. Some picturesque sea-beaches like Radhanagar beach, vijaynagar beach, Harminder Bay beach, Karmatang beach and Ramnagar beach looks alike the heaven on earth. This coastline are exclusive for eco-friendly tourist who desires to check out the lively spots of water monitar lizards, megapode, crocodiles, reticulate python etc.

Beaches in Maharashtra:

A beach tourism in Maharashtra, India, takes beach-lovers into the swirling current of fun and enjoyment. The state's charming destination like the Marine Drive, Ganpatipule beach, Janjira beach, Juhu beach and Chowpatty beach features the various beach activities like building sand-castle, screaming with volley-ball, beach-waking, relishing exotic sea-side cuisines, etc. Besides other nearby attraction like the impregnable forts, parks and fabulous locales are some additional punch to the visitors.

Tamil Nadu Beaches:

The soothing sunshines, the mirror- like sea and the golden sand–Tamil Nadu beaches have it all. This southernmost state in India boast of the second longest beach in the world, the Marina Beach. Highly looked at by the sun-bath lovers, the exotic locations like the Covelong, Elliots, Kanyakumari, Rameshwaram and Mahabalipuram are gaining immense popularity in the Big-Screen fantasy. A visit to the cited beaches offers a golden chance to plunge into the blue sea and comfort the body and soul with the salubrious environment, here.

Goa Beaches:

Goa, one of the smallest states of India is located along the western coast and is 400 kms from Bombay. It is bounded by Maharashtra on the north, Karnataka on the east & south, and by the Arabian Sea on the west. The capital of the city is Panaji. Some of the major beaches in India are:

***Anjuna* Beach:** Located in the north Goa, it is about 18 km from the capital city. The Anjuna beach is a perfect hangout spot for Indian as well foreign tourist and shows a mixture tradition of east and west.

***Baga* Beach:** The Baga beach is an ideal spot for fishing, bathing and picnics. The main attraction of the beach is the medicinal spring whose water is believed to be medicinal.

***Colva* Beach:** This romantic beach is located in the south Goa. It is a 40 km long white sand beach fringed with palm trees.

***Candolim* Beach:** It is another beach in Goa which is less crowded and offers some peace & quite places to relax.

Kerala Beaches:

Kerala is one of the major tourist places in South India. Its diverse geography, a synthesis of mountains, rivers, forests, picturesque beaches, lakes with a rich culture attracts tourists from all over the world. Numerous beaches of Kerala are renowned for its blue water and various water sports activities. Some of the main beaches in the coast of Kerala are:

***Kovalam* Beach:** Kovalam is a small village situated on the Malwar Coast has three fabulous beaches named the Lighthouse, the Hawah, and the Samudra beach.

***Marari* Beach:** The name of the beach is derived from the name of the village Mararikulam – a local fishing village.

***Kumarakom* Beach:** It is a small village and is a cluster of little islands and is an ideal destination for beach holidays in South India.

Mumbai Beaches:

The island city Mumbai is located along the bank of Arabian

Sea on the west coast of India. It is the capital of the state of Maharashtra and due to its port, it is also an important trading and shipping centre. Some beaches in the list of Mumbai are:

***Marine* Drive**: Also known as the Queen's Necklace, the Marine Drive is located in the central Mumbai.

***Juhu* Beach**: Located 18 km north of the city centre, the Juhu Beach is one of the most visited beaches in India along the shore of Arabian Sea.

***Chowpatty* Beach** (GirGaum): Located at the northern end of Marine Drive, this sandy beach is a must-visit tourist place in Mumbai. It attracts tourist and local people on a large scale, especially during weekends and holidays.

Kanyakumari Beaches:

The beach at Kanyakumari offers a wonderful chance to the beach lovers for an exciting beach holidays. The lighthouse at this beach offers a panoramic view of the beach. The beach is also an important pilgrimage destination as the confluence point of the seas and so called the "Thriveni Sangam". The beach at Kanyakumari offers a wonderful chance to the beach lovers for an exciting beach holidays.

Lakshadweep Beaches:

Located in the southwest coast of India in the Arabian sea, Lakshadweep consists of 36 islands and is called the Lakshadweep Island Group. This coral island is just 400 km from the state of Kearala. It is one of the popular beach holiday destinations in the coast of Kerala and known for its marine life, especially exotic corals. Some of the major beaches of the islands are given below.

Kavaratti: Kavaratti is the capital of the island Lakshadweep and offers several adventure activities in its lovely beach. It is one of the best places for beach holiday lovers to enjoy sunbathing, swimming, sailing, windsurfing and other water sports.

Minicoy: Beaches in the Minicoy Island offers water sports activities including bathing huts that make it one of the island beach paradises in Lakshadweep.

Bangaram: This island is popular for its beautiful beach, which is exclusive destination for beach lovers.

Agatti: It is another island in Lakshadweep which is a perfect picnic spot and a perfect place for adventure tourists.

There has been an upmarket trend in the tourism over the last few decades, especially in Europe, where international travel for short breaks is common. Tourists have high levels of disposable income, considerable leisure time, are well educated, and have sophisticated tastes. There is now a demand for a better quality products, which has resulted in a fragmenting of the mass market for beach vacations; people want more specialised versions, quieter resorts, family-oriented holidays or niche market-targeted destination hotels.

The number of foreign travellers to India is on the rise. This is not only due to the increasing number of business trips, but also because of the growing popularity of India as a destination for medical tourism, rural tourism, heritage tours and adventure tourism. More and more Indians too are travelling abroad and within India, for business and leisure. Web-based travel businesses are gaining momentum. Sectors like aviation are witnessing phenomenal activity.

Needless to say, India plays host to some of the major global players in the business; and the travel and hospitality industry is witnessing growth and expansion, like never before. There is a great demand for information pertaining to travel in India.

WILDLIFE TOURISM

Historically and culturally, forests and all forms & wildlife in them, have played a very important role in the Indian way of life. Plants and animals have even been worshipped over the centuries and thus the importance accorded to them. According to estimates the forests, the deserts, the mountains and swamplands of India sustain over 350 species of mammals 2,100 kinds of birds – both local and migratory, 350 varieties of reptile and innumerable insects.

Nature-based tourism and its various subsets can also encompass some particularly challenging, but potentially high spending, special interest market segments. These often comprise socially and environmentally aware, highly educated and potentially demanding visitors who travel both to learn and to achieve personal and social goals. Most of these visitors are serviced and targeted by specialist tourism operators and suppliers who often provide highly expert guides as part of the service.

Wildlife tourism involves travel to observe wildlife in natural environments and preferably the native habitat. It is a further subset of nature tourism and one in which significantly high levels of domestic and international interest exist. Wildlife tourism involves wild and non-domesticated animals and can encompass free-ranging and captive circumstances.

Given the unique character and special appeal of most of Australia's wildlife, this suggests it may represent a tourism opportunity area for some destinations. The Blue Mountains, Barrington Tops, North and South Coast areas and Outback New South Wales possess great potential in this regard given their species diversity and relative convenience as destinations from major source markets and ports of entry.

Internationally speaking, wildlife tourism encompasses the chance to encounter fauna (and flora) in terrestrial, aquatic/marine and aerial settings and to gain some further understanding of a wide variety of species (including viewing kangaroos, koalas, whales, dolphins, seals, fish and birds). Undertaking this activity in a manner that is environmentally responsible is important to ensure less disturbance to wildlife and habitats.

In terms of major visitor trends, 'appreciative tourism' involving observation, photography and interaction with wild animals is large-scale, prominent and growing. Consumptive tourism involving such activities as hunting and (non-catch and release) fishing is also large-scale, but declining.

Ideally, wildlife tourism should include some element of education and an increased appreciation of nature and conservation issues. Potential new models for wildlife tourism in Australia are being developed. These involve wildlife sanctuaries with feral-free habitats attempting to use tourism and other enterprise-based revenue sources as a means to help protect endangered native species and develop recovery plans for the species.

Activities directly related to wildlife viewing, such as scuba diving and whale watching, are experiencing rapid world-wide growth in popularity and it is clear that the concept of wildlife viewing itself is gaining global currency with visitors. It has been estimated to generate $30 billion worldwide in revenues each year.

Wildlife tourism should also seek to maximise the benefits to local communities, while avoiding problems such as disturbance to wildlife and pollution. Types and magnitudes of environmental impacts associated with wildlife tourism vary with the type of tourist activity pursued – some impacts are obvious and easily identifiable while others are indirect and difficult to quantify. The impacts on particular animals should not be considered in isolation from the broader environmental settings and wider animal population.

The conservation benefits of wildlife tourism can include – its financial contribution; practical (in kind) contribution; socio-economic incentive for conservation; and education.

Each sanctuary has several species of mammals and birds but is sometimes known for one particular species. For instance the Sultanpur Sanctuary in Haryana is known for the large contingent of migratory birds from October onwards every year, and Gir in Gujarat for its lions.

Various Wildlife Sanctuaries and National Parks:

About 80 National Parks and 441 Sanctuaries have been created to protect this life from the onslaught of urbanization and rapidly increasing population.

Wildlife Sanctuaries, National Parks:

There are a number of wildlife sanctuaries and National parks all over this vast country which are well preserved. They cover hundreds of square kilometres and the varied wildlife can be observed here in their natural habitat.

Apart from this, the Government of India initiated Project Tiger which covers almost 25,000 sq. km. of space in 15 reserves. This has helped in increasing the numbers of tigers, over the years.

Some of the major wildlife sanctuaries and national parks in India are located in Andaman & Nicobar Islands, Assam, Bihar, Goa, Daman & Diu, Gujarat, Himachal Pradesh, Jammu & Kashmir, Karnataka, Kerala, Madhya Pradesh, Orissa, Rajasthan, Sikkim, Tamil Nadu, Uttar Pradesh, and West Bengal.

- Mount Harriet National Park in the Andaman & Nicobar Islands hosts the Andaman wild pig, saltwater crocodile, turtle and robber crab. The best time to visit is January and February. There is also the Saddle Peak National Park famous for bird and the Andaman teal. Best time to visit is November to April. The Andamans also have Marine National Park.
- Kaziranga National Park in Assam is famous for the one-horned rhinos, of which the park has a sizeable number. Apart from this, there are tigers, wild buffaloes, elephants, barasingha, hog deer, wild boars, leopards and leopard cats, and a large variety of birds. The best time to visit Kaziranga is October to March.
- Hazaribagh National Park in Bihar showcases the tiger, leopard, sambar, chital, and wild boar and the best time to visit is October to March.
- Palaman (Betla) National Park in Bihar, is also a Tiger Reserve seen best between October and May. It was once the homeland of the now extinct Indian cheetah, but one can still view the tiger, leopard, wolf, wild dog, jungle cat and the barking deer, here.
- Bhagwan Mahavir National Park spread across Goa, Daman & Diu houses gaur, sambar, mouse deer, barking deer, flying squirrel, and porcupine. Best time to visit is October to March.
- Spreading over a large area in Gujarat, the Gir National Park (also a Lion Sanctuary) is best visited from October to June for a view of the Asiatic lion, panther, sambar, and the four-horned antelope.
- The Velavadar National Park also in Gujarat hosts the blackbuck and the wolf. Best time to come here is October to May.
- The Nal Sarovar Sanctuary in the state of Gujarat is known for its

flocks of flamingoes and other birds which abound from October to February.

- The Great Himalayan National Park in Himachal Pradesh houses the snow leopard, mountain goat, yak cranes, and brown & black bears. The best time to view them are from April to June and from September to October.
- Some natural parks are Chilka, Nandankanan, Kaziranga National Park, Similipal National Park, Corbett National Park, Dudhwa, Sariska, Sunderbans, Gir, Bandipur, Bandhavgarh.
- The state of Jammu and Kashmir has two national parks namely Dachigain and Kishtwar. While Danchigam is famous for its endangered Kashmir Stag called Hangul, it also has the Himalayan black bear, brown bear, leopard, hill fox, jungle cat, Himalayan weasel, and long-tailed marmot among others. The best time to visit is August to December.
- The Kishtwar National Park is best visited from May to October and includes snow leopard, antelope, wild yak and the Tibetan ass.
- The Bandipur National Park, adjoining the Madhumalai sanctuary in Karnataka welcomes visitors all the year round with its inhabitants comprising the tiger, elephant, gaur, chitals, wild dog and sloth bear.
- The Nagarhole Park also in Karnataka welcomes visitors all the year round and has a host of elephants, tigers, panthers, chitals, sambars, sloth bears, and gaur.
- The small state of Kerala has three major national parks.
- The Eravikulam Park is open throughout the year and houses elephants, gaurs, sambars, lion-tailed macaque,and the famous Nilgiri tahr.
- The Periyar Park has a large number of elephants, gaurs, wild dogs, sambars and can be best viewed from September to May.
- The Silent Valley National Park houses elephants, wild boars, panthers, sambars, and the lion-tailed macaque which can be seen from September to March, best
- In the state of Madhya Pradesh, there are three national parks, namely Bandhavgarh, Kanha and Pench and the best time to visit them is November to June.
- The Bandhavgarh Park spreads over 32 hills and is one of the best places to watch tigers and panthers apart from the chitals, gaurs, sambars and the nilgai.

- The Kanha park spreads over 1,945 sq. kms. and is famous as tiger land. Apart from the tiger, it is home to panthers, barasingha, black buck, barking deer, mouse deer, nilgai, wild dog, chital and sambar.
- The Pench National Park is also a good place to watch the tiger, panther, gaur, chital, sambar and nilgai.
- Orissa also has three major wildlife habitats, out of which one is a National Park and two sanctuaries. While Chilka is an all year round destination, the Similipal National Park and Satkosia gorge sanctuary are best visited from November to May .
- Spreading over 900 sq. kms. of lakes, shore and hinterland, Chilka is part of a large lagoon, separated from the Bay of Bangal by a strip of sand. It is India's largest salt lake and home to a large number of migratory and other birds like flamingoes, duck, bar-headed goose, sandpiper, plover, ruddy shelduck, gulls, terns, and white-bellied sea eagle.
- The Similipal Park, best time for visit between November and June, is home to the tiger, elephant, gaur, leopard, mouse deer, flying squirrel, and the mugger crocodile.
- The Satkosia Sanctuary houses gharial, tiger, sloth bear and the leopard.
- Rajasthan boasts of four National Parks.
- The Desert National Park shelters the stately Great Indian Bustard. Apart from this, are the Blackbuck, Chinkara, wolf, desert fox, hare, and desert cat, and is open all the year round.

The Keoladeo Ghana National Park welcomes tourists round the year for viewing its inhabitants which comprise as many as 350 species of birds including its winter visitors from Central Asia and Siberia. The rare Siberian crane traverses more than 6000 kms every year to reach here in winters. The best time to watch birds here is early morning or late evening. Some of the major species spotted here apart from the Siberian crane are, the cormorant, egret, heron, painted stork, spoonbills, ibis, pelican, barheaded goose, etc. The mammals found here include the wild boar, sambar, chital, blackbuck, fishing cat, mongoose, and also the python and monitor lizard among the reptiles.

HILL TOURISM

World is hub for tourist places or destinations in form of the wide seasonal and cultural diversities which one gets to see in the world. In world, you might find snowfall at one place like Siberia (Russia) or Kashmir and hot weather conditions at others like Ethiopia. Every country or region in the world from India to US is a tourist place as each offers something unique and exciting in its own way to the travellers.

This land of forests, hills, waterfalls, lakes, caves and cottages – India – is full of Mother Nature's benevolence. The woods of Shillong are lovely dark and deep, streams rush down the hillsides, the climate is pleasant and countryside here echo's with tribal songs that sound pleasant to the ears. When you explore its enchanting places, you will realize that your search for eternity and serenity has reached its terminus. Truly, if you are looking to relax and enjoy Mother Nature's bounty, Shillong is the place to visit.

With the highest mountain ranges in the world, the Himalayas, running north to east, Aravalli and Vindhya ranges across western and central India, and Western ghats in western and southern parts, India is full of hill stations and offers some of the most spectacular landscapes in the world.The Indian hospitality industry has seen a major hike in the recent times owing to the astounding industrial growth of the country. Indian hill stations are a traveller's paradise, gifted with snowy peaks, deep gorges, green valleys, misty woods, frothing rivers, azure lakes and flower-filled meadows. These misty, mystical and serene hill stations of India are a perfect holiday option.

Shimla:

In the days before independence, Shimla was the most important British hill station, and in the summer season served as the summer capital. Shimla was first "discovered" by the British in 1819, but it was not until 1822 that the first permanent house was erected and not until many years later that Shimla became the summer capital. The name Shimla derives after the Himalayan Goddess Shamla, a synonym of Kali.

Shimla the capital of the glorious state of Himachal Pradesh is a fabulous hill-station surrounded by dense forests that comprises of oak, deodar, pine and rhododendron forests. Shimla has abundance of natural beauty and the locals are privileged to live in such panoramic locations. This place can enamor anyone with its beauty.

Dalhousie:

In western Himachal Pradesh, It covers an area of about 14 square kms and built on five hills. It is named after the British Governor-General of the 19th century, Lord Dalhousie. The town's height varies between 1525 m and 2378 m, and is surrounded by varied vegetation. Dalhousie has charming colonial architecture, including some beautiful churches. The spectacular snow-covered Dhauladhar Mountains are also visible from this enchanting town.

Shimla has a lot of variety to offer. Shimla is an ideal place for fishing, golfing, skiing, trekking, etc. Adventuring here definitely make one enthusiastic and spirited. For more energetic entertainment, hit the indoor roller-skating rink in Lakkar Bazaar or go open-air ice-skating above the Rivoli Bus stand. There are always amazing things to be explored in its surrounding countryside. Fagu, Kulfri and Naldhera are some of the well-known places for adventuring and camping too.

Dharamshala:

Set against the backdrop of the dramatic Dhauladhar Mountains, Dharamshala is perched on the high slopes in upper reaches of Kangra Valley. It is charming town with elegant bungalows nestling in thick conifer forests. Dharamshala is also the home of Dalai Lama, spiritual head of Buddhists; Little Lhasa is an enchanting world where spinning prayer wheels and fluttering prayer flags spread the massage of peace and universal harmony.

Pachmarhi:

An all-season hill resort, Pachmarhi nestles in Satpura ranges with its enchanting forest glades, giggling ravines and fascinating wildlife. It has its archaeological assets too. There are rock paintings, said to be dating back to thousands of years, in the caves of Mahadeo hills. Pachmarhi was discovered in 1857 by a Bengali lancer. The British developed it as a hill resort. The location has been named Priyadarshini Point.

Ooty:

This green and pictorial Queen of Hill Stations located in South India in the state of Tamil Station is at an altitude of 2240 m. Conifers, pine and eucalyptus trees grow abundantly in this region and make the environment fresh, clean and pleasant. The funnel-shaped lavender-blue flowers bring in radiance to the sloping mountains.

Ooty is huddled in an arena that is generated by four royal hills – Elk Hill, Snowdon, Doddabetta and Club Hill. These majestic hills are fractions of the regal Nilgiri range which forms a congregation for the Western and Eastern Ghats.

Dense forests, lofty mountains, extensive tea and coffee plantation and sprawling grasslands characterize Ooty. Ooty provides ecstasy for trekkers. Trekking here is filled with excitement and pleasure. One can watch nature in its best form and splendor while trekking in Ooty. Ooty has many trek routes to offer. However, they differ in distance, stature and topography. Hand gliding and Angling are other activities that one could participate in.

This eco-friendly land with lush greenery, radiant flowers, deep forests, lakes and waterfall offer a fantastic sight and make your stay in Ooty laudable.

Darjeeling and Gangtok:

Darjeeling and Gangtok are a wonderful combination of tranquility, verdant hills, panoramic views and above all the mesmerizing beauty of the mighty Kanchanjunga. These hill stations are famous for ambience of desolation and they offer magnificent view of the vast plains lying below. Both Darjeeling and Gangtok are famous for beautiful serene monasteries, tea plantations and orchard.

Gangtok, the 'Lofty Hill' or the 'hill made flat', was built with Gangtok Monastery in 1716. Cradled in the manifold splendors of nature, deep within the snow clad Himalayas is Sikkim's capital – Gangtok. Overlooking the city is the hill Lukshyma, 'the mother of pearl' citadel of magic mountain, Khang-chen-dzodnga. Gangtok offers a hospitable base to explore the varied wonders of this highland, its picturesque valleys, monasteries, mountain, lakes and trekking trails.

One of the attractions of Darjeeling is its toy train. Built in the late 19th century, the world heritage Darjeeling Himalayan railway is a technological marvel. Its tracks rise from sea level to an altitude of over 7,500 ft in just about 70 km. Zigzag, reverses and loops were devised to overcome these gradients, the most famous being the Batasia Loop, where the train does a complete figure of eight. It covers about 83 km in six or seven hours, so sit back and enjoy the mountains and the fresh air.

Lachung:

One of the most exquisite valleys in Sikkim, Lachung is resplendent with snow-capped mountains, breathtaking waterfall and all that nature can offer. Its on the North of Sikkim highway – a highway which can boast of being one with the most beautiful surrounding. Lachung is situated at height of 8610 ft. Blessed by the goddess of nature, it is the most picturesque village of Sikkim, where the time stands still. Take one and half hour drive to Yumthang situated at a height of 11,800 ft, gets covered with rhododendron flowers with riot of colours bursting on each other.

Mussoorie:

Mussoorie was originally a popular hill station frequented by the British. This picturesque town with its verdant hills and with a variety of floral life and animals inhabiting the region, the place is really fascinating. Hemmed in by snowy mountain peaks to the northeast and glittering view of the beautiful Doon valley and Shivalik ranges in the south, the town presents a fairyland ambience to the tourists.

Mussoorie is hailed as the queen. It is one of the most beautiful hill stations. The climate of this resort is just wonderful and this is the reason that people enjoy visiting this hill station a lot. It presents a pretty picture during summer.

Mussorrie has really attractive views of the mighty, snow-clad Himalayan peaks. The breathtaking Kempty falls, 11 km away from the town, attracts hordes of tourists daily. Depot Hill, which is another interesting place, is point with highest elevation in Mussoorie and all majestic Himalayan peaks are clearly visible from here on clear days.

Kodaikanal:

Kodaikanal is a beautiful hill station of South India quietly ensconced amidst the green Palani Hills. Kodaikanal has a breathtaking scenic beauty. Its wooded slopes, enhancing waterfalls, mighty rocks and beautiful lakes can captivate any visitor.

Kodaikanal has an excellent climate and it charm attracts tourists all through the year. Bird watchers love this place, as do the people who enjoy solitude. No doubt, Kodaikanal still has its virgin, pristine charm.

Situated at an altitude of 2,133 m, the fruits and plums of Kodaikanal are famous for its taste and freshness. This town possesses many orchards where fruits like banana, plums and lychees are grown in plenty. The Kurinji-flower, which is better known as the pride of Kodaikanal blooms once in a decade. With the blooming of this flower, the mountainous slopes gets magically transformed to a bluish-purplish shade.

Kodaikanal provides ample opportunities for trekkers. Trekkers can choose between the 17 routes that are of different lengths.

Dehradun:

This picture perfect hill station is the capital of the state of Uttaranchal. It is located at an altitude of 2,200 ft. and is surrounded by two sacred rivers – the Ganga and the Yamuna. Dehradun is embedded in the lap of the beautiful Doon valley and is surrounded by the Shivalik ranges. Its pleasant weather conditions throughout the year make it an ideal place for vacationing.

Dehradun's spectacular natural assets like floristic varieties, astounding valleys, breathing panorama, tea plantation and leech gardens have transformed this town into a paradise. Its natural environment has a soothing effect on the minds of visitors. It is a perfect retreat for people of different desires and needs.

Manali:

Manali is the northern end of the Kullu Valley and is the main resort in the area. It is beautifully situated and there are many pleasant walks around the town. Surrounded by towering peaks at arm length, Manali's major asset is its proximity to the snowline, never more than few hours drive from the town nestling at comfortable 2,050 meters. It is the center of flourishing orchard industry, a popular honeymoon destination, and trailhead for numerous treks.

Kullu-Manali is an extremely popular tourist destination. Both these hill stations are a delight to those who desire to spend some time in the lap of nature. The intricate web of beautiful valleys brings gleam to ones eyes. Whether it is under the radiant rays of the sun or under the spell of hazy mist, the valley looks brilliant.

The awesome Kullu valley spreads its charm on both the sides of River Beas. The flower-filled meadows, exciting glens surrounded by the gushing streams and meandering rivulets is enough to make the tourists ecstatic. Kullu provides ample scope for trekkers, mountaineers, artists and others who wish to enjoy the variegated spectacle of the scenic mountains. Just inhaling the pristine air of the majestic Himalayas will help to invigorate.

Srinagar:

Luxurious houseboats, sprawling Mughal Gardens and magnificent golf courses is what sets apart Srinagar from the rest of the hill stations. Srinagar is the capital of the state of Jammu and Kashmir. This town is full of fascinating alleyways and buildings. Just wandering in this intriguing city for a few hours leaves you rejuvenated. Its natural splendor makes Srinagar the most magnificent hill station of India.

Srinagar (1,768 meters) is at north of Delhi via Pathankot, and Jammu. It is on both the sides of River Jhelum and is the summer capital of Jammu and Kashmir, which includes Jammu. Vale of Kashmir, Kishtwar, Ladakh & Zanskar ranges. The God has graced this city with such a beauty, which is often compared to Venice. Walk down Sonwar or Residency Road and you'll see half-timbered houses and brick churches surrounded by magnolia trees in the garden. Enter a houseboat and you are instantly transported to another world.

Sonmarg:

At an altitude of 2740 meters, Sonmarg is at Srinagar – Leh Highway. The town lies in the heart of a beautiful valley carved by the river Sindh, the meadow of gold strewn with the loveliest of alpine flowers and surrounded by towering mountains. Located at Thajiwas Glacier, where snow remains round the year, Sonmarg is known as Gateway of Ladakh.

Gulmarg:

The large meadow of Gulmarg is on southwest of Srinagar at 2730 meters. The name means meadow of flowers and in spring it is just that. Gulmarg is one of the most beautiful summer resorts in the valley. It is also popular for its golf course, which is highest in the world and skiing during the winter season. This is also an excellent trekking base. In winter, it used to be India's premier skiing resort.

Pahalgam:

Pahalgam (2240 meters) is heralded by gushing, silvery streams of ice – water and by densely wooded mountains. As the road winds along, Pahalgam appears round the corner against a background of mountains and glistering glaciers with streams rushing past. Pahalgam is the starting point for many trekking trails, such as to the Kolohoi Glacier, Amarnath, Zanskar and Kargil.

Mount Abu:

It is the only hill resort of Rajasthan, crowning at the highest peak of the Aravali hills at altitude of 1220 meters. It is not only one of the prettiest hill stations in the country, but also a major Rajput centre. Mount Abu was dedicated to Lord Shiva before it became Jain pilgrimage center. The biggest draws for Mt. Abu are Dilwara Temples. The hill boasts of a rich vegetation and thick forest. It stands out like an oasis in arid environs.

Mount Abu is an oasis in the barren desert land of Rajasthan. The cool climate of Mount Abu is due to its extravagant flora which consists of flowering shrubs and coniferous trees.

The massive rocks makes the approach road to Mount Abu curvaceous. Mount Abu is the only hill station of its kind in the state of Rajasthan. The golden tinge that smears over the hills of Mount Abu during sunset makes it a spectacular sight. The grassy plains and deep valleys makes Mount Abu look fabulous, especially during dusk.

Shillong:

This hill station provides a clean and unpolluted environment to its tourists. Shillong, the capital of Meghalaya was planned by the British as a hill resort and remain summer retreat of the British; the beautifully kept golf course and several English country cottages testify to another influence besides the local one. Beautiful lakes and falls, hillside cottages, a large university, and the popular Bara Bazar are quaint aspects of this town. The place, the people and the climate all combine to create an atmosphere to make Shillong an ideal holiday resort throughout the year. Cherrapunjee, one of the wettest place on earth, is only 56 kms away from Shillong.

Coorg:

Coorg is one of the smallest districts of Karnataka in size but is among the most beautiful. It is often called the Kashmir of Karnataka for it's cool weather and natural beauty. This small district is home to 260,000 people and is as well known for its coffee and tea estates, as for its brave and gutty people. Several Kodavas (as the people from Coorg are often called) have actively served in the Indian army and the "Coorg Regiment" is among the most decorated.

Munnar:

Munnar is nature lover's paradise and was the summer resort of British Government in South India. With 1600 m above sea level, sprawling tea plantations, picture-book towns, winding lanes and holiday facilities make this a popular hill station. Among the exotic flora found in the forests and grasslands here is Neelakurinji. This flower, which bathes the hills in blue once every twelve years, will bloom next in 2018 AD. Munnar also has the highest peak in South India – Anamudi, which towers over 2695 m., an ideal spot for trekking.

Vythiri:

Tucked away at the north eastern tip of Kerala, this quaint little hill station, about 1300 m above sea level, is renowned for its coffee, tea, cardamom, pepper and rubber plantations. Mist-capped mountains and breathtaking scenery dominate other tourist attractions.

Nainital:

At 1938 meters in the Kumaon hills, this attractive hill station was once the summer capital of Uttar Pradesh. Nainital is very much a green and pleasant land that immediately appealed to the homesick Britishers, who were reminded of the Cumbrian Lake District. This is certainly one of the most pleasant hill stations to visit and there are many interesting walks through the forests to points with superb views of the Himalayas. Today, the life of Nainital revolves around the lake of Naini. But there are few other lakes around Nainital which are equally beautiful and attractive as the Naini lake.

Ranikhet:

North of Nainital and at an altitude of 1829 meters, this peaceful hill station offers excellent views of the snowcapped

Himalayas including Nanda Devi (7817 meters). It is an important army town and the headquarters of the Kumaon regiment. Unrivalled for panoramic views, it offers added attraction of ancient temples, pretty picnic spots and quiet strolls, exciting treks of Kausani and Dunagiri. Ranikhet is a delightful place to spend some time. Besides, the golf course at Upat offers good golfing facilities.

Almora:

The picturesque hill station, at an altitude of 1650 meters, is one of the few of its type created by the British. Some 400 years ago, it was the capital of the Chand Rajas of Kumaon.

Kausani:

Nestling amongst thick, dense pine forests, atop a narrow ridge and separated from the towering mountains of the Nanda Devi range, Kausani is known for Himalayan snow-capped peaks standing in a stately row of over 300 kms, of majestic glory. The glory of snow covered peaks – Trishul, Nanda Devi and Nanda Kot when the sunrays turn them into crimson and gold at sunrise and sunset can bedazzle any viewer by its scenic grandeur and beauty.

India is truly a great place with lots of diversity and is a unique place in the world. Even after the terror attacks in India and the the economic melt down Indian tourism industry has performed well. India is the perfect tourist destination when it comes to visiting one of its many picturesque hill stations.

India is a beautiful country with great cultural and geographical features. The country has many tourism options to grab the attention of tourists and vacations. Among those hill stations and beach tourism are very popular, with tourists and vacationers looking for fun-filled holiday with great tourism opportunity in India. Hill stations and beaches of India are ideal for family vacation and honeymooning vacation as they offer serene and scenic ambience for peaceful vacation along with some of adventure and sport activities. Exploring beautiful hill towns and beach towns of India is itself a unique experience one would love to cherish forever.

There are many vacation stations and mountain towns in India widely known for hill station tourism. In whatever part of India you will travel, you will find some of picturesque hill stations inviting you with their sectional charm. If you are honeymooners then you will certainly fall in love with awe-inspiring charm of Indian mountain towns. Indian hill stations are also known for adventure and sport activities.

North India is globally famous among tourists and vacations as it has many picturesque hill stations which are gifted with superb natural beauty and serene ambience. Shimla, Manali, Kullu, Dalhousie, Dharamshala, Kashmir, Gulmarg, Sonmarg, Pahalgam, Srinagar, Mussoorie, Dehradun, Ranikhet, Almora, Darjeeling, Kalimpong, Gangtok, etc are some of popular vacation stations in northern part of India you will love to travel and spend your holidays for some days enjoying nature beauty and adventure and sport activities. Southern part of India also has some of famous vacation stations known for exotic nature beauty, adventure and sport activities. Ooty, Kodaikanal, Munnar, Ponmudi, Coorg, etc. are popular vacation stations located in southern India. Munnar is so beautiful that it is often described as the Kashmir of South. Indeed, hill stations in India have a great impact on Indian tourism.

There are also many beaches and beach towns in India appealing tourists and vacationers through out the entire world. Western India and southern India are dotted with many exquisite beaches. Goa and Kerala are widely acclaimed for their breathtaking beautiful beaches fringed by palm-coconut trees. Beaches of India are ideal for fun vacation, family vacation, adventure holiday and honeymoon holiday. Palolem, Colva, Bogmalo, Anjuna, Aguada, Baga, Dona Paula, Miramar, Calangute, Benaulim, Mobor, Arambol, etc. are popular beaches in Goa. Kovalam, Varkala, Beypore, Alleppey, Kollam, Mararikulam, Cherai, Fort Kochi, etc. are popular beaches in Kerala. Goa and Kerala attracts a large number of tourists and vacationers through out the entire globe for beach tours in India and provide them a wonderful opportunity to enjoy beach tourism which is full of delights and cheerful activities.

Well, if you too want to enjoy the charm of Indian hill stations and beaches, it is advisable that you should go with a right package. With a right India tour packages covering hill stations & beaches you will be able to explore the charm of Indian beaches and hill towns in most convenient and cheerful way.

DESERT TOURISM

The desert is bounded by the Aravalli hills in the east, by the fertile Indus, the Nara valleys of Pakistan and the salt marsh of the Rann of Kutch in the west, and by the alluvial plains of Haryana and Punjab in the north.

Area: 446,000 square kilometers, Features: Rolling Sand Hills, Scant Rainfall and Average annual rainfall: 100 to 500 mm.

The Thar Desert is located in western India and southeastern Pakistan. The huge unending expanse of burning hot sand is spread over four states in India, namely Punjab, Haryana, Rajasthan, and Gujarat, and two states in Pakistan covering an area of about 446,000 square kilometres. It lies mostly in the Indian state of Rajasthan, and extends into the southern portion of Haryana and Punjab states and into northern Gujarat state.

The Legend

It is believed that aeons ago, Shri Ram drew an arrow in his bow, targetting Lanka, the island capital where his wife was held captive by the demon king, Ravana. However, such were its destructive powers that the gods pleaded with the Lord to desist from his intended purpose.

But the arrow once drawn could not be pulled back and thus Rama pointed the arrow to a far-flung sea. The heat generated by the arrow dried the sea and and in its place arose a dry, arid and hot desert.

The Origin:

The origin of this desert is a matter of much controversy. Some consider it to be only 4000 to 10,000 years old. Many others believe that the region started becoming arid much earlier.

Another theory states that area turned to desert relatively recently: perhaps around 2000-1500 BCE. Around this time, the Ghaggar ceased to be a major river.

It now terminates in the desert. It has been observed through remote sensing techniques that Late Quaternary climatic changes and neotectonics have played a significant role in modifying the drainage courses in this part and a large number of palaeochannels exist.

Thar desert region of Rajasthan is one of the most inhospitable landscapes on earth. Apart from the huge distances between hamlets and settlements here, the landscape is constantly shifing with the sand, as wind and sandstorms re-arrange the terrain at will. Community workers here live and work in this vast, arid, sprawling and shape-changing environment.

There is a lack of water in such an arid region. In search of water, ancient villagers of the Thar often find themselves migrating on foot across sometimes hundreds of miles towards neignbouring states. This centuries-old way of life continues here against all odds. Life is a struggle here, but the ancient attachment the villagers have to their homes, is strong. The ancient desert is believed to have been a witness to one of the earliest human civilizations

Vegetation

The region has great diversity in vegetation. As many as 700 species of plants are found in the area, of which 107 are of grass alone. The local grasses are generally prolific seeders, and most of the species are palatable, fairly nutritious and rich in minerals, including trace elements. These also have medicinal value and hence alkaloids, used for making medicine, and oils for making soap, are also extracted therefrom.

There is a great paucity of water and hence, the thar desert vegetation is mostly herbaceous; with the trees very rarely dotting the landscape. On the hills, Gum Arabic Acacia and Euphorbia may be found. The Khajri (Prosopis Cineraria) tree grows throughout the plains. Water is very scarce. Land-use in the Thar is dependent on rainfall. In good rainfall years, large areas are cropped, cattle thrive on extensive pastures and substantial amounts of hay are stored for future use. Rainwater is stored in ponds and underground tanks.

As rainfall is very erratic, a pattern of mixed farming has been developed in which human and animal populations benefit from each other.

Natural vegetation of Thar Desert is composed of following tree, shrub and herb species.

Tree Species

Acacis Jacquemontii, Acacia leucophloea, Acacia senegal, Anogeissus, Prosopis cineraria, Salvadora oleoides, Tecomella undulata, Tamarix articulata.

Small Trees and Shrubs

Calligonum polygonoides, Acacia jacquemontii, Balanites roxburghii, Ziziphus jujuba, Ziziphus nummularia, Calotropis procera, Suaeda fruticosa, Crotalaria burhia, Aerva tomentosa, Clerodendrum multiflrum, Leptadenia pyrotechnica, Lycium barbarum, Grewia populifolia, Commiphora mukul, Euphorbia nerifolia, Cordia rothii, and Maytenus emorginata Capparis decidua.

Herbs

Eleusine compressa, Dactyloctenium scindicum, Cenchrus biflorus, Cenchrus setigerus, Lasiurus hirsutus, Cynodon dactylon, Panicum turgidum, Panicum antidotale, Dichanthium annulatum, Sporobolus marginatus, Saccharum spontaneum, Cenchrus ciliaris, Desmostachya bipinnata, Cyperus arenarius, Erogrostis species, Ergamopagan species, Phragmitis species, and Typha species.

The Thar Desert is endowed with some of the best breeds of livestock in the country. Nearly 50 per cent of the country's wool is produced in Rajasthan, and the area has been the main supplier of bullocks to the North.

Climate

The area receives very scant rainfall, with the average annual rainfall varying from 100 to 500 mm. Receiving an annual average rainfall of less than 10 inches, the desert is a largely a sun-scorched region of shifting sand dunes, broken rocks, and scrub vegetation. During the months of July and September, around 90% of the rainfall is attributable to southwest monsoon. There are wide fluctuations in the amount of rainfall from year to year.

The mean average temperature varies from a minimum of 24 to 26 degrees C in summer and 4 to 10 degrees C in winter. Dust storms and dust raising winds blowing at very high velocity are very rampant.

May and June are the hottest months of the year while January is the coldest month.

Desert Soils

Tourist attractions of Rajasthan, Thar Desert, the soils of the Arid Zone are generally sandy to sandy-loam in texture. The consistency and depth vary according to the topographical features. The low-lying loams are heavier and may have a hard pan of clay, calcium carbonate ($CaCO_3$) or gypsum. The pH varies between 7 and 9.5.

The desert soils occupy the districts of Jodhpur, Bikaner, Churu, Ganganagar, Barmer, Jaisalmer and Jalore. The Thar consists mainly of the wind-blown sand. The area is covered not only by sheet of sand but also by rocky projections of low elevations which constitute the older rocks of the country. Water is scarce and occurs at great depths, from 30 to 120 m below the ground level. Some of these soils contain a high percentage of soluble salts in the lower horizons, turning water in the wells poisonous. Being poor in organic matter they show a low loss on ignition. They contain varying amount of calcium carbonate.

The Wildlife

About 23 species of lizards and 25 species of snakes are found here. The thinly populated grasslands support the endangered Great Indian Bustard, the Black Buck, the Chikara (gazelle), and some feathered game, notably the Francolin and Quail. Sand Grouse, Ducks and Geese are common among the migratory birds.

People of Thar Desert

The inhabitants of the Thar Desert, the tourist attraction of Rajasthan have their main occupation: agriculture and animal husbandry. There has been a tremendous increase in human population as well as animal population, in past years. The increase of human and livestock population in the desert has lead to deterioration in the ecosystem resulting in degradation of soil fertility.

The Indian Desert is mainly inhabited by Hindus, Muslims, and Sikhs. The portion in Pakistan is inhabited primarily by Sindhis and Kolhis. There are around 60% Muslims and 40% Hindus in the Pakistani part of the Thar Desert.

A large irrigation and power project has reclaimed areas of the northern and western desert for agriculture. The small population is mostly pastoral, and hide and wool industries are prominent.

The living standard of the people in the desert is low. The people have a great passion for music and poetry.

Tourism in Desert

India is known as the land of diversity and its diversity can be seen in its culture, tradition, and geography. Indian Desert Toursism is an endeavor to provide one an excellent platform for travel to India. Desert Tourism presents one of the richest culture and civilization of the world making one to travel in India. During tourism one has a brilliant opportunity to observe rich culture and civilization of the country.

As one travels to Rajasthan, one explores so many new facets of Royal Rajasthan India including the sand dunes, the massive forts and palaces, and will realize that there is no other place like Rajasthan. For a traveller who is interested in the history, culture and the lifestyle of the people of the Oriental world, Rajasthan is just the perfect tourist destination. Unlike what its barren scenery suggests, it is found that Rajasthan is the most colourful and interesting place inhabited by humans. An exotic land, a dream come true for the Westerners, Rajasthan was home to the Rajputs, the martial races of India known equally for their love for arts and architecture as well as valor and chivalry.

Tourism opportunities in Rajasthan are immense. Rajasthan tourism and tour packages offer a great variety of travel experiences. Whether it is sand dunes, Desert safari, forts and palaces, the colorful tribal life or the fairs and festivals, travellers to Rajasthan are assured of a truly regal experience.

It is better to have a companion who has the first hand knowledge of local area, about people, their culture, tradition, landscapes and other useful information.

And knowledge of local families, camel/horse-men and other skills and experiences in rural travel and riding tourism (horse/camel rides, walking and jeep drive).

Rural Trips and Safaris:

Camel Safaris, Desert Walk and Camping
(Horse Riding-Safaris,Trekking)
Jeep Safaris (bishnoi people+wild life+crafts)
Highlights of Rajasthan (private taxi tours)
Thar Drive (driving through Thar Desert)
Arravali Drive (driving through Arravali Hills)

Types of Accommodation:

Home Stays (family-run guest houses)
Heritage Properties (staying alike Maharajas)
Camping in Desert Countryside (royal tents)
Theme Evening in desert (camel ride+sunset+dinner+ folk music)

Camel, Community and Desert Taste:

Enter in the Thar desert camel-back. Walk up and down with a secular rhythm, between millenaries dunes and get a chance to approach their mysteries.

Here, travellers are welcome to live a real Rajasthani experience. Going to get a chance to discover hosts of Thar desert community who are living with traditional customs and traditions, also detect some flora and fauna unsuspected at first glance. Great

Indian Desert is an immensely desert space, but sparsely inhabited, one can't find the same in world because all deserts are different.

Some harsh travellers find deserts unvaried, but most enthusiast find a supreme happiness. Camel in past, the only one mean for transportation in remote areas, the camel is not an ordinary animal, it is rugged, adapted with climate.

First used as a beast of burden, camel provides its owner with milk, leather and wool. In spite this, in desert, nobody eats camel meat to sustain life there. Here camel has only one hump, in reality it is a dromedary, even if one prefer employed, camel. Dark coat or light coat, it shows haughty in its singular sedate manner and its temperamental mood.

Camel-Back Rides: (Needs to be known before starting)

One can choose between given few example/suggested itineraries to experience authentic desert life.

1. Authentic rural life in Rajasthan: (Itineraries)
   one could get a chance to approach the real local daily life in Thar desert.
2. Experience the difference!
   Maharaja Camp + Traditional Huts home

(A) Well Prepared Trips Includes:

1. A ride between Mewar and Marwar.
2. A Marwaris-horse ride at camp in Aravali hills.
3. A ride between wild life and cultural life.
4. Jeep Safaris
   - Bishnoi village tour
   - Osian temples tour
5. Dream Weddings.
6. Fair and Festival Tour.

Precautions:

- Respect the wildlife.
- Viewing animals from a safe distance is fine; touching, feeding, or cornering them is not.

- Respect endangered species.
- Do not buy products that exploit wildlife, aid in habitat destruction, or come from endangered species.
- Do not litter.
- This is one time when the old adage, "When in Rome, do as the Romans," doesn't apply.
- Even if you see a local person littering, set an example and dispose of your garbage appropriately.
- Recycling is extremely limited or non-existent in most of villages and city areas.
- Avoid products with excess packaging; opt for beverages in glass bottles as they tend to be re-used.
- In desert areas of India, there is a major problem of drinking water, so please make sure about consuming water on trip/safaris.
- Local customs and traditions may be different from our own.
- Take the time to learn what behaviour is acceptable and what isn't.
- Always ask permission to take photos of people and respect their wishes if they refuse.
- If you do take a photo, offer to send copies back to them and make sure to follow through with your promise.
- If your subject wants immediate compensation in return for the photo taken, offering a piece of fruit or cookies, or a souvenir from your home are ways to do it.
- Learn a few local phrases.
- Take the time to learn about the country state, city and village you are visiting.
- Learning about the customs and a few words in the local language can go a long way and is appreciated by the local people.
- It also makes your interactions more meaningful and memorable.
- Discourage offering money to people begging on the streets of some places in country.
- Parents often send their children out into the streets, since a child can make more than their parents make begging on the street.
- This promotes further dependency and encourages more parents to send out their children.
- Support local artists and artisans by purchasing locally made goods.

- Many communities sell handmade crafts that one may purchase while on tour.
- Often guests return home from a trip having interacted with local people and experiencing life in another culture.
- Have a true cultural experience while helping to improve the basic living conditions in remote Bhisnois, bhils-bhopa and rajput communities.
- Today the "Green Laws" of conservation are making people aware of how man and the environment can live symbiotically for more time to come and eco-tourism is the only way to maximize the economic, environmental and social benefits of tourism.
- Everyone is a stakeholder in the process and we clearly need to avoid our past shortcomings and negative impact that they have had.
- In India too, the movement is gathering momentum with more and more travel and travel-related organisations are addressing the needs of the eco-tourists and promoting eco-tourism in the country.

Responsible Tourism Policy:

- Use locally-owned and run services by preference.
- Use locally owned and run accommodation by preference. Recommend a wide variety of home stays in Rajasthan, many cities for those clients who are interested. Not only does the money from home stays directly benefit the community, but clients will also gain an authentic insight into the region/state.
- Aim to, wherever possible, purchase equipment and food from locally produced source.
- Support local income generating and small business enterprises by supporting locally owned transportation, shops and restaurants and also using local guide & staff services.
- Aim to take responsibility for maintaining and improving the environment.
- Provide financial support for local economic and environmental projects that will benefit the local communities thereby actively encouraging local community involvement in tourism project.

Travellers Guideline Code:

- Try to preserve local resources wherever possible.

- Remember to turn off electricity in the room when not using it (particularly air conditioning units) and keep water usage to a minimum.
- Respect the local environment : do not litter, do not pick wild flowers or plants, try to reuse water bottles and recycle what is possible.
- Be aware of dressing appropriately in places of worship (Temples etc.) or significance and don't take photographs without obtaining permission beforehand.
- Be open and willing to learn about the differences between foreign cultures and your own.
- Even more importantly, be tolerant of these differences.
- A few words learnt in a local language can be greatly appreciated and can open the doors to a more "authentic" holiday experience.
- If you decide to give beggars or to children, parents, whose children are regularly bringing home money from begging, are unlikely to want to sent their children to school.
- Take responsibility for maintaining and improving the environment.
- Provide financial support for local economic and environmental projects that will benefit the local communities.

Thereby actively encourage local community involvement in tourism project.

Impact of Desert Tourism:

The impact of tourism on town and culture revealed an interesting distinction in the positive and negative nature of the impact.

They saw positive impact in economic terms while negative impact was seen in social teems. Economic and material gains were the most commonly cited aspects of positive change: more income, more variety of goods available in the market and variety of job opportunities.

The social moral of foreign tourists, especially the women, was cited as the most strongly felt negative influence on the local culture:

- immodest dress and objectionable behaviour in public places,
- Photographing local women,

- Walking into houses and temples,
- Giving money to children,
- Encouraging them to solicit other souvenirs from tourists.

The souvenir shop owners said that most of the craft that they sold came from outside Jaisalmer. Some leather works and stone sculptures were, produced locally.

A local stone mason confirmed that the local tradition of using carved stone decorations on the facade of buildings had been reinforced by local building regulations, and was a boon to his profession. He felt that this was due to the awareness created through tourism.

A sample survey of personnel at these places revealed that they were, by and large, self-taught in their profession and were more opportunistic. Not surprisingly, they were culturally ambivalent and operated in a 'liminal' world, which appeared to give them license to behave differently.

Talking to foreign tourists confirmed another aspect of liminality amongst these cultural brokers: most tourists did not entirely trust them and felt that they were uncouth and behaved badly only with foreign tourists.

The tourists are hassled by touts from the time they get off the bus or train, to the time they leave. This was the saddest insight into the real nature of relationship between the tourists and the host community: the closer the contact between the host and the visitor, the more disappointed they were of each other.

It was surprising to find out however, that while the tourists generally anticipated that they would be cheated in their dealings with local people (at the Guest House, restaurant, Camel Safari and souvenir shops), almost everyone carried back with them a positive impression of the place and people.

The natural pride and dignity of the local people came through even as they tried to make the quick buck.

The havelis and Jain temples were pleasant surprises and reinforced the dominant images they had held of Jaisalmer before they came – colour, desert, the Fort, jewellery, exotic people and the sunset.

One could conclude from these impressions that Jaisalmer in spite of the problems still retains its aura for the tourists: this reflects the depth and resilience of the attractive characteristics of the city and the local people, rather than any positive initiative on the part of the Government to conserve them.

There is no effort to train or educate the tourist-related personnel, the 'cultural brokers' and consequently they offer a negative image of the local society.

The Government has plans to boost tourism at Jaisalmer by improving its accessibility, including the introduction of air service.

Bibliography

Abraham, Sherry, Tourism Marketing Management, New Delhi, Globus Press, 2014

Acharya, Prasanna Kumar, Manasara Series, Vol.1-VII.

Agrawal, Banu, Metalware of Mughal period, Salar Jung Museum Research Journal, 21-22, 1987

Agrawal, D. P., The Copper Bronze Age in India, New Delhi: Munshiram Manoharlal, 1971

Agrawal, Prateek, Hospitality Marketing Management, New Delhi, Mohit Publication, 2014

Agrawal, Prateek, Tourism Planning: An Integrated Approach New Delhi, Mohit Publication, 2014

Agrawala, V.S. The Heritage of Indian Art, New Delhi: Ministry of Information and Broadcasting 1964

Ahmad, Rais, Tourism and Rural Management, New Delhi, Regal, 2013

Amit Kumar, Women and society: the developmental perspective. New Delhi: Criterion Publications, pp 324-355, 1986,

Balraj & George Michell, Human and Divine 2000 years of Indian Sculpture, 2000

Banerji, R D, Eastern Indian School of Mediaval Sculpture: Archaeological Survey of India,1933

Barnard, Nicholas and Gladstone Soloman W E, Masterpieces of Mogul Art: Essays on Miniature Painting and Architecture under the Moguls, Mumbai: 1932

Barnardl Nicholas, Arts and Crafts of India,1993, Conran Octopus Limited, London.

Basham, A. L., The Wonder That Was India, New York: Taplinger Publishing Co., 3rd rev. ed. 1968

Bhandari, Anil K, Tourism in India: An Economic Activity, New Delhi, Har-Anand, 2013

Bhandari, Dhingra, Dr. Vandana, Sudha (1998). Textiles and Crafts of India. New Delhi: Prakash Book Depot.

Bhatia, A K, Tourism Development: Principles and Practices, 3rd rev edition, New Delhi, Sterling Pub, 2012

Bhatnagar, Sanjeev, Handbook of Research Methods in Tourism, Jaipur, ABD, 2012

Cable, Vincent, Ann Weston and L. C. Jain, The Commerce of Culture: Experience of Indian Handicrafts, New Delhi: Lancer International 1986

Campbell, J.M. ed., Muslim and Parsi Castes and Tribes of Gujarat, Gurgaon: Vintage Books. (1990) [1899]

Census of India, 1951, West Bengal: The Artisan Castes of West Bengal and Their Craft, Sudhansu Kumar Ray, Calcutta, 1953.

Census of India, 1961 (Bihar), Selected Crafts of Bihar: Stoneware Craft of Patharkatti Village, IV, Part VII-A, No. 1. Patna, 1969.

Census of India, 1961 (Delhi), Selected Crafts of Delhi: Village Pottery, XIX, Part VII-A, No. 2. Delhi: Manager of Publications 1967

Chaudhary, Poonam (ed), Heritage and Cultural Routes: An Anthology: Global Cultural Routes: Tourism and Socio Economic Viability New Delhi, Shubhi, 2012

Chaudhuri, S., An Exhibition of Folk and Tribal Images of India, New Delhi: Lalit Kala Akademi 1970

Chauhan, S R & N S Chauhan, Tourism and Human Rights, New Delhi, Global Vision, 2012

Chhiber, Neelam, Stone Craft of India, 2 volumes. Chennai: Crafts Council of India. 2004

Dahiya, Neelima, Arts and Crafts in Northern India: From Earliest Times to c. 200 B.C. Delhi: B. R. Publishing Corporation 1986

Dalmia, Yashodhara, Art and religion amongst the Warlis, Art and Life in India: The Last Four Decades, Josef James, ed., Delhi: B. R. Publishing Corp.

Dar, S. N., Costumes of India and Pakistan, Bombay: D. B. Taraporevala Sons & Co. Ltd 1969

Dhar, Prem Nath, Aviation Management and Operation: Element, Dimensions and Trends, New Delhi, Kanishka, 2015

Dhar, Prem Nath, International Tourism: Emerging Challenges and Future Prospects, New Delhi, Kanishka, 2015

Dodd, John & Veena Sharma (eds), Leisure and Tourism: Cultural Paradigms, Jaipur, Rawat, 2012

Dua, J C, Tourism and Handicrafts of India, New Delhi, Kaveri Books, 2013

Dubois, J. A. (Abbé), Hindu Manners, Customs and Ceremonies, Oxford: Clarendon Press, 1897; 3rd ed., 1928

Ganguli, Kalyan Kumar, Folk art of Bengal, All Indian Folklore Conference Souvenir, Calcutta, 1964.

Gupta, R K & S.R. Bakshi, Studies in Indian History: Rajasthan Through The Ages; The Heritage of Rajputs (set of 5 Vols.). Sarup & Sons, 2008

Gupta, K. C., Progress and Prospects of Pottery Industry in India, Delhi: Mittal Publications 1988

Gupta, S K, Tourism and Heritage Resources in Garhwal Himalaya: An Approach to Planning and Management, New Delhi, Kaveri Books, 2017

Guy, John and Deborah Swallow, Arts of India: 1550-1900. Exhibition Catalogue, London: Victoria and Albert Museum 1990

Hall, C Michael (eds) et. al., The Routledge Handbook of Tourism and Sustainability, New Delhi, Routledge Taylor, 2015

Hsu, C H C & William C Gartner (eds), The Routlegde Handbook of Tourism Research, New Delhi, Routledge Taylor, 2012

Jacob, Robinet et.al., Tourism Products of India: A National Perspective, New Delhi, Abhijeet, 2012

Khandelwal, S, Tourist Destinations of India, New Delhi, Sankalp Prakashan, 2015

Kumaric, J Krishna, Budhist Monuments: Their Role in the Development of Tourism in Andhra Pradesh, New Delhi, Readworthy, 2013

Mahapatra, P. K., The Folk Cults of Bengal, Calcutta: Indian Publications 1972

Maity, P. K., Folk-Rituals of Eastern India, New Delhi: Abhinav Publications 1988

Maity, S K, Masterpieces of Hoysala Art: Haledid, Belur, Somnathpur,1978

Majmudar, M. R., Cultural History of Gujarat, Bombay: Popular Prakashan 1965

Manhas, Parikshat Singh, Strategic Brand Positioning of Tourism Destinations, New Delhi, Kanishka, 2012

Manohar, Aashi, ed., Tribal Arts and Crafts of Madhya Pradesh, Ahmedabad: Mapin Publishing Pvt. Ltd., with Vanya Prakashan 1996

Mukhtar, Shahnawaz, Tourism and Pilgrimage: with special focus on Pilgrimage Tourism of Kashmir, New Delhi, Sarup & Sons, 2012

Murugan, Annamalai, Medical Tourism: Potential Prospects and Emerging Issues, New Delhi, Abhijeet, 2012

Nandi, Santibhusan and D. S. Tyagi, Forms of villages - Peasant Life in India: A Study in Indian Unity and Diversity, Nirmal Kumar Bose, ed. Calcutta: Anthropological Survey of India 1967, 1–5

Naqvi, Hameeda Khatoon, Mughal Hindustan: Cities and Industries 1556-1803.Karachi: National Book Foundation, 2nd ed. 1974

Nath, Aman and Francis Wacziarg, eds., Arts and Crafts of Rajasthan, Ahmedabad, New York: Mapin Publishing Pvt. Ltd. 1987

Negi, Jagmohan, Air Travel Ticketing and Fare Construction, New Delhi, Kanishka, 2015

Prasad, P N Girija, Global Tourism Marketing, New Delhi, Akhand, 2014

Ramesh, Ruchi & Sudhir Kumar Singh (eds), Tourism in India: Challenges and Opportunities, New Delhi, Pentagon, 2012

Saksena, Jogendra, Mandana, A Folk Art of Rajasthan. New Delhi: Crafts Museum 1985

Smith, Melanie & G Richards (eds), The Routledge Handbook of Cultural Tourism, New Delhi, Routledge Taylor, 2013

Solanki, Ramesh, Tourism Hospitality and Air Transport: Indian Spectrum, New Delhi, Manak Publications, 2013

Tod, James & Crooke, William. 1829. Annals and Antiquities of Rajasthan or the Central and Western Rajpoot States of India, Numerous reprints, including 3 Vols. Reprint: Low Price Publications, Delhi. 1990

Vidyarthi, L. P., Cultural Contours of Tribal Bihar, Calcutta: Punthi Pustak 1964

Wacziarg, Francis, ed., Arts and Crafts of Rajasthan. Ahmedabad: Mapin Publishing 1989

Walker, Anthony R., The Toda of South India: A New Look, Delhi: Hindustan Publishing Corporation 1986

Zimmer, Heinrich, The Art of Indian Asia: Its Mythology and Transformations, 2 vols. Princeton, NJ: Princeton University Press 1983

Index